Diary of a
Rad Housewife

Diary of a Rad Housewife

Ten Years of Tirades and True Tales

Shannon Drury

Right Fracture Press
Minneapolis

© 2016 by Shannon Drury

All rights reserved. No part of this publication may be reproduced, distributed, or transmitted in any form or any means, including photocopying, recording, digital scanning, or other electronic or mechanic methods, without prior written permission.

ISBN: 978-0-9973750-1-5

Cover by Kerry Ellis

"Morning Song," "Nick and the Candlestick," "Two Sisters of Persephone," and "Child" from THE COLLECTED POEMS OF SYLVIA PLATH, EDITED by TED HUGHES. Copyright © 1960, 1965, 1971, 1981 by the Estate of Sylvia Plath. Reprinted by permission of Harper Collins Publishers.

Right Fracture Press
Minneapolis, MN
rightfracturepress@gmail.com

*To Matt, Elliott, and Miriam,
for whom my love is absolutely
100 percent true.*

Contents

Introduction 1

Not fighting your Mommy Wars 5

A bridge in troubled water 13

Presidential politics is a motherfucker 23

In the kitchen with Rose and Sylvia 41

Health care may be hazardous to your health 61

Triggered 87

A casualty of the War on Women 107

Am I a good mother yet? 137

Intersectionality for white people 153

Getting older, not wiser 171

Introduction

On Thursday, May 4, 2006, I signed up for a MySpace account and entered the following words in the text box:

Testing, 1-2-3... Is this how one writes a "blog"? Am I officially a "blogger" now? Is Miriam crying miserably because her mother is "blogging" instead of paying her mind?

Yes, in 2006, blogging was a concept so foreign to me that I felt it required the clarification of ironic quotation marks. After all, I was a thirty-four-year-old stay-at-home mother of a one-year-old daughter and a six-year-old son, not some popstress hoping to become the next Lily Allen. I signed up for the site in response to the urgings of a few younger friends who thought that the blogging platform would suit me. They already enjoyed the cranky, funny things I liked to blurt out at Minnesota National Organization for Women (NOW) meetings about how my feminist activism collided with my parenting life. Why not share that stuff with the world?

Why not, indeed? Unlike a lot of bloggers who claimed that they didn't think of themselves as real writers, I was an unpublished novelist with about ten credits' worth of MFA work under my belt. I believed I would get to my Serious Literary Writing eventually, once Miriam got out of diapers and Elliott got out of elementary school, but a funny thing happened on my way to the Nobel podium: I discovered that I loved blogging.

I *loved* it! The permission to rant about whatever was in the news that week! The immediate feedback! It was far more rewarding than anything I'd cranked out in a class or in a three-ring binder gathering dust in the attic. And there were *emojis*! Wheee!

I didn't know that I was setting in motion a chain of events that would lead to my first published book—which was not a scorching piece of literary fiction, as I had once planned, but a memoir based on my feminist parenting adventures that shared the same name as my goofy MySpace moniker: The Radical Housewife.

***

Okay, okay, compared to Angela Davis, I'm hardly what you'd call radical. But compared to June Cleaver or Barbara Bush? Totally.

The real inspirations for the name were the activist collectives known as the Radical Cheerleaders, about whom I had read in *Ms.* magazine. They wore black and shook big red pom-poms to feminist chants in a truly brilliant combination of political action and street theater. What would happen, I wondered, if a gang of rebel moms co-opted their style with aprons and rolling pins? Just imagine the world-changing possibilities of Radical Housewives!

To mangle the words of Flavia Dzodan, my feminism will have a sense of humor, or it will be bullshit!

***

In the ten years since I registered that funny name, a lot has changed. My son is a high schooler who finds me annoying, and my daughter is a middle schooler who finds me slightly less annoying than he does, but annoying all the same. MySpace yielded to Facebook, and blogs yielded to Twitter. Polishing up my ranty blogs led to a columnist position with the *Minnesota Women's Press*, and my confidence in those clips led to freelance opportunities in local and national publications. Social media connected me with a world of new readers as well as writers, as I learned that I wasn't the only feminist mama with a computer and a long-simmering dissatisfaction with the status quo.

But many other things remain as stubbornly intractable as ever: sexism, racism, trauma, illness, and death. If you live long enough, you'll experience grief that will drop you not just on your knees but flat on your back. There are days when the sociopolitical climate is so poisonous that you're not sure you have the strength to get out of bed, much less get your fingers on the keyboard.

Online culture, while rewarding in some ways, can also be cruel and disorienting. I ranted, but others ranted right back. Was it worth all the drama to get my page views up? And were my Twitter followers an accurate reflection of my worth? Some bloggers and publishers seemed to think so. Hell, *I* started to think so. That's when I knew that it was probably time to move on.

***

Why gather up all my favorite posts and freelance pieces in one place? Well, why not? I'm a collector, the type of Gen X nerd who likes to have all her Replacements records and Nancy Drew titles organized neatly and chronologically. I am very proud of this work, a lot of which is no longer available, either in print or online. It's amazing how many outlets have folded in the last decade—was it me?

In this collection, I contain multitudes. I am the foul-mouthed babbler who can't help but pop off at the people she finds annoying. I am the frustrated academic applying maternal theory to the works of feminist icons Sylvia Plath and Courtney Love. I am the humorist spinning hilarious tales of sexual embarrassment. I am the clear-headed policy analyst making a rational argument. I am the forty-something American woman reckoning with grief and death. I am the mom of two kids watching this fresh, strange, new world through their eyes.

Taken as a whole, this book is also a pretty interesting record of how the social-media and political landscapes have changed since Dubya was winding down his second term. When I started blogging in 2006, it seemed more likely that Madonna would run for president than that the Defense of Marriage Act would be nullified. A civil rights revolution happened, due in no small part to the revolution in communication that enabled people around the world to share their stories without any gatekeeper to tell them they couldn't. Voices that could never have dreamed of reaching the editorial page of the local paper, let alone the *New York Times*, now found that they had a worldwide platform; all they needed was a Twitter account and a clever hashtag.

This is not a complete record of everything that ended up on MySpace, Blogger, or even TheRadicalHousewife.com. I learned the hard way that some rants are best kept in an analog diary, the kind we used to keep under our beds, with tiny locks and even tinier keys. Also, there are only so many posts anyone can read about the Stupak-Pitts Amendment to the Affordable Care Act of 2010, even a feminist policy wonk like me. I consider this book my Greatest Hits, my Immaculate Collection, my Radical Housewife Gold, if you will.

***

This decade of documenting culture-war craziness wouldn't have happened without the support of my family. Elliott and Miriam, can you forgive me for not making you pseudonymous way back when? Your childhoods are well-documented, for better and worse. I love both of you, no matter what.

Matt, the Radical Hubby, supported me literally and figuratively. Thank you for making 100 percent of a white man's dollar.

I am grateful to all the outlets, past and present, active and shuttered, that published my work, and to each editor who took the time to help me fine-tune my use of the semicolon and the em dash. Particular thanks go to the readers, editors, and publishers at the *Minnesota Women's Press*, where women's stories are truly changing the universe.

Many thanks also to beta readers and moral supporters Veronica Arreola, Gillie Bishop, Sonya Huber, Joan Kinsley, Jessica Trites Rolle, and Jenni Undis.

Last but not least, I have to thank Erin Matson and Kristi Shaw for convincing me to make that account ten years ago. You said I would love it, and you were right! Thank you.

2006
Not fighting your Mommy Wars

It all starts here, with me tapping into a MySpace page that only two people read. By the end of the year, that number would double—or triple, if you include my mom and dad.

Grossed out by pro-choice kids
MySpace, May 5, 2006

This was not my first blog post, strictly speaking, (see the introduction), but it was the first one that told a story of political activism with young children in tow. At the time, no one had any clue that Michele Bachmann would not only win a seat in Congress later that year, but would also become a focal point for right-wing batshittery. Now the fact that she yelled at my kid is a point of personal pride!

A slightly longer version of this tale appeared on the website MOMocrats ahead of the 2008 election. Both are 100 percent true!

Out-of-towners: you should know that state senator Michele Bachmann is a hateful old cow who keeps introducing a constitutional amendment to ban same-sex marriage and any legal equivalent in the Minnesota legislature. And she's decided that poisoning Minnesota politics is not enough—she's running for Congress! Yechhh.

Yesterday I took the children to the capitol to show our opposition to the so-called Abortion Regulation Act, one more law designed to take us a step closer to the dark ages. We were joined by my sister Leah and my nephew Aidan. The boys quickly grew bored with holding "Pro-Choice Pro-Family" signs and wanted more fun, so they began chasing each other around a bronze statue of Cass Gilbert. A pinchy-faced woman approached and nagged, "You should stop them from doing that. That statue is really valuable." As she walked away, I whispered, "You don't have to listen to her. She's *mean*." Yep, it was our pal Michele.

We returned to the cluster of sign holders. Michele returned with one of her staffers in tow. She strode through our group, then turned to look behind her with a classic "Who farted?" grimace on her face. Though she was staring at me and my kids, I thought her look of disgust was probably a delayed reaction to the gentleman displaying a sign with her picture and "HATEMONGER" written across it. As Michele stomped off into the Senate offices, the women behind me gasped, "Did you see that? She was staring at the kids! She was grossed out by pro-choice kids!"

I was so proud. We'll be back soon to destroy that statue, Michele—just you wait!

The perils of showing up
MySpace, May 15, 2006

I won the election handily: no one else ran! I ended up serving six terms, many of them great, though I never did get a free trip to Albany. Perhaps that's for the best.

I finally mailed in my registration for the annual Minnesota NOW conference. Of course I've been wanting to go, to see the whole gang, rub elbows with local leaders, get wired and stuttery on cheap NOW coffee, the whole deal. Yet I put off sending in my registration for fear that showing up will land me on the state board again. Or worse: I might end up state president. Urghhh.

How could anyone fill the sexy, pointy shoes of our outgoing leader, Erin? I couldn't. What's more, I feel confident that my leadership could polish off our chapter permanently. But I have to admit that there are a few perks that might make it worthwhile:

1. I hear we get free trips to important presidential conferences, meetings, and whatnot, and I could really use a vacation. Even if it is in Albany.

2. I think that Robert's Rules give me some sort of superpowers to stop people from talking about stuff I find boring. Don't they?

3. During my vacation (see #1), I could tap [then-National NOW President] Kim Gandy on the shoulder and say, "Excuse me, but Erin Matson said there would be an open bar."

Mmmm, tempting.

More to the point, however, are my feelings of guilt at not contributing more to the Great and Glorious Cause than a couple of checks and a half hour holding up signs for the cheerful honks of passersby. I crab that I'm too busy with my kids, but everyone's busy these days. There must be more I can do. Maybe it starts with just showing up.

The activist parent lives to regret it
MySpace, June 12, 2006

Another ridiculous tale that is 100 percent true.

Elliott bonks his sister on the head and instantly is marched upstairs for a time-out. Five minutes later, he stomps down to the living room, shouting at the top of his lungs,

"HEY HEY! HO HO!

GROWN-UPS HAVE GOT TO GO!"

Matt's eyes grow huge. I try to stifle a laugh but fail. Trying to be supportive, Matt says, "You really ought to be holding a big sign with a picture of grown-ups with a slash through it." Elliott nods; he hadn't thought of that. Maybe next time.

Forget the mommy wars. Let's talk class wars
MySpace, July 26, 2006

The rant heard 'round the…uh, liberal corners of the Twin Cities! I submitted a cleaned-up version of this blog post to the Minnesota Women's Press, *who published it. A year later, I was a regular columnist for the paper.*

This version, straight from my blog to you, is full of all the fucks I had to give at the time.

You've heard about it, haven't you? This deliriously poisonous little book called *Get to Work: A Manifesto for Women of the World*? By a former philosophy professor named Linda Hirshman? No? Could you believe it's yet another salvo in the so-called "Mommy Wars" that every member of the media can't stop slobbering about? Yes. Yes, of course you could.

I haven't read it yet (I'm on the hold list at the library), but I did catch Hirshman on MPR's Mid-Morning program yesterday. Predictably, I felt alternately nauseated and enraged each time Hirshman chuckled at the naive women who called up and tried to defend their choice to stay at home to raise their children. Hirshman thinks we ought to do exactly what the title of her book says: get our spoiled asses off the couch and work for a living. We are betraying feminism if we don't put our fancy degrees to work in corporate or academic settings. This woman actually had the nerve to insist that women who stay at home lead unfulfilled and unfulfilling lives. Yes! *Me!* The Radical Housewife herself! Worth nothing more than a piece of shit you'd scrape off your shoe! Or, to put it more appropriately, a piece of shit you'd wipe off Miriam's ass!

The radio conversation ended with a discussion of the final example in the book, one on which Hirshman feels she can rest her entire argument. A married couple, both doctors, had some kids. The wife decided to stay home and raise the little cretins. The husband felt guilty for working seventy-hour weeks; he complained to Hirshman. When she asked why he worked himself so hard, he replied that he was a pediatric oncologist who was—no joke—trying to cure childhood cancer. Ah. That's all Hirshman needed. He's curing cancer, she tells us in her book, but she (the mother) never will. I could almost hear Hirshman smirking over the airwaves when she told this tale.

You've got to admit, it's one hell of a Mommy War strike. Who's going to argue with curing childhood cancer? That one could stop any radical housewife in her tracks. But think past the smirk for a minute. Is it possible that this gentleman could work less and help with the children more? I thought the days of lone scientists toiling in dank laboratories died with Louis Pasteur. There are usually large research teams behind these sorts of discoveries. And did anyone ever think that maybe, just maybe, a guy with that level of commitment to his work ought not to have children?

Now think about this story another way. Replace "pediatric oncologist" with "short-order cook." Or "drill-press operator." Or "truck driver." Is the argument the same? My father was a garbageman for thirty years. What does she think of his level of self-fulfillment? Again, I have not read the book. Perhaps there are chapters and chapters full of stories about stonemasons and janitors and plumbers, but I doubt it. She doesn't seem to care. Hirshman argues, in her *American Prospect* article that inspired the book, that it's the "educated elite, who are the logical heirs of the agenda of empowering women," who are letting all feminists down by raising their kids. The rest of the teeming underclasses can go fuck themselves.

Hirshman may think she's talking to me. I have a degree from one of the country's most prestigious liberal arts colleges, and I'm at home, raising my kids. I'm just the kind of feminist turncoat who's the reason we don't have a female president right now.

Here's another quote from Hirshman's *American Prospect* article: "A good life for humans includes the classical standard of using one's capacities for speech and reason in a prudent way, the liberal requirement of having enough autonomy to direct one's own life, and the utilitarian test of doing more good than harm in the world. Measured against these time-tested standards, the expensively educated upper-class moms will be leading lesser lives."

But that fancy education was paid for by my dad emptying garbage cans (and my mom crunching numbers in middle management). From my working-class background, I can see these Mommy Wars for what they are: a series of petty arguments to keep us distracted from real social inequities. Caitlin Flanagan can brag all day about how much she pays her nanny—that doesn't change the fact that most working parents can't afford quality child care. And since pay equity still hasn't been achieved by any wave of feminists, in hetero couples the woman's salary is easier to let go.

Hirshman tells women to get to work. But I'm waiting for someone who has the guts to tell the government to invest in children and child care, to pay child-care workers what they're worth, to give tax incentives to stay-at-home fathers, to make that forty-hour work week iron-clad so that everyone, dads and moms alike, knows that people are more important than work, no matter what kind of work you do. That includes wiping kids' butts and curing kids' cancer.

Don't worry, Linda. There's still hope. I'm telling Miriam that she's got to study law and one day run for president. But I'm telling Elliott that he's got to be a daddy who stays home with his children. And I'm going to be very proud of them both.

How did I become the Radical Housewife?
Minnesota NOW Times, September 29, 2006

This essay, published in the Minnesota NOW member newsletter, was the first coherent expression of my feminist-mom philosophy, what I would later refer to as the Radical Housewife's origin story. The editor of the Minnesota Women's Press, *a NOW member, liked it so much that the paper gave me a 2006 Changemaker award.*

I was born feminist and progressive, raised in the *Free to Be. . .You and Me* era by a couple of baby boomers who, while not quite flower children, took to heart the political upheavals of the age. In our house, all people were equal and everyone had unlimited potential. So I took my college education and became an at-home parent (see previous post for that discussion). I could do anything, be anything, and handle anything. Only when my son Elliott was born in 2000 did I realize how wrong I was.

Elliott was not just a colicky baby. He was a screaming, hollering, kicking, squalling-until-he-ran-out-of-air-and-turned-purple baby. For hours at a time my sweet, wanted, loved, adorable baby boy would wail inconsolably, while every cell in my body went into meltdown. I had an epiphany. You've all seen the stories on the news of parents booked on charges of grievous assaults on their children. You see their grainy mug shots and think: how could anyone do that to their child?

My epiphany? I knew.

I knew how such a horrible thing could happen, even though I had nearly nothing in common with the sad adults on the news. I had everything going for me. A safe, monogamous relationship (with a man, so I had access to his health benefits in addition to myriad hetero perks), a middle-class lifestyle that allowed me to be home with my child, good health, a college education, a support network and friends and family, and a child who had been conceived out of love and was wanted. In short, I had everything I needed to get out of my desperate situation. But as I dialed my nurse practitioner, my mother, and my husband for help, I understood how fragile children are and how they suffer when new parents are at risk. Talking about the difficulties and sorrows of raising children, colicky or no, is a cultural taboo; perhaps it's a Darwinian trick that keeps us humans breeding. I love my son very much. But what could have happened if my advantages hadn't been there? What if I had been single? Addicted? Seventeen? A rape victim? Homeless? Uninsured? All of the above?

If the children are our future, we need to take care of everyone today. Even if you don't have children, you have an investment in this too. Who repairs your car's brakes? Who prepares your restaurant meal? Who's answering your 911 call? Someone's child. We all have an interest in being sure that that child was raised with love, compassion, and dignity. Every person's future depends on it.

I joined Minnesota NOW because our multi-issue organization addresses the inequalities that remain obstacles to women and families today. A popular quote says that to be a parent is to walk with your heart outside your body. My motherhood experience has given me that and more; now I can see the hearts on everyone's outsides, and most of them are broken. And that, my friends, has made me radical.

Thirty-five is the new fifty
MySpace, November 28, 2006

An honest assessment of where I'd been and where I wanted to be—and the first mention of my friend Liz's struggle with cancer. Nowhere on this list is "write memoir about being a feminist stay-at-home mom." That wouldn't occur to anyone until 2009 at the earliest.

This fall many of my old friends from years past have been popping up in the local media. One opened her own retail store, another's band made the Picked to Click in *City Pages*, and another provides good quotes for the paper as a local music maven. Minneapolis is small town, but Google can make anywhere smaller. Matt found that an ex of his from college is now running a very important indie record label. My former beaux have much less sexy careers in medicine and the academy. It seems like everyone out there's living the dream. How about me? Hitting thirty-five this October seemed like a good time to dust off that old "Things to Do Before I Die" list and give it a look.

1. Finish the novel.

I finished the first manuscript in the spring of 2004, all four hundred lousy pages of it. I planned to give it a pitiless overhaul but found myself knocked up. Instead I started another manuscript and made it to three hundred pages the morning Miriam was born. My list never said "Write a bestseller" or even "Get a novel published." Lists of this sort require that kind of leeway.

2. Be in a band.

I doubt that either the Elliott Black Attack, noisy and tuneless art-skronk featuring my firstborn on vocals, or the Voltages, my thirteen-year-old cousin's heavy metal project, fulfill this ambition. Though my drumming is getting much better.

3. Meet Paul Westerberg.

I served the man a four-shot cappuccino during one fateful shift at Starbucks in the spring of 1997. I told him that he needn't pay; I had been a great fan for ages. He mumbled thanks, dropped a buck in the tip jar (which I still have), and left. I waited until he was gone to dash to the storeroom to scream. Again, I have doubts that this counts. When I originally wrote this list, my intent was that he and I would have an emotional chat over both our coffees, but maybe that's not a good idea after all. There's too great a risk of being disappointed by one's childhood idol.

4. Have a baby.

Done. And done.

So at thirty-five, even if I haven't hit 'em all, I've come pretty close. But is it enough? I wondered this as I read about my old friends' successes. I wondered this during naptime as I knit, washed piles of filthy clothing, and wrote NOW fundraising letters. I wondered this as I read Dr. Seuss books at bedtime, as I shoved mac and cheese down kids' throats, as I roared at them to give me the peace and quiet a thirty-five-year-old needs to think about these things. I'm so old *old* OLD, I thought, having these mid-life assessments and wondering if my life has been a success. I felt like fifty, not thirty-five. Should I have gone after my goals more actively and finished the books before I had kids? (Unclear.) Should I have been less of a weenie and started that riot grrrl band back in the day? (Yes.) Was I doing enough to deserve the title of Minnesota NOW President? (Probably not.) Thirty-five is the new fifty, I kept mumbling. Thirty-five is the new fifty. I ought to buy myself a goddamn convertible.

Then I heard that my dear friend, a mere child of only thirty-four, was having yet another setback in her desperate fight against cancer. The tumor in her colon was gone, and the bits on her lungs had shrunk away from a course of chemotherapy. But now her ovaries were under attack, and she sounded like her confidence was every bit as weak as her body. I visited her and saw her fear. Mortality wasn't an abstraction that might motivate her to write a stupid goals list. It was real. It was present. It was happening.

Thirty-five is young. Assessments are fine. Goals are fine. But thirty-five is young. Thirty-five can be the new fifty if that means you can stop obsessing and start living, with or without the mention in Google or the fucking convertible.

2007

A bridge in troubled water

This year I wrote five columns for the *Minnesota Women's Press* (four eventually made it into print) and very few blog posts that are appropriate for republication here, because I'm saving them for *another* memoir that starts with me having *another* nervous fucking breakdown. (The first few appear in *The Radical Housewife: Redefining Family Values for the 21st Century*, available wherever better books are sold.) In the meantime, I give you 2007!

American Manhood Idol
MySpace, May 2, 2007

When the editor of the Minnesota Women's Press *let me know that a columnist position was opening up, she asked me to submit two sample columns if I wanted the job. This is one; the other was printed in the paper in July 2007. Though Sanjaya Malakar is certainly no longer a part of the pop-culture landscape, I have reprinted this piece on my blog several times, each time after another mass shooting. After I reposted it in the wake of the shooting of Rep. Gabby Giffords in January 2011, I was delighted to receive a comment from someone who said she was Sanjaya's mother. "I am very proud of him," she wrote. "It made me cry to hear another woman facing the same challenges to raise a boy within a culture that glorifies violent, macho images of young men."*

I am happy to admit it, totally honestly, without a trace of irony: I'm a Fanjaya. That is, I am an honest-to-goodness fan of Sanjaya Malakar, the seventeen-year-old *American Idol* contestant whose wacky hairdos and wobbly vocals made him a target for derision from the web to the grocery tabloids to the network news. I participate in pop-culture silliness as much as anyone (I still have my Spice Girls dolls), but I really do love this kid. In fact, I've had a mom-crush on him ever since his first audition in Seattle, long before he shocked the nation with his pony hawk.

Shall I break for another pop-culture definition? A mom-crush occurs when an adorable kid provokes a powerful desire to pinch the object's cute cheeks and serve him or her homemade cookies. In common usage, one might say, "I hope they never recast the stars of the Harry Potter movies. I have a mom-crush on all three of them." And Sanjaya had the toothy grin and the goofball charm to win over the stoniest mom in America. When he wept openly after his older sister was cut from the competition, I felt a bit teary myself. Who sees a boy cry on television any more, much less out of genuine tenderness and emotion? I loved it. He was my Idol pick, no matter how he styled his hair.

But fellow moms and Idol geeks like my friends Pam and Liz thought I was nuts when I confessed that I was dialing for Sanjaya. "Are you serious?" Pam squawked. "He was terrible!" Liz e-mailed. These are sensitive, loving women who are both certainly capable of some mom-crushing. But I soon realized what could have made them immune to Sanjaya's charms.

Neither of them were mothers of sons.

Now someone else's son is in the news, and for something far more disturbing than off-key singing: on April 16, 2007, Seung-Hui Cho opened fire on his university campus in Virginia and killed thirty-two people before turning the gun on himself. Media coverage after the massacre followed a predictable pattern, with a parade of pundits expounding on gun control laws, why students ought to own guns, pervasive mental illness, the rights of the mentally ill, violence on television, violence in video games, the logistics of campus lockdowns, and more. All of that changed the day NBC announced that it had received a package from the killer himself, containing videos and photographs of Cho decked out in all his murderous finery. In one image, Cho brandishes two firearms, holding them from his ammo-clad body at right angles, his face glowering with rage. It's too perfect. It could easily have come from any grindhouse movie; hell, it could have come from the movie *Grindhouse*. This is not to blame Hollywood, but to recognize the brutal allure of this image. In America, we love power. We need it; we feed on it. The power that comes from violence is the cheapest and easiest available to those who are the weakest among us.

I was pregnant with my first child when the home-video footage made by the two Columbine killers was made public, to be shown 24/7 by news outlets in a desperate attempt to understand what these boys had done. Not long before, a fuzzy black and white ultrasound had shown that I was going to have a little boy of my own. Two television screens, showing two separate images of boys in America. My typical first-time mom jitters gave way to full-blown panic. There was no chapter in *What to Expect When You're Expecting* about this. What on earth was I going to do with my American boy?

Fast forward seven years, and I still don't know. No one else seems to, either. Seung-Hui Cho, despite having spent his youth in South Korea, idolized the Columbine killers as "martyrs." I adore my boy, but I fear for him. No talk show or how-to book is going to sort this mess out. But maybe one boy's spontaneous tears on the country's most popular television show will help.

I know I had best not pin all my hopes on this one American boy, a reality TV star at that. Of all media icons, they tend to have the shortest shelf lives. I have a lot of difficult, ugly parenting work ahead of me, and Sanjaya will be busy just growing up. I thank him for the courage he displayed on the show week after week—and I'm not talking about the spectacularly funny hairdos. It takes guts to be yourself in America these days. It takes strength to take chances, to stand up to criticism, and to cry when it's all over. That's a kind of power that is neither easy nor cheap, but it will last him a lifetime.

I hope his mother is proud.

In search of the perfect diet
Minnesota Women's Press, July 10, 2007

Behold: my first byline as Women's Press columnist! I set the tone for future columns by revealing embarrassing truths about myself and my children right off the bat!

"Hey, fatty!"

My heart dropped from my chest to my gut with a sickening thud. Please, let it be my hearing that's fading in my old age, I thought. Maybe he forgot her name and called her Patty. He couldn't have said that.

The woman asked, "What did you say, Elliott?"

"I said, 'Hey, fatty,'" he repeated.

The woman before us was indeed large, but she was also a treasured member of the staff at our gym. It's almost always the sweetest, friendliest people who are on the receiving end of my kids' fumbled experiments in etiquette. I wished I could disappear. She, however, maintained her composure and watched calmly as I stammered that we don't use those kinds of names, and people come in all shapes and sizes and are special just the way they are. My hot cheeks turned several shades of magenta while she accepted my son's mumbled apology. "It happens," she said and went on her way.

Moments later I hauled Elliott into a quiet corner and demanded to know how he could say such a horrible thing. His face blanked out as I hissed, "Do you have any idea how hurtful that is? How would you feel if someone said that to me?" But he wasn't vacant out of spite or annoyance. He wasn't tuning me out. He had no idea how to reply. No one would ever say "Hey, fatty!" to me, because I'm not fat.

Not anymore. I'm twenty-five pounds lighter than when I graduated from high school and fifty pounds lighter then when I graduated from college. I'm a size 8, the size Valerie Bertinelli says she hopes to achieve in her new Jenny Craig campaign. That blew my mind as I read it in the checkout aisle: She—a woman who had a kid with Eddie Van Halen—wants to be like *me*! What I wouldn't have given to be her in my tween years. Yet here she was, on the cover of *People*, begging for the public's help to get down to size 8 slim.

Somewhere at this point in the column the formerly fat person is asked to share the "secret" to her transformation, her solution to escaping the epithet "fatty" for good. I don't have one. I have several. Pick and choose which most suits your active lifestyle:

The Heartbreak Diet: in which you break up with your unstable boyfriend in a strange town across the country, pound the pavement looking for jobs because he took the car, and subsist on nothing but generic corn flakes and milk in an attempt to hoard rent money. Not recommended for depressives or those with weak knees.

The TMJ Diet: in which the temporomandibular joint in your jaw locks down due to stress (see above), chronic pain nearly derails your life, and you cannot eat anything but oatmeal and soup. Not recommended for anyone.

The Post-Partum Diet: in which the new baby won't stop shrieking, the older child won't stop demanding your attention, and you lack energy to do anything but brew another pot of coffee. Not recommended for those who can afford a nanny.

After each of the dieting experiences listed above, I found myself showered with compliments, rewarded almost daily by loved ones as well as strangers. A friend who is a recovered anorexic says that in the worst throes of her illness she was approached several times by modeling agents. And really, why not? We want our women thin. We don't care what it takes to get them there. We want an easy story of triumph (thinness) over adversity (fat), not a downer of a tale in which the destination wasn't worth the journey.

When college classmates remark on how different I look, I bore them silly by sharing my eventual discovery that my body deserves respect and care, not torment. I tell them that I still believe fat is a feminist issue and that everyone has the right to be his or her own perfect size without hectoring from seven-year-old boys who have no idea that, once upon a time, their size 8 mothers were teased until they cried. I tell them I'm proud to be a member of the YWCA, where people of all shapes, colors, ages, genders, and abilities are welcome as participants and employees.

But, as Valerie Bertinelli herself might sniff, that's easy for me to say. I'm not getting picked on anymore. I can only hope that the woman at the Y that day believed me when I said, "I'm sorry."

The housewife's collapse
Minnesota Women's Press, August 23, 2007

This brutal column was written in the aftermath of the 35W bridge disaster on August 1, 2007, and a bitter rift between members of my family of origin and me. Ouch.

I am an at-home parent. That's how I identify, purposefully avoiding the popular, gender-coded acronym SAHM that implies all stay-at-home moms are the same. I'm not. Another label I created is The Radical Housewife, a moniker that seemed pretty funny when I set up a MySpace page. I'm just that kind of post-hipster, Gen-X irony-laden spouse and parent who wants to reclaim "housewife" from the June Cleavers and Barbara Bushes of American history.

Why the distinction? Why deem it necessary to create a goofball label at all? Not simply to declare my leftist leanings to the world, surely. No, my choice to differentiate myself runs deeper than my political beliefs—it's about the long-suppressed secret of full-time motherhood.

Housewifery really sucks.

But it sucks no more or less than any other job, when evaluated critically. Kissing ass can be as soul draining as wiping ass, but the white-collar worker doing the former lacks the suffocating aura of love and devotion and all-consuming cultural sacrifice of the latter. Back when I slung lattes for a living, I didn't have the world's expectations upon me. I wasn't molding the future, I wasn't anyone's savior, and I wasn't anyone's model of goodness and purity. I made coffee people liked. People liked it enough to buy more. The corporate coffee gods rewarded me in turn. You don't need a radical outlook to miss the simplicity of those capitalist days.

At times, I do like my job. At times I even love it. But lately, I hate it. I suppose this admission is as radical an action as any.

Strip housewifery of its pink aprons and banana-bread scent, and it's a job like any other, with aggravation and burnout and depression or worse. And when we housewives finally implode, it can be spectacular.

It's not too much of a stretch to call moms the neglected infrastructure of our society, taken for granted each and every day. My children certainly careen over me with abandon, caring little of the wear and tear they exact. Whining demands are like rust, intractable demands are hairline cracks, and bellows of "I hate you!" are deep shudders. A child's special-needs diagnosis turns into a fracture that's harder and harder to repair. But it's supposed to be that way, isn't it? We're built to withstand the strain, right? Maybe. Some bridges and moms are built tougher than others. Unlike highway bridges, however, moms aren't subjected to yearly inspections, no matter how flawed. How would anyone know if I were structurally deficient if I didn't tell them so? And I'm not going to. It seems that even radicals cling to outmoded ideals of motherly perfection, in spite of themselves.

Is it any wonder, then, that the horrific 35W bridge collapse affected everyone so deeply and me so viscerally? To me, the fall was a tragedy not only for the people lost and for the survivors whose lives where irrevocably shaken, but for my entire city, and, by extension, me. How else to explain the constant tears and the intense, almost physical discomfort at seeing my city on the front page of the *New York Times*?

I recoiled in disgust watching Matt Lauer's handsome mug reporting from the riverbank. What in hell was he doing here? When the nation's First Housewife and her husband flew in to witness the rubble for themselves, I'd finally had it. Get away! I shouted at the television. Leave us alone! We don't need you! This was wrong, utterly wrong. This was not supposed to happen here. The despair twisting in my gut felt familiar: it was the same churn I had experienced only a week or so before, when my mother had told me, "You are falling apart from stress, and you need help."

How did I reply to her? To the woman over whom I had run roughshod in my own way so many years ago? Get away! Leave me alone! Some things never change. Until they have to.

For when we are unsupported, we will fall. Cracks and fractures happen; they are part of life and as such are easy to ignore. If only our deeply held myths were as vulnerable. If a mother weren't held up so high and trod upon so often, all the while supporting the desperate hopes of so many, maybe her collapse wouldn't be so unavoidable. And maybe, just maybe, if a wounded community can accept the scrutiny of the entire world, one mom can too.

That would be radical.

An abuser in the House
Minnesota Women's Press, October 2, 2007

This is not just a story about one awful Minnesota legislator; it's about the larger issue of how we hold people accountable for the crime of domestic violence. Mark Olson wasn't kicked out of the Legislature after his conviction—he was re-endorsed by local Republicans for his 2008 race! I bet that made a lot of women in Big Lake feel just great! Thankfully, voters in that district were smarter than their GOP leadership and got rid of him.

Women of Minnesota, it's time to clean House.

Last July, Rep. Mark Olson (R-Big Lake) was convicted of one count of misdemeanor domestic assault with the intent to cause fear. Sherburne County District Judge Alan Pendleton sentenced Olson to two years' probation and required him to pay $400 in fines as well as court costs for repeatedly pushing down his wife Heidi during an argument.

That seems like a pretty light sentence, you say. A person convicted of a domestic-assault charge ought to draw a stricter punishment, you think to yourself—and you're not alone. In December 2006, not long after the charges against Olson were filed, Governor Tim Pawlenty went on record saying that Olson ought to resign if he was found guilty.

So what happened? Nothing. Olson won't quit. Last fall his Republican caucus dumped him, but no one in the party has made another peep about wanting him to resign.

You don't need to be a state officer of a national feminist organization (as I am) to hear this news and want to puke. You don't need to be a victim of domestic assault or know someone who is (as most of us do) to feel repulsed. You just need to give a damn about the people of Minnesota to know instinctively that Mark Olson has got to go.

Would a representative convicted of real estate fraud be allowed to serve in a body that determined the laws governing such transactions? If dear Governor Pawlenty, heaven forbid, had a file full of speeding tickets, would we want him wielding his veto power over a bill that would put such repeat offenders in prison?

The budgets of women's shelters and domestic abuse education programs are determined by the legislature. Should Mark Olson be allowed to have a vote when such a bill comes before him? Would you trust him with that kind of power?

It wasn't that long ago that a friend admitted to me that the breakup of her long-term relationship had been caused by her partner's abuse. "Some feminist I am," she said, laughing bitterly. My response then was that it's not anti-feminist to be abused; abuse can and does happen to anyone. Victims aren't defined by their class, race, gender, sexual orientation, or even political orientation. "It's feminist to leave," I said, and I still believe that now.

For all the endless hand-wringing over what is and isn't feminist (Lipstick? *Sex and the City*? Hot pink iPods? Heterosexuality?), let's all agree on one thing: It's feminist to speak up and speak out. Even a hater like Ann Coulter enjoys the right to press charges against a partner who beats her up, and she has a hundred years of feminists to thank for the privilege.

Yet for every single woman who speaks up, hundreds of her sisters remain silent. And why not? Put yourself in the Crocs of a housewife, radical or no, sitting in her living room one evening last summer as she watches the local anchor deliver the news of Mark Olson's conviction. As part of the story, she sees Olson report that he'll remain in the Minnesota Legislature and that the Republican leadership will let him. She has to move the ice pack from the bruise on her cheek; it's getting soaked with her tears. If a public person like Mark Olson won't have to pay for his crime, how will her partner? She might just change her mind and not file that police complaint after all.

Each of us must call our legislators to demand that Olson be brought before the Ethics Committee at the start of the 2008 session. Another suggestion: if you're reading this and you live in his district, do not hesitate for a moment. Run against him.

Love can't build a bridge
Minnesota Women's Press, November 13, 2007

Another column on the theme of collapsing infrastructure in our cities and our hearts. Though the new bridge was built in a record fifteen months, the rift with my family took much longer to mend. My friend Liz died three days after this column was printed; I'm still gluing together those broken pieces. In 2011, the city of Minneapolis opened a lovely memorial and garden to the victims of the disaster, a gesture much nicer than the outcome I imagine here.

In a previous column, I compared the cracks in one housewife's interior to the flaws that triggered the collapse of the 35W bridge. Forgive me while I continue to use (some might say abuse) the metaphor. Such catastrophic events happen so rarely that they are irresistible to writers. The book *The Onion Presents Our Dumb Century* nailed it when they composed the classic fake headline for April 1912: "World's Largest Metaphor Hits Iceberg."

Jokes aside, what's left of the bridge remains in the dirt-brown waters of the Mississippi, available for viewing by all who care to see. Upriver, caring local citizens display messages of hope painted on old bedsheets. "A bridge over troubled water," said one. "Love can build a bridge," announced another. Sorry, folks. I'm here to claim otherwise.

Victims' bodies were still in the water when Governor Tim Pawlenty announced an ambitious plan to erect a bigger, better bridge within fifteen months. Minneapolis Mayor R.T. Rybak bickered with him over whether a rail line could be squeezed in. Within two weeks of the collapse, MnDOT officials elbowed their way into the press conference fray to announce that they were accepting new design entries. Why?

We are a nation of fixers, of builders. If something breaks, you repair it. If something crashes down, you build it up again. We're also a culture of relentless improvers: thus the constant refrain that the new 35W bridge be bigger, better, faster, more. Built bigger and faster, engineered better and safer, so your commute will be quicker and nicer. Perhaps a shiny bronze plaque will be drilled into one side to memorialize the thirteen people whose lives ended on August 1, 2007.

The housewife didn't crumble quite as quickly as her bridge did, but those who surrounded her demanded fixes just as hastily. It's an impulse bordering on instinct to offer advice to someone whom you believe to be hurting; my biological family members made the claim, "I only say this because I love you." They ran a press conference on my quavery mental state, with lists of fixes discovered from extensive research on Google. Many tips were thoughtful; some were inappropriate. Some were bewildering in the extreme. I imagine the raging Mississippi herself wondering if she couldn't get a bit cleaned up before all the shiny new plans were made. Of course, our river's been so thoroughly defiled over the years that she's sure no one gives a damn about her feelings anymore. Don't worry, Ole Miss. I do.

Love can't do anything; nor can it do everything. Invoking love's name cannot soften judgement or criticism. Similarly, love can prevent normally honest people from admitting serious truths. For example, I love my children so much that I'm afraid to admit that sometimes I can't stand being around them. Any parent knows the emotional damage a child can cause. And vice versa.

I offer an alternative. Let's try a slow-fix. Let's take a moment and honor the twisted wreckage in the water. Let's back away from the finger pointing, advice giving, and blame laying.

But "life goes on," you know. "If you fall off, just pick yourself up and hop on again." Why? To fall down once more?

It's no crime to want to lie in the water just a little bit longer. But it is embarrassing and inconvenient. Acknowledging grief runs counter to two centuries of American cultural programming. Not-doing seems illogical or worse in a nation whose myths rest on a boat full of busy worker bees who carved Plymouth out of unspoiled wilderness. The key word there is unspoiled. The Pilgrims spoiled it, as the Wampanoags and Narragansetts know too well.

I suggest that we try it the slow way. Hold a memorial, not only for the people who died on that horrible day, but also for the faith we lost when the structure gave out. The housewife will also rebuild, in time. For now, though, she'd like room to grieve the dream she lost: namely, that parenting and radical housewifery would ever be easy.

Bridges can't be built with love alone. They need time, care, expertise, and as much as four hundred million bucks. Let love be only a beginning. A necessary start, but not the whole story.

2008

Presidential politics is a motherfucker

Some people might remember 2008 as the year that Barack Obama won the presidency, the year that a former *Saturday Night Live* regular ran for United States Senate (and won!), or the year that Michael Phelps earned more gold medals at a single Olympics than anyone ever had.

I remember it as the last year that I blogged on MySpace.

Just kidding! I remember it for Sarah Palin, of course! If John McCain hadn't plucked her from the obscurity of the Alaska tundra, I would have had to invent her to serve as my bizarro world twin, the doppelgänger who opposed everything that I supported—*and* she had an abstinence-only teenage daughter who was pregnant! Amazing!

But before I met Sarah (and I do feel like we're on a first-name basis), I would encounter my first real trolls, a special rite of passage for every blogger. Between the political drama in my nation and in my neighborhood, I had no shortage of writing topics, and my output exploded.

Media catnip
MySpace, March 10, 2008

In 2008, my son's public school decided to participate in a new anti-LGBT bullying program designed by the Human Rights Campaign called Welcoming Schools. Readers of The Radical Housewife *should be familiar with the following scene, one of my proudest parenting moments! I love that I captured my immediate reaction on my blog.*

I have often claimed that kids at political events = media catnip. Now there is Fox 9 News video proving my point.

When Elliott heard that I was going to attend a school meeting to show my support for the new Welcoming Schools curriculum, he said he really wanted to join me. He was horrified to think that some parents might not approve of measures that would keep his buddy Morgan (and his two amazing mommies) from being a target of bullying. The news camera couldn't get in his face fast enough!

This clip doesn't accurately represent the level of support for the curriculum, which was huge. *Huge.* I love South Minneapolis. And, most importantly, I love Elliott's principal. Lisa, the nutball mom who gets face time in this clip, crabbed at the mic that presenting same-sex couples as, ahem, "normal" was against her religion. The principal stood up in the front of the room and barked, "But that's your religion. THIS IS A PUBLIC SCHOOL." I would like to have that on tape.

What *is* on tape is one of the proudest moments of my life. The last word in the clip belongs to my incredible son Elliott, putting into words what all kids know in their hearts. "People are people and love is love."

And how I love him!

Imagine a pro-vagina world
Minnesota Women's Press, April 16, 2008

All credit for this inflammatory title goes to my Women's Press editor, who cooked up something much better than my uninspired "On White Guys." A piece with the latter title couldn't have drawn the ire of lefties and righties alike! A discussion on how soundly this piece got me flamed followed this column's republication in The Radical Housewife. *I think the column is worth re-republishing, and you'll soon learn why.*

When I first started thinking about a Democratic presidential nominee for 2008 (sometime after the weeping stopped in November 2004), my criterion was simple: *not* another white guy.

I have nothing against individual white guys, mind you. My charming husband happens to be one, and before long my eight-year-old son will be one too. But it's as Sister Suffragette put it in *The Sound of Music:* "We agree that, as a group, they're rather stupid."

Not only stupid, but entrenched. They've been running things since the dawn of humanity, despite a handful of anthropological studies that show that matriarchies did exist, before patriarchies squashed them like bugs (*lady* bugs). So imagine my thrill when Hillary Clinton and Barack Obama looked like my party's choices for 2008. Joy! Rapture! Why, back in the old days of ought-seven, discussing the candidates was sheer pleasure. No one argued. Everyone gasped, *"Oh my gosh, aren't we lucky?"*

Then the calendar flipped to 2008. I wore my Hillary pin at the new Richfield SuperTarget and got looks as dirty as I've seen in any campaign season. I attributed this to suburban conservatism. Imagine my surprise when at my precinct caucus, deep in the heart of the People's Republic of South Minneapolis, I felt the sting of being in the political minority. I haven't had that experience since I wore my homemade "Dump Reagan" pin to my classes at Edina's South View Junior High. Suddenly, political discussions were making my stomach ache.

Why? Was it *so* hard to have people not agree with me? What happened to the nicey-nice? Usually, when I listen to Rush Limbaugh (for research, people), my heart sings when I hear a candidate like Obama labeled a "tax-and-spend liberal." Why did I feel so disappointed by his success?

I realized that I wanted a woman to be the nominee much more than I had thought. I wasn't satisfied with Obama, who is not white. He's still a guy, and I am sick of guys.

Yet when I announce this, I am accused of being not only sexist but also racist. No, I don't mean me personally, mostly because I am too mousy to stand up in the public square and talk about how sick I am of men (though my supportive husband encourages this). I should defer to the royal "we" here, because when Gloria Steinem wrote about the subject in a widely read opinion piece in the *New York Times*, you better believe my heart sang.

But many women writers in the blogosphere whom I respect and admire called the essay sexist. And racist. And they said very hateful things about women like me who support Hillary Clinton, including that they are sexist and racist. One commenter on Feministing.com called it "pro-vagina selfishness."

Oh, dear. No more nicey-nice.

My daughter Miriam will be three years old in May. Let's imagine, shall we? Say Hillary Clinton is elected in 2008 (my best-case scenario), proves utterly ineffectual in office (worst case), and is defeated in 2012 by George P. Bush (whose mother is a native of Mexico). My daughter grows until adulthood with a woman president as historical fact, not a figment of her imagination. Any jerk messing with her self-esteem will get a sassy retort about President Hillary from my tough little girl, who is already known in her neighborhood for not playing princess. When my daughter puts on a tiara, she knows to be queen.

By all accounts, Barack Obama is almost as cool a guy as my husband and son. If he's the nominee, I will happily support him. But these days when I see him on camera, I'm always peeking over his shoulder, thinking, *Hmm, that Michelle is one smart and accomplished woman. Why didn't she run? Damn.*

Is wanting a woman to run the show selfish? Yes. I acknowledge that it is. So is wanting 50 percent of the members of Congress and at least three more Supreme Court justices to be women. I also want 50 percent of the parents watching their kids at the park to be men. I want what any parent wants. I want a pro-vagina world for both of my children.

Perhaps the most important lesson of the campaign is that untangling gender, race, class, and so many other of the big "–isms" is far more difficult than anyone thought. The shouters on both sides exhort us to vote blind to them all, to cast our ballots on issues alone. Okay. I took one of those candidate surveys on the Internet and was given my perfect match: Dennis Kucinich.

Never mind.

My first troll!
MySpace, April 23, 2008

I remember this day well, my friends: the first appearance of a troll who would haunt me off and on for the next three years. On a blog post that I marked private, I shared with my readers the entirety of his tirade against me. Of course, I can't do that here, because this gentleman, whom I will call by the pseudonym Nathan, has already threatened me with legal action . . . but more on that later. Under fair use, however, I can reproduce a handful of the words that Nathan uploaded to WordPress after he read my "pro-vagina world" column.

"Decline of Western civilization. . . . stupid. . . . President of the Minnesota National Organization of Women Wimmin Wymyn. . . . Shannon Drury is a racist, gynocentric, matriarchic supremacist."

Pretty cool, huh? I think so now, but at the time I was gobsmacked that anyone could possibly have such a hate on for li'l old me. I understand thinking that my column was ill-informed, but that I was a "matriarchic supremacist"? I had never heard of such a thing—but I liked it!

Of course, a big, brave man like Nathan didn't have the guts to write under his own name. With a little research and a little more googling, I was able to uncover his identity. What would I do about it? Read on, fellow gynocentrics, read on!

What would *you* call a welcoming school?
Minnesota Women's Press, June 1, 2008

Katherine Kersten, a notoriously reactionary columnist for the Minneapolis Star Tribune, *was tipped off about our school's plan to talk to children about family diversity . . . er, to liberally indoctrinate nine-year-olds. I raged about this for days until I remembered that I was a columnist too—I could write a piece in support of Welcoming Schools myself! This column was also reprinted in its entirety in* The Radical Housewife. *Forgive me—2008 was a weird year.*

In the twentieth century, it meant the squat brick building down the block that took your kids when they were six and popped them out into the world when they were eighteen. Parents said thank you; the schools said you're welcome.

Today, in the post-everything age, even the task of signing a kid up for kindergarten is a highly fraught endeavor, including paperwork and assessments. But in the end, a school is selected, the child is registered, and the parents toast with juice boxes and hope for the best in the fall. As an admittedly anxiety-ridden parent with a tendency to overthink just about everything, I found the whole process grueling. In the end, our community school, the squat brick building named for patriot Nathan Hale, welcomed our son in September 2005.

I should mention that at no time did my husband and I consider a private school. We live in Minneapolis purposefully, and our commitment to this community extends to our son's education. As he grows older and his needs change, perhaps we will reevaluate. But we're convinced that the only education a young kid needs is in how to get along with other people. There's no better place for that than the Minneapolis Public Schools.

Every school in Minneapolis has a pie chart that breaks down the racial makeup of a school, as well as the percentage of families who qualify for free or reduced lunch. District statisticians can spout the number of children who are classified as English Language Learners and those who receive special education services. But none of these numbers can fully capture the rainbow of diversity that kids encounter at a public school. Children and adults at Hale bring an array of thoughts, backgrounds, and experiences that contribute to my son's real education every single day.

But now, there's a different kind of rainbow that's bothering some parents at Hale. It's the capital-R Rainbow, the official symbol of the civil rights struggle of gays, lesbians, bisexuals, and transgender folks. The principal at Hale, Bob Brancale, announced to the Hale community that our school had an opportunity to participate in a new curriculum designed by the Human Rights Commission, the nation's leading GLBT rights organization. The curriculum, entitled Welcoming Schools, addresses family diversity and bullying. Brancale stated in his letter to parents that he had lobbied to get the program at Hale because of the continued use of anti-gay slurs among students. The family-diversity component merely reflects the increasing number of GLBT families in the district.

At a March 6, 2008, community meeting, some parents objected to the curriculum's sponsor, a political action group. Some argued that instruction time is too precious to spend on this topic. One frustrated mother said that opting her kids out of the program would subject them to bullying. Then have them take the curriculum to learn that bullying is unfair, said a district representative. But no, the mother spluttered. No, *no*, NO. Then the truth came out: this curriculum would undermine her parental authority. The children would learn something was *okay* at school that they learned was *wrong* at home. What was that something? Well, gee. Gay people.

My first impulse was to shout, "Go ahead and home-school 'em, lady!" But I'm glad that good sense prevailed. For what better place for her children than a public school? What environment is *less* diverse than the family home? And unless these kids live at home with the TV turned off and the windows nailed shut, they are going to meet some different people. A few gays, too.

That was March. Now, as the school year winds down, the battle is heating up. The *Star Tribune*'s resident loose cannon, Katherine Kersten, weighed in on the topic, arguing that the curriculum is political indoctrination. The district has been threatened with legal action from Arizona's Alliance Defense Fund, and Brancale has been targeted by the Minnesota Family Council, both (shocker!) political action groups. Finally, an anonymous blog is now accusing Brancale of exaggerating Hale's discipline problems: the word "lies" comes up often.

Enough. I'm all for diversity of opinion, but the above just smacks of bullying (ironic, isn't it?). Stop panicking, Kersten et al. Get to know

Minneapolis, and you'll find that our diversity is our greatest strength. Hale parents, let's keep talking. Don't take your kids from our school. I like them. They are different from my kid, and that's good.

Rage, rage against the morons on the right
MySpace, June 11, 2008

Lisa is a pseudonym for the fiercest opponent of the Welcoming Schools curriculum, the mother who "spluttered" in the column above. When she went on the record, her opposition to the curriculum was misguided but never insulting. When she wrote anonymously for a blog she called Stop Welcoming Schools, *however, she made outrageously offensive and totally unsubstantiated claims about Machiavellian tactics at our kids' school. She was sloppy, though, and I was able to verify that she was behind the site. Finally, I got so fed up that I lashed out. I was right about the coming revolution though. Sorry not sorry!*

The *Twin Cities Daily Planet is a local aggregator of independent regional media that picked up my Welcoming Schools column from the Women's Press.*

Oooooh. I am really losing it now.

The *Twin Cities Daily Planet* has been inundated with comments from the well-organized group of parents who oppose the Welcoming Schools curriculum. Unlike the Women's Press, where my editor rules the comments with an iron hand, I don't believe the *Daily Planet*'s comments are closely moderated.

Where is my organized fan club? Why does someone as icky as Lisa get a Greek chorus to follow her every move? She has five or six parents pouncing on Welcoming Schools everywhere it pops up in the media, in print, or online. Where is Shannon's Army, I ask you?! Where?!!

"Breathe," says my therapist, who is not Chinese but believes that Qi Gong is the answer to everything. Breathe, dammit.

On the Daily Planet site, I wrote that I appreciated the fact that a fellow school parent's comment was unusually respectful. But I also noted how frustrating it is that he doesn't make the connection between his biracial daughter's teasing and the plight of children from LGBT families. I would expect otherwise, as anti-miscegenation laws were on the books as late as 1967, when the Supreme Court finally struck them down. The plaintiff in that case, Mildred Loving, issued a comment last year, on the fortieth anniversary of the decision, that read in part: "I believe all Americans, no matter their race, no matter their sex, no matter their sexual orientation, should have that same freedom to marry. Government has no business imposing some people's religious beliefs over others. Especially if it denies people's civil rights."

Yesterday Lisa posted a comment on the Daily Planet in which she admitted that "my religion does not recognize [same-sex relationships] as good behavior." Well. Finally. Team Lisa has been whining for ages about how they've been painted as a bunch of bullying homophobes. Now Shannon's Army can coalesce around her twin bombs:

1. She is imposing her religious views on my kid's public school education.
2. She has admitted that she doesn't think same-sex partnerships are "good."

I know I should be thrilled that I have some hot ammo, but really, all this mudslinging is taking an emotional toll. I'm tired of finding a new attack on me and my school every single goddamn motherfucking day. And I'm a boring old heterosexual housewife! Christ, how would I feel I were one of those folks whom Lisa found aberrant?

Thanks to the magic of MySpace, I do know: my intensely fantastic friend Christine announced on her blog that, on the twentieth, she and her longtime girlfriend have plans to visit the San Diego courthouse, when the two of them will get married. *Married!* I have tears in my eyes whenever I think about it. And not because I am the boring old housewife who bawls at any wedding, even if it's just on *All My Children*. In fact, I have a rather jaded view of the wedding-industrial complex that can wait for another blog.

My happiness is not only for the two of them, but also for my kids. This is more than a marriage; this is a civil rights revolution. I am going to share this story with my adult children one day, watching their faces drop when they realize that there was a time without marriage equality. "Wow, Mom," they'll say. "That is fucked up!"

I just reread Christine's announcement, and I'm getting teary all over again. The mudslinging will go on, and it will be worth it. Congratulations, Christine!

Say "fuck" like you mean it!
MySpace, June 13, 2008

Imagine my surprise when I saw that I, your very own Radical Housewife, was the next subject of a post on the Stop Welcoming Schools *site! The headline: "Does Shannon Drury need anti-bullying training?" All because I used the f-word. Personally, I find homophobia a more dangerous trait, and I said so.*

Hey gang! Guess what? I write my *personal* thoughts on my *personal* blog!

But, darn it, it was my own fault that I printed Lisa's last name so she could find herself on a Google alert. Sorry, Lisa. Won't happen again.

My buddy Lisa has decided to "out" (pun intended) my potty mouth and penchant for lowbrow humor. She's also let the world know that I think that two lesbians getting married is the best thing ever. Here's what she wrote on her *Stop Welcoming Schools* blog:

[The blog is long gone from the Internet, but I still don't want to open myself up to copyright infringement by quoting it here. Her major complaint was that I used vulgar motherfucking language and that I said she was "icky."]

I get that on my MySpace page, I am able to use swear words that the *Minnesota Women's Press* would never print. Why? Because swearing is fun. It's *really* fun! If it weren't fun, people wouldn't do it.

Naughty words aside, I don't see what my personal blog has to do with my reportage for the Women's Press or that paper's support of free speech. After all, Lisa, you and I both know that any idiot with a computer and the Internet can start a blog. The two of us are proof of that. Let us cast aside any illusions that the Internet hews to the same rules of decorum as a community newspaper. The rule here in cyberland is that there are no rules.

That being said, I earned my newspaper column with my talent. I am a good writer with important things to say. If I may quote my all-time favorite newspaper columnist, the incredibly talented and thoughtful Dan Savage, "If you don't like it, get your own fucking column."

In addition to a column with my name on it, I have a blog with my name on it. Lisa, you can't even admit that you are the voice behind yours. I really don't think I need to submit to anger-management counseling because I said you were icky. As I replied on your blog (should you post it), I know that you think I'm icky, too. No big. Really. That I can handle. I get mad when you start going after my school and my friends. That's not okay.

And if you read more, you already know that, in addition to having this wonderful blog to vent my frustrations, I have a therapist and a continuous supply of Paxil. What's your excuse?

A million thanks to everyone in Shannon's Army!
MySpace, June 27, 2008

Finally, at long last, a post of hope!

The Stop Welcoming Schools site is not only inactive; it is done. It's finally closed to all but "invited readers." Which is as it should be: Lisa and her buddies can gab with each other all the damn day long without pretending that they represent parents who are actually concerned about Minneapolis Public Schools.

Lisa directed her followers to the blog of the Minnesota Family Council, which has been inundated with snarky commenters. Snark is an excellent weapon against a site that continues to pretend that they love the sinner, but hate the sin. Who do they think they're fooling? A clever poster has listed the many wonderful sins listed in the Bible that aren't quite worthy of the MFC's hatred, such as allowing ladies to speak in church and eating shellfish.

Best of all, I have been contacted by people who saw my flaming on the old site and wanted to offer support. Additionally, at a Rainbow Families meeting on the subject last night (that I couldn't attend), Matt was identified as "Shannon's husband" and told that my army really does exist.

Thank you. You have made me happy. Thank you!

The color of protection
Minnesota Women's Press, August 19, 2008

The state of Minnesota is 85 percent white. I am 100 percent white, which means it's on me to be aware of how racial bias shapes news stories, including what is deemed worthy of making the news at all. By now you are really getting a sense of how deeply I loathe Katherine Kersten, aren't you?

A girl was groped by a gang of boys at Valleyfair this past Fourth of July; her father was there to protect her; he failed. Unpleasant. But the fact that the boys then beat the father to a pulp made it a Big Deal. We expect daddies to protect little girls. But rumors that the girl was white and her perpetrators were black pushed it beyond Big Deal and into the realm of Serious News. Suddenly the radio talkers, opinion writers, and newscasters kicked into overdrive. It seems that the appetite for frightening tales of black-on-white crime, particularly black-male-on-white-female crime, can never truly be sated.

Don't believe me? Consider the resounding shrug given to the police report that the victims and the perpetrators were all black. All of them, even the girl whose body allegedly triggered the whole thing. Listen for the sound of crickets chirping after Shakopee police revised their initial statement: the girl was sixteen, not twelve (therefore more woman than child), and she was swatted on the head, not the derriere (therefore more annoying than sexual). Yawn.

Don't misunderstand: I would like gropers of children to be punished. I would like their booking photos printed on the front page of the *Star Tribune*, thank you very much. On second thought, forget the Strib. It continues to employ accomplished race-baiter Katharine Kersten, who didn't miss the opportunity to write a hysterical column about how narcissistic hip-hop musicians like Pharrell Williams and Snoop Dogg made those Valleyfair boys want to grab a hunk of tasty girl flesh.

Except maybe they didn't. I don't know. It sure sounds to me like a bunch of bullies were trolling Valleyfair looking to beat up just about anybody, and then they did. Don't misunderstand: I would like those who commit physical assault to be punished too. But like the proverbial onion, this story just stinks worse the more you peel it back.

Two weeks after the Valleyfair attack made local news, *Time* magazine published a piece on a lavish Purity Ball held in Colorado Springs. The girls' dresses were as frilly and sweet as wedding cakes, which was probably the point. Fathers snuggled reverent daughters in their arms and claimed to the *Time* reporter that they were not simply defending these girls' virginity; they were shielding their integrity from the likes of . . . well, let's be honest: Pharrell Williams and Snoop Dogg.

The skin of the girls and men in the *Time* photographs was uniformly pink, which is not to suggest that no brownish people were present. Rather, it suggests how little anyone cares.

For the protection of white girls is still a cultural imperative in 2008 America. This fascinates me all the more because I happen to have one of these precious little girls in my house. The Perfect American Girl is not an abstraction: she kisses me good night. My three-year-old daughter is pink-skinned and blue-eyed and boasts a full head of butter-yellow curls. These will all come in handy, I realize, should she meet the fate of doomed blonde daughters such as Jon-Benet Ramsey or Natalee Holloway, both of whose cases consumed tabloids and police departments to the possible detriment of lost girls of a different shade.

White girlhood has a protective advantage: people care. But it seems to me that we've gone too far. My daughter's hymen is not my property, nor is it her father's. A young pink body is not the manifestation of all things hopeful and innocent, no matter what the blogosphere says. Misguided assumptions do more widespread damage than the fists of angry teenage hooligans.

My daughter's brain is no one's property either. She can think what she wants. She may very well end up wanting a fluffy white dress should she marry, and I'll have to accept it. I'll just try to educate her, and I'll continue to remind her of her white privilege. My responsibility is to enable her to use it for good, not evil. Just look at the latest from uber-blonde Paris Hilton, who struck back with a hilarious video on the website Funny or Die when John McCain implied that his black rival shared her inherent fragility.

And you'd better believe that when Paris spoke, people listened. I sure did. Her dad must be so proud.

"Amoral and nihilist"
MySpace, August 27, 2008

I no longer get my kicks by baiting people online; the thrill is totally, completely gone. I don't even retweet at the weirdos who try to bait me. Adulting!

Al Franken's run for Senate was dogged by people claiming that his humor writing for Playboy *magazine made him a misogynist creep. If there's anything I can't stand, it's feminists of convenience.*

For some time, the Minneapolis E-Democracy Forum has been boring. Lots of talk about foreclosures and property taxes, both of which are extremely dull subjects that are best left to the wonks we elect to serve us on the city council. But things picked up when a cranky white dude wrote a dainty little post inquiring about a recent Women for Franken event. Golly, he wondered, did anyone on the list go? He was just so gosh-darned curious about the whole thing.

I took the bait—and it was delicious. I figured it was my civic duty to make that damned message board lively again. This man went on a furious tirade about how Al Franken is a pornographer on the scale of Larry Flynt, how could a woman of principles support him, how dare I call myself a feminist since he is an expert on the subject and would never define me as such, and on and on. I gently reminded the group that the Republican Party in this state has just endorsed a man convicted of domestic assault for a state Senate seat (that would be Mark Olson, about whom I wrote in October 2007). Does that square with the feminist values that all these white men claim to share?

For an extra bit of fun, I introduced abortion into the debate. I mentioned it as a core feminist value, and the boys went apeshit. Dictionaries and Wikipedia were consulted as the word "infanticide" was deconstructed. Ultimately, one of my longtime fans was drawn out of the woodwork and duly left the following post:

"Mrs. Shannon Drury, a self-described 'feminist' who writes for the *Minnesota Woman's Press*, believes that a child in utero can be aborted for any reason whatsoever . . . Mrs. Drury's beliefs are nothing more than amoral and nihilist."

Yes, friends, Nathan is at it again. But this time, armed with research, I am overwhelmed with hilarity and not panic. For Nathan is no intellectual threat; rather, he is the type of knee-jerk hysteric who screams "BABY KILLER!!" and "ANTI-SEMITE!!" at the words abortion and Palestine, respectively.

Also, he called me "Mrs. Drury," which is not my name but *is* funny as hell.

And to read this at seven-thirty in the morning, after taking my first gulps of coffee after feeding two whiny children and parking them in front of PBS, to sit here at the dining room table in my jammies and open my Yahoo inbox to find myself described as "amoral and nihilist" is really the funniest way to start my day.

Thank you, Nathan! THANK YOU!

Palinmania
MySpace, September 3, 2008

At this time in world history, everyone was just starting to get their heads around all that was mystifying, maddening, and downright amazing about the heretofore-unknown governor of Alaska. Every day she brought about a new scandal! I probably owed the greater portion of my blog readership to people googling "Sarah Palin feminist" and finding me complaining about her.

Sarah Palin, you are taking over my life. You have crowded Brangelina from the tabloids and from PerezHilton.com. Okay, okay, I give; you are probably the natural mother of baby Trig. Now we trade one scandal for another: your seventeen-year-old daughter is pregnant by a somewhat dim-witted hockey player. What could tomorrow bring?

You repulse me, yet you fascinate me. You named a child "Track." Why? It boggles my mind. *Time* magazine claims that you asked the Wasilla librarian how you could go about banning objectionable books. What book would you ban? *Beyond Jennifer and Jason*, the baby-naming book? Certainly not Harry Potter, because those kids don't even kiss until they are sixteen.

Your politics are totally repugnant, yet I defend you for being out on the campaign trail, because John Edwards didn't get shit in 2004 for running while he had two little kids at home. Did I mention that your politics are horrendous? Almost stupefyingly idiotic?

I am writing my new column about you, and it's not even due for two weeks. Please do me the favor of digging in your high heels for that long and refusing to let cooler heads prevail. DO NOT LET YOURSELF GET DROPPED FROM THIS TICKET.

Senatorialism: A primer
MySpace, September 25, 2008

When MinnPost, *a local online news site, announced a political satire contest, I knew it was my chance to sparkle, Shannon, sparkle! Even my cover letter was funny, as you'll see here. Norm Coleman was the slimy Republican who only won his Senate seat in 2002 because the beloved incumbent, Senator Paul Wellstone, died in a plane crash two weeks before the election. Removing him from the Wellstone seat made it even easier to campaign for Al Franken, who did have a hand in writing a* Saturday Night Live *sketch that sent up John McCain's dirty campaigning.*

In the end, MinnPost *declared no winner in the contest, because "no entry was as funny as the real elections." What a crock of poop! My blog audience was more enthusiastic.*

Editors:

Below is my submission for the *MinnPost* satire contest, featuring my take on Norm Coleman's "more senatorial than thou" baloney. This will no doubt test your "no foul language" rule, as much of the piece revolves around a funny word for fecal matter. I can only blame this on the fact that I share my home with an eight-year-old boy.

"Senatorialism: A primer," by Shannon Drury

Norm Coleman and his compatriots raise a mighty fuss every time Al Franken is caught doing what he does best: being funny. To them, the business of being funny is not funny at all. Humor, they claim, must be separated from an elusive quality that Stephen Colbert might call "Senatorialism."

What is Senatorialism? Navy suits. Gleaming shoes. Combed hair. That which famed satirist Bart Simpson described as "walkin' around like your poop don't stink."

Hee-hee. I wrote "poop." You laughed, I bet. You laughed because it's funny. Are you going to deny it? Whole dissertations have been written on the psychology of humor, but I lack the room to go further than this: exposing taboos and hypocrisy is funny.

But humor doesn't fit the self-image of those committed to the ideal of Senatorialism. To the Senatorialists, teeth are bleached sparkling white to reflect the pop of a flashbulb at a photo opportunity, not to waste on wit. Senator Norm Coleman is perfect at this. He hasn't laughed since 1998, when he got fewer votes than a pro wrestler. Which is a shame, really: the man's veneers are *flawless.* Senatorialism, it should be noted, also requires the money to get caps of the highest gloss and quality.

So for those keeping score, we have six items on our list of Senatorialisms: suits, shoes, combs, unscented poop, teeth, and money.

But there's one more quality that no Senatorialist can be without. Stronger than poop, shinier than polished shoes, whiter than the teeth of God himself—what could it be?

Moral outrage, kittens. It's the accessory no candidate can be without these days. It hugs the body with the silky confidence of Hugo Boss's finest suit. Phony moral outrage has made the aforementioned star of *The Colbert Report* a more trusted newscaster than anyone currently on CNN. Even phonier moral outrage is on display every time a Norm Coleman flack taps a microphone and asks if anyone ever heard of the book *Rush Limbaugh is a Big Fat Idiot*, and if they have, dontcha think that's a mean thing to say about somebody and you should be ashamed. Why, Mr. Limbaugh sits in his money bin and cries every time he thinks about it. It really *hurts*—the names, not the money.

Moral outrage is what fires up the oppos in their cubbies when they get wind of Al Franken's hand in a *Saturday Night Live* sketch that ribbed John McCain's television ads. "My God, Claire," shouts Intern #1, "Did you hear the word PEDOPHILE in that sketch?!" "Yes, Parker, I did," Intern #2 whines, "and I also heard the word BLACK, which means the same thing as RACISM." Before long, Parker and Claire clutch each other for dear life, tears soiling their cashmere cardigans, joyous in the discovery that they can now craft a press release in which the Coleman campaign can fairly accuse Franken of "joking about things like pedophilia and racism."

Moral outrage, gang. It happens every time candidate Franken opens his mouth. He's been known to rain spittle on the unsuspecting folks in the front row when he's really worked up. And why not? There's plenty to get worked up about these days. Do you *know* how much the value of my house has plummeted in the last week? I don't either, because I'm too frightened to find out. The financial crisis has me scared to pieces. I feel like a bunch of unregulated white guys in New York City have taken what little I own and pooped all over it. I'm pretty upset about that, actually. And I'm getting morally outraged that all of this is happening on Senatorialist Coleman's watch.

Let's recap:

Racism = not funny.

Pedophilia = not funny.

Poop = funny. I really cannot stress this enough.

What the above facts have to do with Al Franken's qualifications for the U.S. Senate = nothing.

Senatorialism = my ticket to an appearance on *The Colbert Report*, but not before I score a visit to the Coleman family dentist. My teeth are as dirty as my mouth, *honest to fucking God*.

He guessed wrong
Minnesota Women's Press, September 30, 2008

I could not wait to write about Sarah Palin in my next Women's Press column! Here's hoping that a Palin-Spears ticket happens in my lifetime.

What do women want?

Freud's not the only "wrinkly, white-haired dude" to tackle that dilemma. John McCain is just the latest person to try and fail.

Friday, August 29, was a strange day for politically engaged feminists. That morning I shared coffee and donuts with a fellow activist. "He did it," she groaned. "He put a woman on the ticket, and Obama didn't." As we worked through the Mel-O-Glaze bag, we realized that McCain wasn't going to give up Hillary Clinton fans to Obama without a fight. Good for him, we thought, for trying to find out what women want.

That evening, I shared cocktails and brownies with a group of neighborhood friends (I'm an aging riot grrrl, not a diet girl). By then a fuller picture of Palin had appeared, and McCain was no longer getting our credit: he was reaping our scorn. Palin opposes abortion rights, one of the cornerstones of the modern women's movement. Even women who might not call themselves capital-F Feminists don't want Palin's nose anywhere near their wombs.

I recently engaged in an online debate over whether reproductive freedom ought to be a centerpiece of our movement. I offered what I thought was the simplest answer: as long as women are the ones getting pregnant, women will consider reproductive decision making to be a cherished civil right. Therefore, Palin's addition to the Republican ticket can be seen as a slap in eighteen million hopeful faces.

Many male politicos and bloggers were quick to jump to Palin's defense, claiming that it was time for Hillary fans to put up or shut up. Women, they argued, wanted a woman, and they got a woman. When feminist women started to raise a fuss about Sarah Palin's views or qualifications, these men became as agitated as any of Carrie Bradshaw's ex-boyfriends. "But you *said* you would vote with your vagina," they whined. "You *said* you would, and we believed you!"

It's hard to predict the behavior of the woman voter. The Al Franken kerfuffle earlier this year was just one example. Many thought that an old freelancing job for *Playboy* would dash his Senate hopes, since women don't want men to be in the same room as that magazine, much less read it. For the few under a rock who missed that controversy, the hysterics on the right made sure that their message came across: we know more about sexism than you do. And these days it's become de rigueur for Fox News anchors to proclaim Palin a victim of the same sexist stereotypes that may have had a hand in scuttling Hillary's presidential bid.

It's an ironic stand for the right wing to take, given the fact that they are the ones who shoved Supreme Court Justices John Roberts and Samuel Alito down our throats. The latter wrote the 2007 majority opinion that negated Lily Ledbetter's successful gender pay-discrimination case. Anyone would find that pretty damned sexist, no matter where you land in the abortion debate. And of course, Alito and Roberts are no fans of *Roe v. Wade*. McCain has already promised to appoint justices made from their mold.

I wrote a column last April about my desire for a female president. Am I being inconsistent by opposing Sarah Palin's candidacy? When my column was printed, I was taken aback by how enraged folks were by the idea of casting a gendered vote. You'd think I supported the candidacy of Britney Spears, not a well-qualified woman of leadership and accomplishment. I considered Obama and Clinton, found both to be excellent candidates, and went with my gut—or rather, my genitalia. At no point did I express the wish for just *any* gal in the White House. I don't want Britney Spears, and I don't want Sarah Palin's reactionary agenda.

Indeed, that makes McCain's pick all the more painful. Did he truly consider the eighteen million votes for a staunch supporter of women's rights? Women of deliberation and critical thought won't blindly vote for lipstick. On a pit bull or a pig, it makes no difference.

And about that lipstick. Some women want it, and some women wear it. That Sarah Palin wears it has no place in the discussion of her politics. As for me, I haven't worn anything stronger than strawberry Lip Smacker in fifteen years, but you won't see me trying to outlaw Cover Girl. I said I was pro-choice, and I meant it. I'm not like Palin, who'd make sure even rape victims bear their attackers' babies. That is what John McCain thinks women want. And like Freud before him, he got us terrifically, spectacularly wrong.

Let's put the "social" in socialism!
Minnesota Women's Press, November 11, 2008

One of the funnier images I've ever created in a column has to be "my parents whispering 'trickle-down is a failure' in my crib." Ever since I explained to my children that the reason our local library's hours were slashed was the fact that our governor was a fervent believer in Reaganomics, they have been socialists themselves. In 2008 they were still too young to understand what on earth "the Great Recession" was, even though it made their parents weep every time they opened a mortgage statement.

"Our long national nightmare is over," said one former president as he spoke of another, though he could just as well have been describing what America puts itself through every leap year: madness and anarchy culminating in what is always The Most Important Election in Our Lifetime, except when it isn't. No one knows until the textbooks are printed and the verdict is complete.

By the time this column is printed, we'll have a new commander in chief. You'll be thrilled or brokenhearted. Not much will change in the short term; maybe your phone will ring less. The television will certainly shout less about the virtues of people and will return to selling the virtues of products, but will anyone notice? I consider myself as politically versed as anyone, and even I can't tell anymore. Sarah Palin will keep your hair sleek and glossy in any kind of weather! Barack Obama will lower your cholesterol by twenty points in two weeks!

One thing that probably won't change after November 4 is new interest in an old idea: socialism. To listen to right-wing radio is to learn that just the word "socialism" is so dirty that it shouldn't be used in mixed company. Smearing Obama as a modern Mao is the order of the day. But if no less a capitalist grandmaster than Alan Greenspan can admit in public that the current economic crisis is proof of a "flaw" in a solely market-driven economy, you know that we'll all be talking about this well into 2009.

I remember learning the basic framework of these economic systems in junior high school: capitalism, democratic socialism, and communism. This was in the mid-eighties, mind you, when Reagan's powerful manipulation of Cold War anxieties gave kiddos like me nightmares of Soviets charging into our homes to confiscate our decadent Duran Duran records. As fearsome as that seemed, I still connected with the idea of Western European-style socialism.

Why was there a minimum wage but not a maximum wage? Why not see health care as a right and not a privilege? My future as an at-home parent was years away (in 1985, the plan was to spend my thirties writing for *Rolling Stone*), but even then I believed in some form of compensation for home-based caregivers.

To me, this stuff seemed obvious. But other thirteen-year-olds questioned not only my sanity but also my patriotism. This puzzled me. What on earth did an economic philosophy have to do with my allegiance to my native country? I had no interest in moving to Moscow, despite their repeated urgings to the contrary.

Perhaps we are drawn to certain systems by personality, not politics. I can't recall my parents whispering "trickle-down is a failure" into my crib, yet I felt it instinctively. When said parents were in a generous mood, they acknowledged my artist's temperament; when they were grouchy, they cursed my laziness. That I grew up to admire the French should surprise no one.

Some folks achieve like mad. Why can't I prioritize my life around writing books? I am willing to trade in my need for lots of shiny new stuff for that privilege. I would just like to be sure I have a space to live and something to eat. I don't need to pull myself up by my bootstraps. Is it wrong to think that society might grant everyone a decent pair of boots?

This is not to imply that capitalists are solely interested in shiny new stuff or that socialism is inherently as godawful as talk radio would like you to think. Rush Limbaugh scared the bejeezus out of my kids when he warned on our car radio that Obama wanted to steal their Halloween candy. I reminded them that if anyone was gonna steal their Milky Ways, it was gonna be me. They felt better.

In November we think not only of elections but also of Puritans, who were kicked out of Europe for their obnoxiously busy ways. They gave America a tradition of industry (early to bed, early to rise, etc.) and judgment (thy lazy bum!). We live with this legacy every time the question "Spare some change?" is answered, "Get a job." It's not for nothing that those Puritans wore only black and white. Today, things are complicated and colorful.

So righties, cool your jets. You have nearly four hundred years of entrenched culture on your side. And lefties, giggle along with me when you imagine THE HORROR of universal health care. *Pain au chocolat*, anyone?

2009

In the kitchen with Rose and Sylvia

Though Sarah Palin was defeated in November 2008, Proposition 8 wasn't. Remember Prop 8? That's the amendment to the California constitution that banned same-sex marriage there, just six months after the California Supreme Court ruled that the existing constitution recognized marriage as a civil right. My friend Christine, who wed her girlfriend in that window of opportunity, found herself in legal limbo.

Prop 8 pushed the question of marriage equality to the forefront of the national conversation, and reaction to its passage paved the way for *United States v. Windsor*, the Supreme Court case that killed the Defense of Marriage Act, meaning that Christine's marriage would soon be legal in every state in the union!

But let's not get too ahead of ourselves, shall we? In 2009, same-sex marriage and health care reform were such hot topics that you'd think the fate of the republic rested on whether Christine's wife could rely on Christine's insurance to pay for her urgent-care visit. Thanks, Obama!

2009 is also notable for being the year that I abandoned MySpace forever. Like millions of other people in America, I switched to Facebook for day-to-day navel-gazing and LOLcat posting. My blog, at its own domain, was now a separate entity, focused less on the minutia of my life than on feminism, politics, parenthood . . . and, admittedly, more than a little navel-gazing.

This is about the time in my writing career that Matt took a look at my output and asked me why I still considered myself a novelist. Wasn't I more of an essayist now? And what would be easier and more fun to write than a memoir of my adventures as a feminist stay-at-home mom? I mean, that shit writes itself! And so *The Radical Housewife* book was conceived, by two parents who loved each other very much. Like a baby, it was a painful and expensive undertaking, and it made me cry. Unlike a baby, it gestated for five long years and wouldn't mow my lawn. Actually, my teenager doesn't do that now either . .

The price of inequality? $9,000
Radical Housewife blog, February 12, 2009

Minnesota banned same-sex marriage by state statute in 1997, one year after the federal Defense of Marriage Act was passed. Conservatives voiced support for an amendment to our state constitution that would stand up to threatened lawsuits, but our Democrat-controlled legislature squashed it every time. A small, grassroots group called Marry Me Minnesota formed around this time to start building momentum toward suing the state for marriage rights. They sponsored a rally at the capitol building just before Valentine's Day that year, and I was invited to speak on behalf of Minnesota NOW. On my blog I posted a transcript of my remarks.

I'm proud to say that my tax-stressed friend was in the audience, cheering for me as loudly as anyone! I'm very grateful that she gave me permission to share her story.

It was bad enough, my friend thought, that she had to check the TurboTax box marked "single" when she'd been happily partnered for eighteen years. That was just one psychological price to pay for being a lesbian in Minnesota. Another was the fear of meeting the fate of Kristen Boyne, the Minneapolis woman who was beaten into unconsciousness in January by two men regaling her with anti-gay slurs.

But as she finished filing her taxes, she wondered: is there another price, a measurable price? With the easy TurboTax program, she ought to be able to find out. She went back and made one simple change. She checked the box marked "married." How much was she being penalized by not being able to file jointly with her partner?

The amount: *nine thousand dollars.* She nearly fainted at her computer. Then she called me.

She called because her family and mine are very much alike. Both consist of two parents and young children. Both sets of parents include one wage earner and one at-home caregiver. The wage earners earn comparable salaries, affording their families a solidly middle-class lifestyle.

The difference? In my family, the wage earner is a man. In 1999, this man and I entered into a civil marriage contract with the state of Minnesota. Since then, the state has extended us the privilege of filing taxes jointly, in addition to many other tax perks that only an accountant and TurboTax fully understand. The result is a system that not only denies a committed couple the opportunity to marry, but charges them $9,000 besides. That's not fair.

As long as marriage confers civil benefits, it must not discriminate.
Ever.
Thank you.

Feminist housewives reclaim the kitchen
Minnesota Women's Press, February 25, 2009

In 2009 the Minnesota Women's Press *transitioned from a biweekly newspaper to a monthly magazine with themed issues. The new editors asked if I would consider writing a feature article on the topic of "home." I think they could hear my excited screams across the river at their offices in St. Paul. Any time I can connect feminist analysis to pop culture movements to my own family, I'm in my element.*

This essay was picked up by the national independent news aggregator AlterNet. *On the latter site, a disgruntled second-wave feminist objected to my use of the word "housewife," which she found offensive. I was a "homemaker," she corrected, just like Sue Ann Nivens. Whatever.*

When my beloved Grandma Rose died in 2003 at the age of 89, it made sense that my eulogy at her memorial service opened this way: My grandmother is the smell of butter.

For she was. Even today, when I smell onions browning in the stuff, or I get a bite of a homemade cookie baked with the real thing, not Crisco, I think of her. Grandma Rose was my first model of a twentieth-century housewife. She raised six kids, cooked and baked like a champ, sewed whatever needed sewing, gossiped with the neighborhood gals, and scrubbed everything in her path to a squeaky, sparkling clean. But, as much as I adored her, I never wanted to do what she did for a living.

I saw other housewives in action on channel 9's late-night rerun lineup: *I Love Lucy, Dick Van Dyke,* and *Mary Tyler Moore.* The shows' respective housewives, Lucy Ricardo, Laura Petrie, and Sue Ann Nivens (who adopted the moniker The Happy Homemaker despite being unhappily unmarried), were all completely nuts. In fact, one could watch the latter two shows and imagine the feminist trajectory of Mary Tyler Moore, as she dumped her boring kitchen in New Rochelle for the independence of paid work in Minneapolis. I sure did. I didn't go to Carleton College for my MRS degree, thank you very much.

But guess who ended up in Rose's profession anyway? Me. I'm a housewife, too.

There are essential differences between us, however. Easy access to effective contraception limited my brood to two. I thaw most of our family's meals, but my homemade banana bread is the envy of the neighborhood. My sewing is limited to replacing buttons. I adore gossip in all forms, but I do less of it over picket fences than I do online.

And online is a terrific place to argue the merits and limitations of the next generation of at-home caregivers, SAHMs (that's stay-at-home moms), and homemakers, happy or otherwise.

Where else can you angrily debate The Right Thing To Do? Whether Linda Hirshman, whose 2006 book orders women to *Get to Work . . . and Get a Life Before It's Too Late,* is a prophet or a kook? (For the record, I put her in the latter category.)

Phony or no, the mommy wars are here to stay, due in no small part to the exalted place that the mother plays in American cultural mythology. When we think of that iconic mother, we don't see her in a power suit. We see her in an apron.

My grandma Rose sewed her own. So does Charlot Meyer, a Woodbury-based graphic artist who sells her recreations of vintage aprons in the online marketplace Etsy. Said Meyer of her aprons, "I like the idea of [the apron] moving from a utilitarian garment to a fashion accessory. Women today are busier than ever at home and work. There's no reason why we can't have fun and be fashionable in our family life." But one woman's necessity (Rose needed to keep flour off her dress) is another woman's ball and chain (legendary women's libber Betty Friedan) and another woman's fashion (Meyer's customers today). How can a few pieces of fabric say so much?

Historian Glenna Matthews suggests in her book *"Just a Housewife": The Rise and Fall of Domesticity in America,* that the emotional loading of motherhood was a necessary byproduct of the new consumer culture of the early twentieth century. Thanks to technological advances, basic household functions were now done by machines, not hands. Thus a great portion of the housewife's justification for existence vanished. Matthews argues that women had to be newly convinced of their emotional utility to the American family. By 1920, any idiot could buy a machine-sewn apron from a retail store, and advertisers knew it.

In 1963, New Jersey housewife Betty Friedan's book *The Feminine Mystique* sounded the alarm that domestic complacency was doing just that: turning women into idiots. You know what happened then. Friedan kick-started feminism's second wave, and millions of women threw their emotionally loaded aprons into the trash.

How fascinating, then, that the third wave of feminists, the women of Generation X and the riot grrrl movements of the 1990s, never met a womanly art they didn't like. The quintessentially third-wave magazine *Bust*, whose founder Debbie Stoller holds a PhD in women's psychology from Yale, has hipster fashion spreads, celebrity interviews, and sex-toy ads sharing space with craft tips, apron patterns, and comfort-food recipes from the staff's mothers and grandmothers.

Many of the new wave of women stitchers and bakers see kitchen work as the reclamation of a lost culture that belonged only to women. The clothing follows suit: what a dashiki might be to a Black Panther, an apron might be to a feminist blogger of the twenty-first century.

I wish I could ask what my grandma Rose would think of all this, but I can't. My sadness over losing this part of my "herstory" could explain why I find myself inexplicably drawn to aprons as lovely and familiar as Charlot Meyer's.

"[My aprons] evoke memories of my grandmother, who never was seen without an apron," Meyer said, "and my mother, who owned a sewing shop and made most of my clothes when I was young."

One of my favorite cookbooks, *How it All Vegan*, was written by two Canadian women who pose on the cover in adorable vintage housedresses (full disclosure, neighborhood: this book is the source of my banana-bread recipe).

Coauthor Sarah Kramer accentuates hers with a double strand of pearls, several large tattoos, and a lip ring. The look is a conscious attempt to link the DIY ethos of the punk movement with the gotta-do-it-yourself reality of the mid-century housewife. Ladies, we can have it all!

Veganism is something my Grandma Rose just couldn't get. As I mentioned before, butter was the woman's natural milieu; I think she probably dabbed it behind her ears. She was born in 1914 into a North Dakota farm family where home cooking wasn't a lifestyle "choice." The only choices she knew were to cook or starve. Rose left North Dakota during the Great Depression, when the latter option seemed increasingly likely.

Grandma Rose loved her family, but we all knew that she hadn't opted out of paid work, as Hirshman tells you I did. Rose never had the opportunity to opt *in*. I often wonder whether she'd be proud of me or just really confused. With so many career options, she might wonder, why on earth would Shannon choose this one?

One part of my job involves taking my three-year-old daughter, Miriam, to a park-board dance class. I recently witnessed two moms put the staff through its paces about the amount of trans fat lurking in the park's popcorn machine. Nowadays it is not enough to cook; one must cook *properly*. Their sons, Parker and Hunter, cannot be allowed to eat that kind of poison, no matter how much they crave it.

Grandma Rose made popcorn better than anyone. A huge iron pot soaked in vegetable oil popped the corn, then melted the stick of butter that she'd drizzle onto our bowls. She handed us terrycloth towels to wipe off our fingers. Yummy.

Cultural movements, like everything else, are cyclical. Rose was at the beck and call of her large family, making popcorn when they wanted it the only way she knew how. My working mom, a second-wave feminist, taught us to toss prepackaged bags into the microwave if we were hungry after school. Today those bags are known to be unhealthy at best and carcinogenic at worst. Hunter's mom will cook him homemade popcorn with organic everything. Which way is the Right Way To Do It? I don't know. Friedan and Matthews suggest that our culture has a stake in keeping us doubtful about every choice we make, even going so far as to obscure whether or not we have one.

For as far as Friedan's movement has taken us, statistics don't lie. [White] women's paychecks are still short twenty-three cents for every dollar earned by a [white] man. Child-care costs in Minnesota are estimated to be as high as $11,000 per year. Mathematics proves that our playing fields still aren't level.

Yet I'm proud that I could put all my college writing skills to work eulogizing a woman who was one hell of a grandmother and housewife. In that eulogy, I noted a truth that would seem shocking if uttered about a mother of a different generation: I can't remember Grandma Rose ever telling me she loved me. That stern North Dakota mien never left her. She showed me, though, in her amazing cooking. I returned her affection by eating.

The perils of procreation
Radical Housewife blog, April 9, 2009

Nicholas Hughes, son of the writer and feminist icon Sylvia Plath, hanged himself in his Fairbanks, Alaska, home on March 16, 2009. I was fascinated by discussions surrounding his suicide, especially the idea that people suffering from mental illness ought not to have children. I even went back and reread Ariel, *but more on that later.*

Even before I scored Sylvia Plath on the "What crazy bitch are you?" Facebook quiz, the recent suicide of her son has been on my mind. The good ladies of Jezebel.com used the occasion of Nicholas Hughes's death to open a discussion on whether those with mental illness feel that it's appropriate to have children, given the likelihood of the disease being passed on. The commenters fell out predictably.

PRO-KIDS: Good lord, no one knows what combination of DNA you'll pass on. Don't be so hard on yourselves. Parenting is a big fat crapshoot. So breed if you want to and don't worry about it!

ANTI-KIDS: Good lord, I am miserable enough without taking on this load of guilt. No way would I hang this noose around my own child's neck. This dies with me.

It should be noted that Nicholas Hughes left behind no partner and no children. Sylvia, on the other hand, had been suicidal since her college years and still had two kids. Why?

I suppose I picked a side when I had a biological child nine years ago, but the decision was not an educated one. Would I have listened to a reasoned argument on the matter, though? Did someone try to talk some sense into Sylvia Plath? She seems like a pretty clear-cut argument for not procreating. But who am I to judge what makes a life worth living? Sylvia's daughter seems to be doing okay. Nicholas Hughes seemed okay too, until he quit his professorship to become a potter, then hanged himself.

Parenthood is so terrifying.

Bristol needs a condom for her mouth
Radical Housewife blog, May 22, 2009

This week in history, Sarah Palin's eldest daughter appeared on the cover of People *magazine in her high school graduation gown, cuddling her son Tripp like he was a gift someone had dropped off at the ceremony. I don't doubt her love for her child, but her hypocrisy was stunning then, and it's even funnier now that she's given birth to her second child outside the bonds of holy matrimony! I sure hope she's figured out how condoms work by now.*

Am I reading this magazine pull-quote correctly? Did Bristol Palin really say "If girls realized the consequences of sex, nobody would be having sex. . . . trust me. Nobody."

So. Much. Wrong. Where to begin?

My first beef is with her statement, which reinforces the age-old stereotype of the girls being the ones in charge of stopping hockey players from coming all over them. HEY, BRISTOL! It's the twenty-first century. Boys can take care of their needs the old-fashioned way—the blue-ball story is fake. Boys are also perfectly capable of going to the Rite Aid and buying a pack of Trojans themselves.

Which leads me to my second beef. Bristol, after all you've been through, are you still going to tell your peers that they should just say no? Wouldn't it be more responsible to say, "Look everyone, I realize how horny teens can be. If you're too embarrassed for mutual masturbation, how can you be too embarrassed to buy some condoms at Rite Aid? Wake up!"

But alas, Alaska's First Teen Mom has chosen to have it both ways: to act like she's a lesson in what not to do while using her cute baby as a fashion accessory. If Bristol wants to keep it real, she should be on the cover with baby Tripp squirting yellow shits all over her J. Crew sweater. She should have a photograph of him gnawing her tits bloody to get a drink of milk. To judge by this photograph, a plump baby boy is what all Alaskan teens are carrying with them at their graduation ceremonies! After all, they're much cuter than corsages!

A Court like our country
Radical Housewife blog, May 27, 2009

I admit it—at one time I was a fairly regular listener of Rush Limbaugh. He was such a great source of blog ideas! This particular post was inspired by how offensive it was to that old white man that Obama did not *nominate an old white man to the Supreme Court when old white man David Souter announced his retirement. I no longer listen to Rush, not even for opposition research, and my health is the better for it.*

May I reiterate a point I've made in the past? Those that cry, "I'm not a racist" the loudest are the biggest racists you'll ever meet. Those who wail, "I'm not sexist" are often worse.

I'm hearing so much bullshit on the air and on the web about how Sonia Sotomayor is a pawn in Obama's hands and how Obama is pandering to the country by appointing a justice who is both female *and* Hispanic. Sotomayor herself has admitted that her gender and ethnicity color (pun intended) her opinions, striking terror in the hearts of white men everywhere.

For once and for all, people, this is *not* pandering! It is completely fair to expect that my governmental institutions look like my country. The 2000 census reported that 12.5 percent of Americans identify as Hispanic. What's 12.5 percent of nine?

Don't ask *me*. I was an English major!

One bit of math that my pretty little head *can* calculate easily is the ratio of men and women in our society. I guesstimate that it's somewhere around. . . oh. . . fifty-fifty. Sonia Sotomayor will be the third woman in the history of our nation to serve on Supreme Court. When she's appointed, she will be Justice #111. There's that math again. . . what's three out of 111, percentage-wise?

Oh golly. I wish that white man I married were here so he could explain it all to me.

Connecting the dots in the culture wars
Radical Housewife blog, June 5 2009

On May 31, 2009, Dr. George Tiller was shot to death in his Topeka, Kansas, church by Scott Roeder, a known domestic terrorist who announced that his actions saved *"preborn children."* Never mind that Dr. Tiller had four *post-born children of his own*, as well as ten *post-born grandchildren*. Those facts never seem to count with antiabortion wackos.

Today, what started as simple clenching of my jaw over how impossibly sexist and racist people can be in the twenty-first century has turned into a deeper examination of my own furious impulses.

Specifically, how much I want to join an army of fierce radical feminists who will show Pat Buchanan exactly what it feels like to be oppressed. First we will cripple his self-esteem with a tape loop telling him how dumb and ugly he is, then we will hint that if he doesn't dress a certain way, he'll get raped. This will scare him to pieces and render him a powerless, anxiety-plagued mess. Hee-hee.

But good sense has prevailed, and I will not be forming such an army after all. I think it will make a better comic book. Feminist artists may contact me on this site anytime.

I picked Pat as my fantasy target because his terror over a Hispanic woman on the Supreme Court is palpable. But it's also infectious. Do you think someone like Scott Roeder was in his audience that day? His mug shot is terrifying. His eyes look defiant. He's even clenching his jaw, poor guy. Poor *oppressed minority* guy.

While abortion clinics and their staff and patients are targets of harassment, no one has died in the abortion wars in a decade. Why now? Why did Scott Roeder decide to kill Dr. George Tiller? Why *now*? Let's see....

Pat Buchanan: Sotomayor "practices race discrimination against white males."

Glenn Beck: Sotomayor is a "racist" who is "not that bright."

Rush Limbaugh: Sotomayor is a "reverse racist" and a "hack."

G. Gordon Liddy: Sotomayor is a "racist" who bleeds monthly and doesn't die.

All of this commentary, mind you, started pouring from the mouths of white men in the days following Sotomayor's nomination on Tuesday, May 26. George Tiller was assassinated in his church on the morning of Sunday, May 31.

Scott Roeder has furious impulses—you can see them all over his face. What *could* have set them off?

What we don't talk about when we talk about health care
Radical Housewife blog, August 9, 2009

Everyone agreed that the United States needed to reform its health care system; no one could agree on how to do it. Americans are loathe to talk honestly about death and economic class, even when the stakes aren't as high.

The high school friend I mention here passed away in 2012. I have yet to attend the funeral of anyone in my age group who died of heart disease.

Not long ago, Matt looked up from the newspaper and said, "It says here that heart disease is the leading cause of death in this country. If that's true, then why do we know so many people with cancer?"

Good question. I wondered if it was because of our demographics—as thirtysomethings, we tend to hang with folks whose cholesterol profiles have not yet caught up with them. We eat cheese and drink beer with abandon. "That still doesn't explain all the cancer," he grumped.

This weekend Matt is on the East Coast visiting a good friend and cancer survivor. It is a trip I made several times myself before my own East Coast friend succumbed to the disease in late 2007. This week alone we experienced both of cancer's violent extremes: a diagnosed family member received wonderful PET scan results, while an old friend from high school had a five-hour operation to remove a tumor from her brain.

I'm at a breaking point. I AM QUITE LITERALLY SICK TO DEATH OF ALL THIS CANCER. It doesn't help that the national nightmare that is health care reform in this country has brought end-of-life care and medical rationing into the debate.

I keep having flashbacks to the one time I accompanied Liz on her chemo day at the Dana Farber Cancer Institute in Boston. One tiny positive through her whole ordeal was the fact that her insurance picked up the tab for all her treatments. Avastin alone, she gasped, would cost over a hundred grand to someone who didn't have insurance. Liz had Avastin and a seemingly endless string of chemo drugs in addition to radiation, several surgeries, and many long hospital stays.

Liz was 33½ years old at the time of her diagnosis. She died two years later. How much did those two years cost her insurers? I don't know. What would it cost *not* to pay for them?

Take a guess. It's been nearly two years since she died, and I can't type this without feeling the too-familiar panicky clutch in my chest, the stinging tears welling up in my eyes. I would do anything, *anything*, to have her back again.

I think about her a lot. At times I smile when I think of the venom she would spew at those who believed that a single-payer system would limit access to the treatments that kept her alive—she knew that these treatments were out of most people's reach already! Liz knew that our health care system was a moral disgrace. She had no doubt that thousands of other people with colon cancer would have *loved* to sit in her chemo chair at Dana Farber but couldn't.

She knew those people would die more quickly, less hopefully, and certainly a hell of a lot poorer than she would.

Of course, she never planned on dying at all. I last spoke to her in October 2007, when she called from her hospital bed to wish me a happy birthday. She sounded frail, both physically and mentally. I was too afraid to ask about this strange thing called "end-of-life care," and she never mentioned it. All I could tell her was that I loved her, and that would have to be enough. She died two weeks later.

What *don't* we talk about when we talk about health care? Death. Money. Economic class. Equality or the lack thereof. Fear. Mortality. Losing the illusion of control that we all hold so dear.

I can't think about "health care reform" and not think about *all the fucking cancer*. I can't hear "end of life" and think that death is going to happen to someone else. Death is coming, and death is real. Death is in the future for you, me, my children, President Obama, Rush Limbaugh, and everyone who panics at the idea of a single-payer system. Death is a certainty. No one can escape it. The existence of death ought to humble us and make us more respectful of life. After all, if a dying woman can muster the strength to give a shit about the uninsured, why can't everyone else?

"We the People, in order to breed more well-armed Citizens…"

Radical Housewife blog, August 18, 2009

Momentum was building for marriage equality, both in Minnesota and across the country, and conservatives were getting very nervous. Even libertarians had to invent reasons why the government had to intervene. This was just a preview of the poisonous culture war that Minnesota would endure before making history in 2012 . . . but we'll get to that in time.

As I've written before, I like listening to right-wing talk radio. I live in a safe, liberal bubble here in South Minneapolis, and I feel it's important to peep outside my comfort zone from time to time.

My favorite right-wing nut is Rush Limbaugh, of course, but on yesterday's drive to Target, the host was the Twin Cities–based conservative who fills in for Rush on occasion, the one and only Jason Lewis. I find Lewis fascinating. He's an avowed libertarian, and I have no problem with libertarians: I find them to be a remarkably consistent bunch, and consistency is something I respect. To libertarians, a small federal government will keep its nose out of your health care AND your personal life.

So I was somewhat shocked to hear Lewis contort all reason in his attempt to justify the federal Defense of Marriage Act. He acknowledged that the act infringed upon the rights of states to determine how they wish to recognize civil marriage, and libertarians *love* them some states' rights. I stayed glued to my radio in the Target parking lot while Lewis declared that civil marriage for heterosexuals existed because the state needs to offer this benefit to give folks incentives for having children. The state, he argues, offers this carrot to heterosexuals because a mommy and a daddy are just naturally better at raising kids.

Did I miss something in American history class? "We the People, in order to breed more well-armed Citizens, shall offer Tax Breaks that are significant, in addition to Inheritance Rights and Health Coverage (through Employers only) to one Man and one Member of the weaker Sex entering into a civil Marriage Contract with this federal Government. Amen."

I have heard a lot of stupid ideas on the radio, but this one really took the cake. I thought about my neighbors across the alley from me, who have enjoyed the benefits of civil marriage for twenty years without producing a single new taxpayer. I thought about the millions of children removed from the homes of abusive, neglectful, heterosexual parents, many of them married! Mostly, I became blind with rage when I thought about my two best friends and the insinuation that that they can't raise their three kids as well as Matt and I raise our two.

I remember well the time Kelly sat in our living room and recounted with exhaustion the years, tears, and big bucks she and her partner had gone through to become parents. "And all *you two* have to do is screw!" she laughed, but I understood her bitterness. Gays and lesbians have to work a hell of a lot harder to become parents: they have to *want* it. Practically speaking, a child would do better to be raised by an adult for whom parenthood is not a surprise, but a considered life choice.

Speaking of choice, I became far more convinced of the mantra "every child a wanted child" when I had a squalling infant at home. If you're not mentally prepared for the pure hell on earth that is caring for a baby, you're going to fuck it up. I daresay that the obstacles facing gay and lesbian parents make them better qualified for the job than quite a lot of breeder parents. They have to *want* it.

In other news, some more nuts are unhappy that the Obama administration is not taking procreation into account in its defense of DOMA. Others, like me, are pissed that the Obama administration is defending DOMA at all.

I think it might be best to turn off the radio for a while, crawl back into my bubble, and hide.

Summer babies

Radical Housewife blog, September 5, 2009

Every fall there's a new crop of summer babies entering colleges large and small. It's hard to believe that most of the children who heard me speak on that panel are now U of M alumni, and even harder to believe that I'm already getting mailings about attending my twenty-fifth Carleton reunion. In my mind I remain a hormonal nineteen-year-old—just don't ask me to make you a Spotify playlist or whatever kids do these days. Mixtapes forever!

Yesterday, in my role as Minnesota NOW President, I participated in a panel discussion on "Gender, Sexuality, and Equality" as part of the University of Minnesota's Welcome Week. These three fascinating topics were completely overpowered by the combined hormonal energy of one hundred eighteen-year-olds.

The whole of the student center was about to go nuclear from the potent mix of naïveté, fear, curiosity, and horniness they radiated. Some of them had parents trailing along in their wake, carrying heavy suitcases and overstuffed bags from the bookstore and looking every bit as shell-shocked as I was. It's exhausting just to be around them.

When I was safely back in my car, the one that's mine and not my mother's, I decided to visit my own college nostalgia via iPod. Pavement's *Slanted and Enchanted* seemed the obvious choice. "Summer Babe" was a song that led off two separate mixtapes made for me by two different shy, brown-haired boys during my college years, only one of whom was rewarded with some foolin' around for his trouble. The other never got a chance, because by the time I met him in person (long story) I was happily dating a different shy, brown-haired boy. It was in college when I realized that I had a type.

When Matt and I met in 1997, I made a mixtape for him, but he didn't like it and told me so. This is when I realized that there was more to a relationship than sharing the same taste. Hell, there was more to it than horniness, more to it than true love even. Matt respected me, so he told me the truth. This blew my mind so intensely that I had to marry him.

A woman on yesterday's panel from OutFront Minnesota joked that passing a "Do you like me?" note in fourth grade is one way of questioning one's sexuality. She paused and added, "Do people still do that anymore? I guess you all just text each other nowadays." I don't need to go back to Coffman Union to find out that kids these days don't do mixtapes. Where would you buy the tapes? The players? The only player in our house is in Miriam's room, part of her Hello Kitty CD player. I use it to play the few cherished tapes I saved from my youth, including one that kicks off with "Summer Babe," then continues with a heady mid-nineties swirl of shoegazers, Britpop, and Uncle Tupelo. I looked for its maker on Facebook but couldn't find him.

While I was educating these teenagers on the finer points of feminism and social justice, I kept thinking about how I had felt during the New Student Week I went through nineteen years ago, and how much I had hated every minute of it. My first year of college was an unmitigated disaster, and not simply because my boyfriend that year was blond. That was the year I did absolutely everything wrong. I wish I could say that the following year I did everything right—it's closer to the truth to say that I got extremely lucky that year when I met the friends I still cherish today.

Oh, summer babies! You who wear the maroon and gold shirts emblazoned CLASS OF 2013! Who am I to tell you anything? You won't listen.

You'll fuck up as badly as I did. Then you'll pick yourself up, make a few MP3 mixes about it, and get on with your life.

Good luck.

On 9/11
Radical Housewife blog, September 11, 2009
My "Where were you that day?" post. I was correct about Bush and Cheney, but I take no joy in it.

I can honestly brag that on September 10, 2001, I was one of the few Americans who knew about the Taliban regime in Afghanistan. A back issue of *Bust* had given them an entire page, an odd thing in a magazine that celebrates fashion more than politics. The tone of the piece mixed horror and outrage with confusion, as though the author wasn't quite certain that this was for real, that the regime hadn't been invented by a sci-fi writer as a post-apocalyptic cautionary tale. I mean, shit, women couldn't even show their eyes in public! Margaret Atwood's Handmaids could do that!

The next day, my eyes burned from the horror of watching people die on live television. I was grateful that Elliott was only eighteen months old and I wouldn't have the additional burden of explaining this madness to him.

After we put our son to bed, Matt and I sat in the basement to watch TV so that my sobs and our collective howls of outrage wouldn't reach the crib on the second floor. By that night the word was that this horrific violence was the work of some creep with a funny name who was associated with the Taliban. "I hope we burn that country to the fucking ground," I growled, until file footage of Afghani women came onscreen. They looked like aliens, truly. But underneath, they were women like me. I cried even harder when I realized what my statement of anger would mean for them. How could I wish suffering upon them? There was far too much pain in the world already.

That Christmas, instead of family gifts, Matt and I made a substantial donation to the Revolutionary Association of the Women of Afghanistan (RAWA), the group mentioned in the *Bust* article. If you go to RAWA's website, you'll see that today they have two enemies: the Taliban and the United States. From a December 2007 press release: "…the U.S. government first of all considers her own political and economic interests and has empowered and equipped the most traitorous, anti-democratic, misogynist, and corrupt fundamentalist gangs in Afghanistan."

The ongoing war in Afghanistan has split the already fractured American feminist community. A RAWA member took Eleanor Smeal's Feminist Majority Foundation to task this summer for its outspoken support of the U.S. military's so-called peacekeeping forces (an oxymoron if I ever heard one). And others, many far more eloquent than I am, have pointed out that September 11, 2001, was an opportunity for worldwide healing that got lost in a heated rush to consolidate power. My children will understand George W. Bush and Dick

Cheney as two of the most ruthless, despicable people in the history of our nation. Of this I have no doubt whatsoever.

People lose their lives, families lose their loved ones, and people lose hope for a future that can be just and humane. I could lose my mind if I write any more.

Reclaiming Mama Plath: A new review of *Ariel, The Restored Edition* and *The Complete Poems*
Literary Mama, November 22, 2009

The culmination of hours of brooding over Sylvia Plath, her children, and her legacy is this long essay, published in the online journal Literary Mama. *It's another one of my favorites.*

It took the tragedy of Nicholas Hughes's March 16, 2009, suicide to bring his mother Sylvia Plath back to the popular spotlight. The media buzzed with what it was all about—famous parents and the shadows they cast, mental illness and its inheritability, and whether anyone, gifted or not, can escape the demons of the past.

When I read Nicholas's obituary, my heart broke. I had forgotten about how much Sylvia Plath's writing had once meant to me, let alone that she had been a mother of two children when she died. Nicholas was barely past his first birthday when Plath sealed him and his sister into their bedrooms so the poison gas wouldn't hurt them.

I decided to read the poetry of Sylvia Plath, this time as a mother. I found a whole new writer, a whole new person coming to life in her words. I saw my own demons being wrestled into submission on one page but emerging victorious on others. I saw my children's flesh and mine, the blood and guts and tears and passionate love and sorrow: in short, I saw all the stuff of motherhood boiled down to incredibly moving art.

As a teenager, I had been moved by her work for other reasons. As had hordes of sensitive girls before me, I devoured the stars of the Plath canon: *The Bell Jar*, *The Collected Poems*, and especially *Ariel*. In the novel, I recognized Esther's profound alienation as my own. I was no middle-class princess, either, and I also failed to connect with the handful of my school's nerdy punks who ought to have been my friends. I sensed early on that the inexplicable rage I possessed was not welcome anywhere. In *Ariel*, I saw rage as a thing of beauty, careening from mournful to manic and back again, Plath's voice by turns vengeful and funny, breaking and broken. As much as I adored Holden Caulfield, his obsession with phonies shriveled beside *Ariel*'s power. I loved it.

The legendary backstory of *Ariel*'s first publication in 1965, two years after Plath's suicide, also appealed to the black-and-white perceptions of the typical teen. Plath was separated, but not divorced, from her philandering husband Ted Hughes at the time of her death, so her literary estate became his. As the story goes, Hughes found the original manuscript of *Ariel* so horribly unflattering that he reedited it to his liking. In an even greater affront to Plath fans, he burned the journal she had kept in the final month of her life. Whether or not Hughes's self-absorption had destroyed Plath's life could be debated; less debatable was the fact that this same narcissism had destroyed her art. This jibed with my experience of the world; teenage boys were heartless, egotistical creeps.

But by the ripe old age of nineteen, I sensed my world changing. I assumed I must abandon drama so that my intellectual self could flower. Plath's books gathered dust at my parents' house while I studied literature at Carleton College. I wrote dispassionate papers on Hemingway's neutered male heroes while blasting Bikini Kill, whose singer Kathleen Hanna referenced Plath's suicide directly in a song called "Bloody Ice Cream" that challenged the idea that "to be a girl poet means you have to die."

The riot grrrl movement rejected the romanticism of self-destruction that had so thrilled me as I read "Lady Lazarus." Hanna, riot grrrl's de facto spokeswoman, urged her fans to point their rage outward, not inward. Third-wave feminists had no use for Sylvia Plath, for we maintained that feminist art must have destruction of the patriarchy, destruction of the self, as its goal. Anyway, Plath-style anguish felt so dull and old-fashioned in the Clinton era—it was more fun to critique sexual roles in Madonna's "Express Yourself" video. No wonder I left my books at my parents' house so long that they gave them to Goodwill.

Much has changed since Plath killed herself, and much has not. Mothers have lots of options, including tearing each other apart in a little cultural clash known as the Mommy Wars. Anyone with a laptop, a modem, and a WordPress account can call themselves a writer, and mothers of young children are no exception. But the crap we plow through every day isn't any easier forty years on. Children fail to complete us; spouses behave like jerks; mental illness courses through a great portion of our population; emotional bravery is still ridiculed while cold snark is king.

The Sylvia Plath story deserves redefining. Moms, I suggest a fresh riot is in order: a movement to reclaim Plath's poetry, to use her art as a tool in our search to reach the truth about our own fractured lives.

I didn't realize until after the death of Plath's son that the momentum behind *Ariel* and her final poems had risen from Plath's conflicted emotions about domestic life. I had to hit up the library to reread Plath again, and there I found that in 2004, Plath's daughter Frieda Hughes had authorized a new edition of *Ariel*, with the poems arranged in the order her mother had left behind.

As grown-ups, we understand shades of gray at work in our relationships. Still, it's hard not to hate Ted Hughes a little for his fumbling attempts to reframe their life together. Their messy marriage provided a lasting archetype for scholars of feminism's second wave, for whom Sylvia was a martyr to compulsory heterosexuality and its pitiable consequence, motherhood.

As a teenager, I never thought about this. Frieda and Nicholas, as children, didn't really exist; they could have been extended metaphors, for all I knew. Rereading the poetry makes me feel very stupid indeed. *Ariel*, in both versions, begins with the poem "Morning Song." Its opening stanza is as follows:

> *Love set you going like a fat gold watch.*
> *The midwife slapped your footsoles, and your bald cry*
> *Took its place among the elements.*

In the image I saw my newborn daughter Miriam's bloodstained body being kneaded into her first breath by the team of doctors who feared that meconium could be lodged in her throat. She gasped for air; she gagged; she began. My god, I gasped at the page beneath my hand, Sylvia's writing about childbirth! Even the term "midwife" had failed to jog me out of my insulated teenage stupor. Sylvia as mother hadn't existed any more than Lady Lazarus herself had lived outside of the poet's prodigious imagination.

Today I am thirty-seven, six years older than Plath at the time of her death, and I am an at-home mom myself, trying to keep up my writing while I raise a son and a daughter. *Ariel* and *Collected Poems*, read through the lens of motherhood, reveal far more than the either/or paradigm common to teenagers and second-wave scholars. A close reading of her early poetry cannot fail to reveal her deep longing for love and for motherhood, a need that cannot be dismissed in solely political terms. If today we understand homosexuality as biologically based, we might give heterosexuality the same break. Sylvia Plath wanted to marry Ted Hughes, and she wanted to have children with him. At the same time, she wanted to be a world-class poet. She needed these things, and she fought like hell to get them.

But I get ahead of myself—so-called "choice" feminism of the postmillennial age still doesn't apply to the Hughes family, created as it was in the dark years before *The Feminine Mystique* (published exactly eight days after Plath's suicide in February 1963). Her husband's intellectual equal, Sylvia was nevertheless expected to raise the babies and type his manuscripts while balancing her own work in the little time left over. Sound familiar, gentle readers?

I'm neither gifted enough to earn a Pulitzer nor mad enough to stick my head in the oven. My feminist husband does dishes and laundry. Still, her rage is once again my own. I love being a mother, and I really fucking hate it. I struggle daily to balance the intellectual requirements of a writing career with the brain-sucking boredom of peanut-butter sandwiches, nose wiping, and *Barney*.

Any reader, be she teenage, motherly, feminist, or otherwise, understands that Sylvia Plath's poetry confronts ugly realities. Her gift to us today is speaking the scary truths of motherhood four decades before memoir gags such as *I Was a Good Mother Before I Had Children*. Plath wanted a baby, but not simply for its own sake—she lapped up baby myths as well as any Yummy Mummy. In

1956, four years before Frieda's birth, she wrote "Two Sisters of Persephone," in which one luscious, fertile sister "bears a king" from the seed of the sun. The other?

> *The other, wry virgin to the last,*
> *Goes graveyard with flesh laid waste,*
> *Worm-husbanded, yet no woman.*

Years later, in baby Frieda's "Morning Song," Plath notes the change in her body (she is "cow-heavy") but laments that she has not undergone the expected transformation of her soul:

> *I'm no more your mother*
> *Than the cloud that distils a mirror to reflect its own slow*
> *Effacement at the wind's hand.*

Two days later, as dated by *Collected Poems*, Plath would write a scathing rebuttal to her own insecurities entitled "Barren Woman." She obsessed over what made a woman true, no more or less than readers of *Cosmopolitan* or Feministing.com do today. In "Persephone" and other early poems, she imbued the condition of motherhood with mystery that no baby could hope to recreate. We postmillennial feminists grapple today with the fact that babies don't make a woman "normal," prevailing cultural attitudes notwithstanding. Babies make a woman a mother, neither good nor bad. Babies withhold judgment. Their job is to get their primal needs met without delay, not to make us feel good about ourselves. Lesser minds than Plath's have been utterly confounded, if not destroyed, by this.

As much as I had adored the prickly wit of "Lady Lazarus" and "Daddy," I had seen fit to hang just one of Plath's poems, "Child," on the wall above my teenage desk, the place where I scribbled out my own contributions to the high school literary magazine.

> *Your clear eye is the one absolutely beautiful thing.*
> *I want to fill it with color and ducks,*
> ...
> *Not this troublous*
> *Wringing of hands, this dark*
> *Ceiling without a star.*

I had loved this poem when I was a child myself, if a sixteen-year-old can be called that; at my desk in the basement, I had felt my life to be ceilinged and starless, due in no small part to the chronic mental illness ravaging my own mother. I had adored this poem and must have seen it every day, but until I flipped through the dusty library copy of *Collected Poems*, I had forgotten it completely. I had also failed to notice that this poem had been written only two weeks before Plath died, on January 28, in a single day of intense creativity that also produced "The Munich Mannequins," which opens with the following declaration: "perfection is terrible, it cannot have children." In one day, the author swung from existential mothering despair to the self-righteousness typical of the worst combatants in the Mommy Wars. I hear Plath telling herself, again, that motherhood, with all its imperfections, will give her the psychic energy to rise above Holden's phonies. As always, the level of her desperation reveals the depth of her doubt.

Today, my mother and I are estranged. She clings stubbornly to her version of my youth, in which I danced among rainbows, free of troubles and care, ignoring completely the effect her illness may have had on our family. Her revision of our history continued into my adulthood, until the ensuing dissonance became too oppressive to endure. The heartbreak of discovering the depth of the chasm between expectations and reality is at the heart of Sylvia Plath's finest poetry.

Frieda Hughes, the "fat gold watch" baby, introduces the restored *Ariel* with an essay seething with hostility toward the scholars who've explained her mother for so long. It's certainly understandable. Would you want an anonymous graduate student to explain the mystery and motivation of your mother? To tell you that rigid political structures made her abandon you, even though you needed her so? Children never like it when their parents are revealed to be active humans with a consciousness separate from theirs, any more than parents enjoy it when their children pull away. Mothers and children lose each other every day, in ways both dramatic (gas ovens) and subtle (dishonesty).

Now Frieda's brother is gone, too. The temptation to write Nicholas Hughes's post-mortem in his mother's poetry is irresistible. Sylvia expressed so much hope for him in her poems, as though the hypnotic rhythm of her verse could create the safety that she failed to secure for him.

O love, how did you get here?
O embryo

Remembering, even in sleep,
Your crossed position.
The blood blooms clean

In you, ruby.
The pain
You wake to is not yours.

Later in this poem, titled "Nick and the Candlestick," she declared her son to be the "solid the spaces lean on, envious." That's what motivates so many parents, though we dare not admit it: we create babies who will connect us—to our partners, our families, and society as a whole. We lean upon these small people heavily, much more so than any of us care to admit.

Frieda Hughes, the subject of the poem "Child," continues her "troublous wringing of hands" over the forced surrender of her mother to the outside world, but this is an inevitable consequence of genius. Plath creates a perfect screen for projection because, in her *Ariel* voice, she was able to do what so many others attempt to do but fail: speak the truth in a wildly inventive and unique way. Smart and sensitive women will always be drawn to Plath's words, and what they search for, they will find. This includes mothers, too. The next time you're at the library, Mom, tuck a copy of *Ariel* in with the Dr. Seuss books. If the teens eye you suspiciously, just shake your head and say, "You have no idea."

2010

Health care may be hazardous to your health

If you thought 2009 was nutty, check out 2010! Only in America could there be a "debate" over whether or not more people should have health care coverage—and only in America could said "debate" result in people being literally kicked in the head at fall campaign rallies. The kickers in question were supporters of Rand Paul, a real live medical *doctor* who ran for Senate because he was so appalled by the broadening of health care coverage.

Jesus H. Christ on a cracker. 2010 was a mess!

It gets worse! No thanks to Obamacare backlash, my formerly bright-blue state legislature reverted to Republican control for the first time in nearly forty years, setting up a "family values" nightmare that would last into the foreseeable future . . . but we can worry about that later.

There were some moments of light. My writing found a home in several new outlets, including *Minnesota Public Radio News*, *HipMama* magazine, and feminist-themed websites *Femomist* and *Feminist Review*. And by December, no one gave a damn about Tim Tebow.

2010 was also the year that I finally, at very long last, read Rep. Shirley Chisholm's 1972 memoir *Unbought and Unbossed*. Rep. Chisholm was a trailblazer and a badass in her day, and she remains a source of inspiration during very trying times. If you haven't read the book yourself, toss it in your library bag or Amazon cart immediately. You're welcome.

Should shy people have children?
HipMama, Issue #45, winter 2010

HipMama *magazine, founded by hippest-of-all-mamas Ariel Gore, was the one place where a freaky pinko mama like me could find something resembling a community. In the late aughties–early teenies, Gore sold her interest in the magazine to a group of Portland mamas who did their best to survive in the cutthroat world of analog publishing, and this piece was published during their tenure. Two years later, the mag folded. In 2014 Gore relaunched the magazine with a Kickstarter campaign to which I was happy to contribute, if only for the "Print Lives" hoodie that I wear almost every day.*

I submit the above question in all seriousness, struggling as I have for over nine years to reconcile my introversion with the external demands of parenthood. If I do not wish that my right to procreate be taken from me, I *do* want to start a dialogue about the whole miserable thing. Put simply, I want to know why someone didn't have the decency to warn me about this!

But it was ever so—in America, the shy are suspicious characters, unworthy of such an advantage. At best, we're aloof, snobbish, or above it all. At worst, we're shut-ins, nutcases, or crazy cat ladies. Even a creative genius like Emily Dickinson is best remembered by middle school English students for her freaky agoraphobia, not her writing. The fact that these twerps sing her poems to the theme of *Gilligan's Island* is a humiliation I'm happy she never knew.

Some might argue that I can't compare myself to Ms. Dickinson because my prose lacks her music and she lacks my guts. After all, I left my house long enough for pregnancy to be an option. It wasn't long after I met Matt, the shy, punk-rock, computer dork of my dreams, that we knew we wanted kids. O! as Emily herself might declare, how very foolish we were.

Any opinion we had on the age-old nature-versus-nurture debate was erased the minute our son slid down the birth canal and introduced himself to the floor nurses. This infant was more naturally gregarious than his parents were after a couple six-packs—an extrovert through and through. I hoped this would bring much-needed balance to our family, but the opposite was true. When your two-year-old works a room like a tiny Bill Clinton, you are not going to be able to go anywhere without the eyes of the world upon you. I felt like the hot blush of embarrassment on my cheeks would be burned there permanently.

Most children grow into stranger anxiety, the Baby Whisperer wrote, and we rejoiced. But for Elliott, this phase never came. We still had to pull him away from grown-ups at the park and hiss in his tiny ear: *Please stop talking to people! Please!* He didn't get it.

I purchased a copy of *The Berenstain Bears Learn about Strangers*, in which Sister Bear is shown a shiny red apple that is revealed to be rotten and wormy inside. We told him this was for his own good, but in truth it was for my sanity. For when Elliott introduced himself to a grown-up at the park, I was the one stuck making chitchat while he ran off to the swings. *I* wanted to be on the swings, dammit. Blabbering about my son's developmental stages with another stay-at-home mommy was so mentally taxing that when we arrived home, I had to have a cup of chamomile tea before I could be bothered to shake the sand out of his shoes.

What extroverts don't realize is that the shy have limited stores of outward energy. Imagine a gauge labeled "For Other People" that gets drained throughout the day, to be refilled only during time spent alone. My son and my husband sip at my energy; strangers at the park drink deeply from it. Nobody had told me that with a kid in tow, I would suddenly be fair game. No parent can live in a bubble, because no kid is quiet enough.

Still, I wished for a child who *was* shy and retiring, a child whom I dreamed would curl up with me on the squishy chairs in the library to read peacefully, without needing to alert every person in earshot that we were doing so. When the shock of Elliott's arrival finally wore off, we had another. My daughter delighted me with her habit of sucking on her fingers whenever a stranger approached. *Aha!* Matt and I crowed. Things would be different with this one.

Our hopes vanished soon enough. My daughter happens to fit perfectly the current American ideal of little girlhood. Her butter-yellow curls, rosy cheeks, and wide blue eyes are a homing beacon to grandmothers and supermarket checkers. I appreciate the sentiment behind their fussing, but when Miriam sticks those pink fingers in her mouth, I'm the one left holding the bag. At least, by the time he turned seven, Elliott realized that he could carry on a conversation better than his mother, and he would dive in to save me. When we must attend school functions, Matt and I argue over who gets to accompany our convivial third grader instead of our bashful doll-child. Still, the girl will do in a pinch, which is what we do to her when our social thermometers plunge dangerously and we need to make a speedy escape. We never hurt her, mind you, but we annoy her enough to make even extroverts wish we would go away. Success!

I guess children are of use to the shy after all. I asked a childless and sympathetic friend if I would have been better off with a dog, but she looked at me like I was crazy. She asked what I would do when my dog took a deep whiff from a stranger's crotch. I saw her point—not even Elliott has tried that.

Not yet, anyway. O, how I am dreading puberty.

What's so funny about Stupak-Pitts?
Minnesota Women's Press, January 1, 2010

For MWP's humor-themed issue, I wrote on the continuing controversy over abortion coverage in Obamacare, as well as the hoary stereotype that feminists aren't totally fucking hilarious. Rep. Stupak withdrew his amendment after President Obama agreed to an executive order promising that no federal money would go toward abortion care. Pppppbbbbttttt!

The moment during the fourth season of *The Simpsons* is brief, but memorable: half a dozen dour, frumpy women walk a picket line, their signs reading "Equality Now!" Under a shower of Duff Beer, however, these Gloomy Gussies transform into Girls Gone Wild, rejecting feminism for booze-fueled fun. A show can't be popular for twenty years without a good grasp of the zeitgeist: everyone knows that feminists are no fun.

I decided to test this stereotype last November when I invited a group of feminist women and men to my home, where the merlot and craft beer (no Duff, thank you) flowed freely. Neither clothes nor humor were lost—this despite my other, less amusing motive for the event: a discussion of the Stupak-Pitts Amendment to the Affordable Health Care for America Act.

Stupak-Pitts, if you haven't heard, would effectively eliminate private insurance coverage of abortion for millions of American women and become the largest restriction on abortion access in a generation. Its successful passage under the leadership of a pro-choice, female Speaker of the House shocked feminists to the core. In a fine example of feminist humor, we used to crack that the only Bush a woman could trust was her own; we never expected to need to start punning on Pelosi, too.

Perhaps this explains the rush to UrbanDictionary.com, where wits thought they would hit Rep. Stupak (D-Michigan) with the same tactic that had doomed homophobic former Senator Rick Santorum (whose first Google hit is a noun too filthy to reprint here). One definition equates *stupak* with imposing religious views on others, as in "I can't believe these creationists want to *stupak* my kid's biology class." As of this writing, the most popular new definition of *stupak* is "life-threatening septic shock resulting from a botched illegal abortion"—totally unfunny because it may prove accurate.

Several women sipping pinot noir at my party were veterans of feminism's second wave, women able to remember a world before *Roe v. Wade*. My friend Barbra showed off a pin she had worn to a march on Washington that read "No Womb for Compromise."

"I was pregnant with my son at the time," she said proudly, and we laughed. Funny! Then she added, "Today he's a father, I'm a grandma, and I'm still fighting the same fight!" Not funny!

If feminists seem a somber bunch, it's because constant threats to women's health and safety have made it so. The number of women who could die of *stupak*, while horrific, still pales beside the number of women who have been killed by their lovers, and that number looks tiny compared with the millions upon millions of American women who will endure sexual violence at some point in their lives. Any sane person considering all this would scowl, too. She might get so angry, in fact, that you might confuse her rage for humorlessness.

Fortunately, this regressive amendment wasn't sponsored by Representatives Johnson and Smith or other common surnames of no use to street picketers. Many slogans were suggested as my party warmed up: *Drop Stupid-Gits!* was my favorite, though some pointed out that the use of cockney slang might be lost on Senators Franken and Klobuchar. *Stupak is Wack!* though of American origin, might have the same effect. *Kiss My Pitts!* seemed an appropriate nod to the feminist veterans of the seventies, while the simple *Stupak is Stupid!* though infantile, captured our frustrations perfectly.

After all, the man who got us all into this mess, Rep. Stupak, shares his first name with a member of the aforementioned Simpson family and one of American culture's most enduringly obnoxious little boys: Bart.

Ay, caramba! That's funny.

Unbought, unbossed, and unbelievable
Radical Housewife blog, January 24, 2010

January is truly Minnesota's cruelest month. The cold, snow and darkness are just as bad as in December or worse, without the sparkly fun of the holidays to take the edge off; instead, the usual January tradition is to get sick. Infections on top of infections confine us to our beds, where we contemplate the sweet release of death or get some reading done.

In 2010 I read a book that introduced me to a real-life wonder woman, Shirley Chisholm. I've been quoting her ever since! Take Root Media published a fortieth-anniversary edition of the book, but it seems to have gone out of print again, which is all kinds of wrong. Every library and home in America should have a copy.

Warning to all frazzled parents: do not wish for a sick day, convinced that all will be quiet and glorious, your children and spouse rubbing your feet and bringing you milkshakes. I can only handle Gatorade and toast. And the screaming, my god, the screaming . . . only half a day until these three freaks get the hell out of my house.

On a positive note, while confined to the couch I have been able to finish Shirley Chisholm's *Unbought and Unbossed*, her phenomenal 1970 biography. I don't think I can adequately express how moved I've been by this book and this woman, not simply because every other sentence is a quote so fucking righteous that I want to run to tweet it, but also because *forty years ago*, she was railing against the same crap that is plaguing Congress and the Democrats today.

In 1969, when Rep. Chisholm was named honorary president of NARAL, then known as National Association for the Repeal of Abortion Laws, she noted the flack she caught from her colleagues in Congress. Did she buckle under pressure, as many Congressional leaders did when Stupak-Pitts loomed?

"I decided to shake them up a little with a feminist line of counterattack. 'Who told you I shouldn't do this?' I asked them. 'Women are dying every day; did you know that? They're being butchered and maimed. No matter what men think, abortion is a fact of life. Women will have them; they always have and always will. Are they going to have good ones or bad ones? Will the good ones be reserved for the rich while poor women have to go to quacks? Why don't we talk about real problems instead of phony ones?'"

I know, right? Swoon! I love her!

Elsewhere she says that the Democratic Party, with its endless compromises made in the name of expediency and graft, keeps infuriating her, but she does not yet want to leave it. And a short Wikipedia entry reveals that she stayed in the party until her retirement in 1982. What would she think about what's happening today? Would she be in a tiny liberal coalition with Dennis Kucinich, hoping that maybe my very own representative, Keith Ellison, would gather up the nerve to join them?

The next book on my bedside table is *The Good Fight*, Chisholm's account of her quest to win her party's 1972 nomination for president. I don't care that she failed; I care that she tried. She paved the way for Keith, Hillary, and Barack, but there are far too few people who know her name.

When I get healthy, I want to change that.

Whose family values?
Radical Housewife blog, January 27, 2010

The retrograde "family values" group Focus on the Family took advantage of the heightened attention to abortion politics in the Obamacare debates with a Super Bowl ad starring the evangelical quarterback Tim Tebow. His mother, Pam, had been advised to abort her fifth child when she became dangerously ill during her pregnancy. The fact that a future Heisman winner might have been aborted (GASP!) was seen by the anti–choice side as a political touchdown! A local radio station contacted me for the feminist position on the matter, which was that CBS shouldn't have taken money from an organization that supports quack therapy meant to "cure" homosexuality.

Ironically, I wasn't able to best articulate my anti–Focus on the Family position, because I was tending to my sick preschooler. This never happens to Phyllis Schlafly! I wrote this blog post in case any listeners bothered to google my name.

In my role as Minnesota NOW President, I was just invited on a local radio station to discuss why on earth anyone would object to a Focus on the Family ad airing during the 2010 Super Bowl. Radio interviews are tricky, especially when you do them at your kitchen table. While I spoke I kept one ear out for Miriam, who had been barfing her guts out only a few hours earlier and seemed comfortable on the couch watching *WordGirl* but could very well begin screaming at any moment, thus making me look like a big doofus on one of the Twin Cities' most popular radio stations.

But would that have been so bad? I do like to remind folks that I'm a mama too. Extreme conservatives like Focus on the Family and the dreadful antiabortion blogger Jill Stanek act like we are shriveled crones who eat small children with our soy lattes for breakfast. According to Jill, when thousands of Catholic schoolchildren are bused in for a pro-life rally, it's American youth bravely speaking out. When I bring my children to Planned Parenthood on Good Friday, they are "props" that are "disgusting" and "grotesque."

In Jill's eyes, Miriam and Elliott are not whole human beings but are just "kids I didn't kill." She states that feminist moms like me "would be just as happy to see little [Miriam] dead." Talk about grotesque.

Of course I support the choice of Pam Tebow to give birth to her baby boy Tim. Why not? I love families! I love 'em so much that I have one! Whether Pam Tebow aborted her baby is none of my business. It's hers and hers alone.

The feminist movement asks that the same array of options be available to every other woman on this planet. No one should confuse one woman's outcome, in one very specific set of circumstances, with every woman's in a million different situations. The movement for reproductive civil rights seeks justice and freedom for every woman, not just a privileged few.

Ain't that a family value?

Rights, not choices!

Minnesota Women's Press, May 1, 2010

As a middle-class white woman, I have always been able to exercise control over my reproductive health, which is why the label "pro-choice" never struck me as problematic. I am grateful to the work of SisterSong and other feminists of color who illuminated how few choices are actually available to the majority of American women. Now I identify as pro–reproductive rights, pro–reproductive justice, and even pro-abortion!

A cursory understanding of the modern women's movement might boil down to one word: choice. The choice to wear pants. The choice to cast a vote. The choice to enroll at Princeton or enlist in the Army. The choice to enter the workforce. The choice to use contraception. The choice to terminate a pregnancy.

This is the What Women Want issue, so I'll share what I want: the removal of this word from the feminist vocabulary. It's no longer useful in advancing women's rights in the twenty-first century, for its message has been cleverly diluted, if not co-opted, by those who oppose feminism's goals. Pam Tebow had a choice to carry her baby to term (except she didn't, because abortion is against the law in the Philippines, where baby Tim was conceived). Bristol Palin had a choice to have a baby at seventeen (though many kids feel so desperate about their similar circumstances that they would hire someone to kick them in the stomach for $150, as a Utah girl Bristol's age did last year).

I suggest that women quit claiming that exercising our civil rights under the law is a matter of personal choice. When the Nineteenth Amendment was adopted, suffragists didn't say they won the "choice" to vote, though casting a ballot each November is not required by law and fifty percent of eligible voters choose not to do it.

Rights belong to all—choices belong to a few. This was made clear during the debate surrounding the Super Bowl ad featuring Pam Tebow's story. Like Pam, I gave birth to a son, but that doesn't mean I think Elliott will someday win a Heisman. Why, then, should I also expect that every woman who pees on a stick will be as thrilled as I was to see the positive result? The experiences of Pam, Bristol, and yours truly are ours alone and cannot be expected to set the standard for every other woman across the globe.

Rights assume differences, while choice implies similarity. Note that the current debate over health care policy also uses the language of choice, as in "Rush Limbaugh had the choice to pay out of pocket for high-quality cardiac care." That statement implies that you have that choice, too. Do you?

I don't. A health care provider I trust recently recommended that I visit a highly regarded specialist, but to see this specialist, I would have to pay $375 per hour out of my own pocket. According to Rush logic, I could choose to visit this specialist, though that might make it impossible to pay my car insurance bill. I wonder how Allstate might react? They might insist on their right to get paid. A state trooper might also insist upon her right to issue me a citation for breaking Minnesota law. Interesting!

Choices assume personal responsibility for every aspect of our lives, while rights assume that not everything will turn out as planned. Rush didn't intend to have a heart attack last January, did he? The health care compromise brokered by Nancy Pelosi asks women to plan ahead for abortions they may never need. Why?

Because the rhetoric since Roe has centered on a woman's choice to seek abortion, making it easy for foes to layer subjectivity and moral judgment upon the procedure. Imagine the riots if barriers were enacted to make it all but impossible for overweight male smokers like Limbaugh to access cardiac care!

This What Women Want issue offers myriad choices for businesses and services to support. Patronize them or don't—it's your right. Don't take it for granted.

A clash of family values outside Highland Park clinic
Minnesota Public Radio News, May 5, 2010

This account of how my family celebrates Good Friday was my first personal essay published by Minnesota Public Radio. The online editor liked that the photo I sent was a selfie with two kids and messy hair. How else to capture the spirit of modern feminist motherhood?

As a typical nonobservant American family, my husband, kids, and I celebrate holidays once rich with religious meaning: we exchange gifts at Christmas and nibble on chocolate bunnies for Easter. But unlike most secular Americans, we also observe Good Friday.

Though we are in the company of family on Good Friday, we do not attend church. This year we spent April 2 on the sidewalk in front of the Planned Parenthood in St. Paul.

Other clinics in the metro area offer surgical abortion services, but the others lack the name recognition of Planned Parenthood and therefore make poorer targets for Pro-Life Action Ministries, the organizer of the massive demonstration that occurs nearby. Hundreds of passionate people opposed to abortion turn out every Good Friday, singing, praying, and occasionally shouting their message to the smaller crowd in front of the clinic.

On Good Friday, I appear at the clinic with my two children by my side. My son and daughter, I explain to those present, are evidence of planned parenthood in action. Antiabortion protesters target me, for I look different from the young college students in their adorable, hot pink pro-choice t-shirts. I'm the one in the sweater stained with apple juice, scolding my son for swiping more than his fair share of doughnuts from the box we brought from Supervalu. Those who oppose abortion demand to know why I would bring my children to a place they consider incompatible with what they consider "family values."

I respond that my family reinforced my already strong commitment to reproductive freedom. As a stay-at-home mom, I experience frustration, exhaustion, and anxiety at every turn, and I'm one of the lucky ones. I'm as lucky as Bristol Palin was lucky to have financial and emotional support in place for her to consider parenthood at seventeen. I'm as lucky as Pam Tebow was to have given birth to a healthy baby boy.

Bristol, Pam, and I are fortunate, indeed, to be three middle-class white women. We also have sons in common, but I don't expect my doughnut-stealer to win a Heisman, and I'm sure that Bristol harbors no illusions about little Tripp. Our experiences are ours alone and cannot be expected to set the standard for every other woman across the globe.

Bristol, Pam, and I did not have abortions, but our circumstances are not the only ones that matter. Families, like all other structures and systems, function best when they develop deliberately. No one would open a small business without significant preparation, and the stakes in that gamble are nowhere near as high. According to a report by the Minnesota Department of Human Services, approximately 5,400 children in our state experienced abuse and/or neglect in 2008. Forty-five of those abused children received injuries that were life threatening, and seventeen children died due to maltreatment. Seventy percent of the abusers were the child's birth parents.

These numbers reveal a truth too painful to be soothed away by prayer alone. Parents aren't the ones who suffer under familial dysfunction—children are.

This Friday on the calendar is Good to many but ambiguous to many more. Because I believe in families; in mothers, fathers, and children; and in supporting planned parenthood every day of the year, I spend Good Friday on a St. Paul sidewalk, my own family at my side.

Radical homemakers vs. radical housewives

Radical Housewife blog, May 12, 2010

So many people contacted me about Shannon Hayes, author of the book Radical Homemaking: Reclaiming Domesticity from a Consumer Culture, *that I felt I had to address where our philosophies diverged. Hayes has yet to comment on what she thinks about me! She's probably too busy working her farm to give a crap about the other radical Shannon.*

"The Opt-Out Revolution" was a 2003 New York Times Magazine *piece by Lisa Belkin that remarked on the curious phenomenon of posh Ivy League grads leaving high-powered jobs to be stay-at-home moms and what it could possibly mean for The Movement, as if feminism existed only to cater to the needs of wealthy white women. Yuck.*

A note from one of the publishers at the Women's Press reminded me of my long-delayed intention of talking a bit about a fellow radical Shannon out there. Namely, Shannon Hayes, she of the *Radical Homemaking* book and a series of articles in *Yes!* magazine. I appreciate her ideas (for the world needs *more* radical Shannons in it, not fewer), but she and I have totally different practices and goals.

Hayes's subtitle is "reclaiming domesticity from a consumer culture." As a committed pinko, I like anything that questions the status quo. Capitalism exists to make us all desperately unhappy sheep. The short-term consequences are increased L'Oreal and Bud Lite sales—long-term consequences are entrenched classism, racism, and sexism.

Hayes's press releases announce that that *Radical Homemaking* is "the story of pioneering men and women who are redefining feminism and the good life by adhering to simple principles of ecological sustainability, social justice, community engagement and family well-being." On the book's back cover, she writes, "in essence, the great work we face requires rekindling the home fires."

And that's where we part ways.

It starts with the word "homemaker," one that I have always found problematic. How does one *make* a home? I haven't a clue. Is it by washing the floors? Baking from scratch? Quilting? Gardening? Reading bedtime stories? Nurturing relationships? I clean my home. In the interest of sustainability, I recycle and compost like a maniac, carry my cloth bags with me, bike it up, etc., etc. But I don't think that keeping a coop of chickens or canning the beans from my garden is the way toward a more just world.

For one thing, "rekindling the home fires" implies turning inward, reaffirming the family as the basic unit of society, just like the folks at the Christian Coalition. Now, I don't know if Shannon Hayes is religiously motivated. But once you start turning inward, toward a unit that looks like you, talks like you, and thinks like you, you start getting out of touch with the complex systems that conspire against the people who *don't* look like you!

Feminism is about fighting oppression in all its forms. That means we must work outward, not inward. This is why I must place Radical Homemaking on the Mommy Wars spectrum, despite its fine intentions. The only examples of "radical homemakers" that the book mentions are well-off, highly educated, white women. Remember "The Opt-Out Revolution," anyone?

A discussion on the subject at *Bitch* magazine led me to the blog Vegan Burnout, where I read the brilliant comment: "To frame the choice between working a soulless 9-to-5 or building a backyard chicken coop and learning to can tomatoes as the only feminist options is reductive and insulting." It's easy to choose your choice when you have so many choices to choose from, so that when you *do* choose, your choice is automatically the best one! It's the Opt-Out argument from 2003 all over again.

So why did I pick the Radical Housewife moniker, then? Because I find the word "housewife" really funny. That's why. When I'm asked to fill in the box marked "occupation," I say I'm a writer and an at-home parent. The damn home can make itself, for all I care.

Sorry, Radical Shannon. I just don't buy it (anticapitalist pun intended).

The mother of online reinvention
Femomist, July 2010

Femomist *was a new online venture meant to celebrate "the radical notion that moms are people." Its founder, a reader of my blog, asked me to contribute, so I sent in a couple of pieces that reflected my obsessions at the time: online identity and Pixar movies. Like so many new sites,* Femomist *didn't last long, and these essays had to wait several years to be reinvented here.*

Being a Radical Housewife and not just another mommy at home with her kiddos means embracing a version of what Lester Bangs once wrote about the soul of the punk-rock movement: "reinvent yourself and everything around you constantly." When Bangs wrote these words in the late seventies, this was a far greater challenge than it is now, when all one requires for transformation is a DSL connection and a Wi-Fi card.

The constant redefinition of self at work in the world of *teh interwebz* amuses and fascinates me. Creaky old groaners in the *New York Times* may lament that no one online is who they claim to be, but I like that. I spent years of my life striking a pose in the real world to no avail: my mousy-nerd soul was far too easily revealed. Now I can safely be the über–hipster bitch of my dreams, just in time for the people I hated in high school to find me again.

In the mid-aughts, I joined the MySpace hordes at the behest of two connected under-thirties whom I consider authorities on all things trendy and irreverent. These qualities constitute the Holy Grail to me, a thirty-eight-year-old mother who flees from the word "mother" and all it implies: *Oprah* on TiVo, high-waisted pants, minivans, "girls' night out," Josh Groban records, moral authority, etc.

On MySpace, I discovered the joys of from-the-hip blogging, which, to use another anatomical cliché, came back to bite me in the ass. In my mad rush not to be one of the mommybloggers on WordPress, I became a spiteful MySpace child who dropped copious f-bombs about people I found annoying. The inevitable result? Six pointless hours with a family therapist, a breakup letter in my (literal, not virtual) mailbox, and thinly veiled threats from parents of other kids at my son's school.

I might as well have loaded up a picture of myself on LOLmoms with the caption *Reinvenshun—ur doin it wrong.*

I was greatly relieved when my young friends signaled that the trendies were dropping MySpace in favor of Facebook. I hustled over and created an account. Unlike MySpace, this site insisted upon the use of your full name. I relented, figuring that using circa-1993 Courtney Love as my profile photo might be a form of Internet privacy, despite the site's stern warning against copyright infringement. Let them kick me off, I gloated, as Courtney would have. I'm a hipster bitch, remember? No glowing pictures of me with my apple-cheeked children, no sirree! That's what *mothers* do.

I should have posted a fake high school and college, though, because I found myself suddenly awash in requests from the bullshit that "Shannon Drury" thought she'd left behind.

I received a friend request from woman whose last contact with me was when her fist had met my stomach at the intersection of Fifty-Eighth Street and Chowen Avenue in 1982. The increasingly creepy People You May Know box soon featured the profile of my former best friend, another of my many disgruntled MySpace readers. The box reported that "You and Amy both live in Minneapolis," but so do four hundred thousand other Facebook users (I checked). I wondered if I was part of a *Twilight Zone* meets *Punk'd* episode in which all the angst from my past is downloaded straight from brain to computer. How can I reinvent myself if Facebook keeps reminding me of everything I once was?

Made vulnerable by all this, I accepted a friendship request from an insufferably self-important high school classmate. In real life, I would never associate with an Ivy League Republican who posts links about our president's plot to create an American "nanny state." Now there's a phrase I find far more repulsive than what got me into trouble on MySpace (colorful variations on "motherfucker," if you're curious). When the "nanny state" is invoked, it is used to imply a nation of emasculated, diaper-clad, white men crying over being dominated by the Mary Poppins from hell. He even snarked at a *Rachel Maddow* link on my wall only a day after his wife give birth to their third son. Why wasn't he wiping that kid's butt instead of hassling me?

Before I hit "remove from friends," though, I wondered: could this guy be reinventing himself, too? His challenge was not to improve upon his past but to live up to it, as the student council president at a suburban high school during the Reagan years. Could he be too cowed to admit that his twenty-first century self prefers cuddling his children to the harsh world of mergers and acquisitions?

Nah.

Curiously enough, the drama hasn't driven me off the site. Last spring, celebrated momista Alexandra Jacobs lamented in the *New York Times* style supplement that Facebook was turning even her beloved Upper East Siders into a bunch of tasteless troglodytes, proving that online reinvention is happening everywhere, all the time. Today my profile photo is Jessie the Yodeling Cowgirl, my favorite *Toy Story* character. Maybe tomorrow it will be Shirley Chisholm, Margaret Atwood, or Lady Gaga in a bra that shoots fireworks.

I am a mom; I contain multitudes. I have the online accounts to prove it.

Toy Story 3 and reviews that review the reviewer

Femomist, July 2010

I really, really love Jessie the Yodeling Cowgirl and will always defend her as a feminist role model. Since this piece appeared, Pixar wised up and finally started releasing movies with female leads: Brave *(2012),* Inside/Out *(2015), and* Finding Dory *(2016).* Toy Story 4 *is due in 2018, the year my firstborn graduates from high school. You better believe I'll be dragging him to the theater with me!*

It has come to my attention that there are some mommies out there (read: this site's editor) who do their damnedest to avoid all things Disney. If I'd just walked out of a screening of *The Lion King*, I'd agree with you—that was the biggest pile of patriarchal crap ever to be foisted upon unsuspecting children, which, in a genre that also includes *Snow White*, is really saying something. But only a year after girls worldwide learned that "the circle of life" excluded them, Disney's Pixar division knocked out a winner with the first *Toy Story* film. Admittedly, this movie had no female characters of consequence. I get that. But it didn't say that girls weren't allowed, which helped, as did the fact that it was engaging, witty, and fun.

Even better was *Toy Story 2*, the 1999 sequel that finally added a girl to the mix—and what a girl! Jessie the Yodeling Cowgirl was tough yet sensitive, sassy but loyal, fearless and frightened: all the things that make any character, male or female, click. As a mother of two young kids, you can only imagine how many times I've watched this movie, but I never tire of it. I'd put it right up there with *Rushmore* and *Eternal Sunshine of the Spotless Mind* as one of my favorite movies of all time.

So you can imagine my excitement in the months leading up to the premiere of *Toy Story 3*, as well as my frustration. Where, I begged the marketing gods, WHERE were my Jessie dolls? I couldn't walk five feet into the Mall of America without a Buzz and Woody onslaught: *where* was their girl buddy? I out-tantrummed the small children in Target's toy aisle. I WANT MY JESSIE DOLL! As a feminist, I know that representation is everything.

Except when you're lost in a hugely entertaining movie like *Toy Story 3*—then all care for the rogues' gallery of –isms fades away. Yes, it's that good. I laughed; I cried. I hugged my kids tighter as the lights went up. Later that week, I read the *Ms.* magazine take on the film, "Third Time Still Not the Charm for Toy Story's Female Characters," sighed deeply, and asked my family when they wanted to see it again.

The *Ms.* writer looked for sexism and found it, both in Jessie's diminished role in the film and in the treatment of Barbie and Mrs. Potato Head. I agree that *Toy Story 3*, as wonderful as it was, is fair game for feminist critique. Unfortunately, what a critic seeks, she shall find, in a process that tells us far more about the critic than the film itself. For example, my nemeses at the Minnesota Citizens Concerned for Life wrote a blog post a week after the film's opening that thrilled to the "fact" that its message was anti-abortion. Hmmm . . . I watched pretty closely, and I don't remember Barbie fretting over a missed period.

The more effective analysis would be an essay on Pixar Studios' stubborn adherence to a strictly male point of view. Pixar has created numerous dynamic female characters, including the wonderful Jessie, the very relatable mom/superhero ElastiGirl (aka Mrs. Incredible), and the dim but loyal Dory who helps find a fish named Nemo. Why can't one be the star? WHY, Pixar? WHY?

Films do open up discussions on cultural values and systems, of course, and that's where things get interesting. Unfortunately again, it's been sixteen long years since I sat in a screening room with my cohort of twenty-one-year-old media studies majors. Today I screen films with a son who keeps interrupting for more popcorn and a daughter who watches so deep in concentration that she chews her fingernails until they bleed. And they fuckin' loved *Toy Story 3*, which made me happy. This says a lot about my priorities, too. I fight the good fight in my state capitol, on the campaign trail (clashing with the Minnesota Citizens Concerned for Life more often than not), and at Target when my daughter asks for a nonexistent Jessie toy of her own. When I'm in a dark movie theater holding their sticky little hands, I want the joy of transcendent fantasy, not the weight of the world upon me. I have twenty-two other hours in the day left for that. Five stars.

Candidate confidential
Minnesota Women's Press, August 1, 2010

I regret to report that in the years since this column, my friend Maren has not changed her mind about running for school board. Neither have I!

When the news broke last spring that three members of the Minneapolis School Board weren't running for reelection, I thought of my friend Maren. A mom to three kids in the district, the cochair of a district advisory board, a graduate student in the education program at St. Thomas—she would be perfect for the job. I told her so, and she laughed. When I explained that I was serious, she laughed harder. "What about *you*?" she asked. "Why don't *you* run?"

I'm a feminist activist, not a school activist, I said. "So?" was the tart reply.

I thought of this conversation when I learned that Minneapolis activist Farheen Hakeem was preparing to announce her candidacy for Minnesota governor. I'd been pestering her to run for months, but she worried that a gubernatorial campaign (after unsuccessful bids for Minneapolis mayor, county commissioner, and Minnesota House) might be seen as a publicity stunt. My response: "So?"

I regretted being so flippant as soon as I logged on to Minneapolis's E-Democracy website, where a post about Hakeem's candidacy devolved into whether or not the unmarried candidate may be addressed as "Miss." (I'm totally serious.)

Women have made tremendous strides in politics since the Nineteenth Amendment was passed, but for every Pelosi or Klobuchar, there are hundreds of women like Hakeem who are considered irrelevant from the moment they file. And there are millions upon millions of women like Maren and me who don't even consider running. Why?

My friend Laurie Olmon has some ideas. She wishes that her only obstacles were being called "Miss": since her election to Nowthen City Council, she's been subject to the harassment that every pioneer fears. And then there was the death threat.

A death threat? 'So,' indeed!

You'd be crazy to run for office in that climate, but run she does, today as the Democratic-Farmer-Labor (DFL) candidate for state representative in District 48A. "I have always said there is a thin line between courage and crazy," Olmon told me, "and it's what you do when you're riding that thin line that counts." She assured me that "moms can do this; regular activists can do this"; *all* women have what it takes be a part of the political process.

Her husband, Phil, an Iraq War veteran, inspired her first steps into activism as an advocate for military families. After attending a training program with the White House Project, Olmon took a good look at the requirements to run for the City Council of her town of Nowthen. "I had the same qualifications as any man running or any man that had run and won."

Ahh, those pesky qualifications. Did Olmon need to be a lawyer or a millionaire? A man? Nope. She needed to be a local resident and an adult. That's it. (Since I know you're reading this, Maren, those are also the requirements for school board. Just sayin'.)

In running for office, she said, "Men feel entitled, and women need to be asked. I was asked in several subtle ways to include myself," including a not-so-subtle hint from Phil (after hearing her scream at the TV) that amounted to his own version of "So?"

Olmon said she's convinced that women's leadership is needed at every level of government. Women, she believes, understand that "to make rules to reign in the few, we need to concentrate on society as a whole," which includes "consistency in how children are taught in public school systems," among other things.

This brings me back to Maren, who, unlike 99.99 percent of the Minneapolis population, actually attended a school board candidate forum, yet still thinks *I'd* be the better candidate.

This game of chicken should be concluded sometime in 2012.

Sin in Linen's Tattoo Flash Print Dishtowels
Feminist Review, September 16, 2010

When the site Feminist Review put out a call for contributors, I thought for sure I'd be asked to pontificate on Audre Lorde reissues or at the very least, new Le Tigre records. Surprise: my first assignment was to review a set of dishtowels! Though I'm tough on them here, I have to admit they are in good shape six years later.

Sin in Linen, purveyor of retro and punk rock patterned household goods, sent Feminist Review and this feminist reviewer a pair of its new Tattoo Flash Print Dishtowels. I'm not sure what to review: their utility? As Courtney Love once sang, "I don't do the dishes, I throw them in the crib." Do I test them for feminist purity? Included among the sacred hearts, horseshoes, and flames are bikini-clad pinup girls, one of whom strikes a squatting-at-the-strip-club-in-platforms pose that is less Bettie Page than Jenna Jameson. Ew.

Lest you accuse me of typically second-wave prudery, I assure you that I do like vintage pin-ups. My husband knows that *Playboy* is verboten in my house not because naked ladies are bad, but because naked ladies who are shaved, starved, and siliconed into looking like pneumatic twelve-year-olds are bad.

My husband, incidentally, is our household's usual dishwasher, and he approved of the Tattoo Dishtowels. "More absorbent than the crap we got at Ikea," was his take. Unfortunately, when he draped the towels over the oven door to dry, my five-year-old daughter and ten-year-old son got an eyeful. She liked the mermaids and butterflies; he wondered why on earth there would be women in bathing suits on the new dishtowels. I told him I didn't know.

I see the appeal of applying tattoos to household products instead of human bodies; the consumer remains *au courant* while avoiding the inconvenience of a lifetime commitment. What I fail to understand, continually, is the use of voluptuous pin-up girl as shorthand for "I am *different*. I am *alternative*." When I gaze at the designs on the Tattoo Dishtowels, I think of an aging Korean War vet's meaty forearms. A dishtowel of tattoos for the new millennium might feature Japanese kanji, Celtic knots, or Shiloh Jolie-Pitt's name in Sanskrit.

But the purpose of these towels is not to celebrate the history of tattooing, it is to send the following message to the neighbors on laundry day: I am no ordinary housewife. This is precisely what I conveyed last week when I attended both kids' school open houses in rumpled jeans and a pair of maroon Chuck Taylors, so I understand this impulse completely. I just don't agree that a half-naked babe, however luscious, is the best way to do it.

Now if that bikini babe were in the company of the shirtless Old Spice guy, then we'd really be cooking (pun totally intended). Equal-opportunity objectification could be all that's needed to unite feminism's many waves—even if it's only over the kitchen sink.

Girls need the right to confidential reproductive care
Minnesota Public Radio News, October 5, 2010

Here is one of my favorite pieces on the subject of "parental authority," that bugaboo used to justify all kinds of restrictions against the privacy rights of teenagers.

To enroll my daughter Miriam in kindergarten this fall, I signed many official-looking forms to confirm her attachment to me. Now that school is in session, the paperwork continues: her teacher sends home permission slips with regularity. One would think I own her.

The issue of parental authority casts a long shadow over the ongoing abortion wars, with the Minnesota Citizens Concerned for Life recently taking gubernatorial candidate Senator Mark Dayton to task for issuing conflicting statements about his position on laws requiring minor girls seeking abortions to procure the consent of their parents. The Minnesota Citizens Concerned for Life organization calls Dayton "confused," an accurate description of any parent faced with a young daughter's unplanned pregnancy.

As a U.S. Senator, Dayton cosponsored the Freedom of Choice Act, which would essentially codify *Roe v. Wade* into federal law, yet he says he supports Minnesota's parental notification law. I, too, suggest that Senator Dayton make up his mind, this time in favor of eliminating barriers to reproductive freedom for all women, regardless of age.

Khalil Gibran wrote a passage on parenthood in *The Prophet* that begins thusly: "Your children are not your children." It is a difficult truth for even the most sensitive of parents to grasp. "You can house their bodies but not their souls," Gibran continues, "for their souls dwell in the house of tomorrow, which you cannot visit, not even in your dreams." Ouch.

Minnesota law, however, views Miriam as my property. As the logic goes, parents are required to give permission for ear piercing, so why not an abortion? I'd have to sign a raft of forms to approve my daughter's tonsillectomy, so why not her abortion? For starters, there is no stigma around the earlobes or other body parts visible to all at Lake Nokomis in July. Tonsils don't sell motorcycles or light beer. Like it or not, American culture is simultaneously obsessed with, disgusted by, and confused about human sexuality.

Contemplating our children as sexual beings feels creepy; we don't want to do it. Some take their unease to unrealistic extremes, refusing to address the need for comprehensive, science-based sexual education in homes *and* in schools. Voters in Delaware support a Republican candidate, Christine O'Donnell, who thinks even masturbation is a sin, yet a Guttmacher Institute report released last January found her state to have one of the highest teenage abortion rates in the country.

We ignore teenage sexuality at our peril. Here at home, the rates of sexually transmitted infections are rising at an alarming rate: Minnesota Department of Health statistics show that rates of HIV infection rose by 13 percent in 2009. The "true love waits" message isn't working; neither is ignoring the problem, hoping it will go away.

Would I want know if my daughter wanted an abortion? Of course. Every parenting decision I make is guided by my desire to build trust and respect in our family. I would want to know about her abortion; I would want to know about her pregnancy; I would want to know that she was sexually active. Do I have the *right* to all this information? No. I work to earn her trust, but I can't force her to give it to me.

Antiabortion activists say that notification laws are especially necessary so that parents will be informed about cases of rape and incest. I say that if the girl hasn't shared her trauma with her parents already, she probably has her reasons (shame and stigma remain a fact of life for sexual assault victims, which is why these crimes are dramatically underreported). No law can force a trusting relationship that doesn't exist. Even the American Academy of Pediatrics supports this view, stating, "Legislation mandating parental involvement does not achieve the intended benefit of promoting family communication, but it does increase the risk of harm to the adolescent by delaying access to appropriate medical care."

I respect Senator Dayton, the father of two sons, for his support for the Freedom of Choice Act. I hope that he'll reconsider legislation that will guarantee the health and safety of our daughters, too.

Terror hits home
Radical Housewife blog, October 27, 2010

2010 saw a continuation of the political violence that had begun with the murder of Dr. George Tiller the year before. The meteoric rise of the Tea Party, with its brazen racism and extremism, scared the living shit out of everyone, and for good reason.

My friend Laurie Olmon, whom I featured in my Women's Press column "Candidate Confidential," just shared some distressing news with me: last weekend, persons unknown vandalized her campaign signs with the slogan BABY KILLER. In lipstick, an interesting choice.

At first, I reacted as I would to any friend who'd been bullied: with words of support, all very "You go, girl!" I wasn't worried.

Hours later, I watched the video of the MoveOn worker getting her head stomped on by a Rand Paul supporter in Kentucky. I clicked links that would allow me to download Rachel Maddow's documentary *The Assassination of Dr. Tiller*. I started to worry, and I remain worried. Very, very worried.

Obviously, this vandal knows that Laurie does not literally kill babies. I've been called this name a few times myself—in the presence of my two young children, no less. No, the term "baby killer" is not meant to be a literal accusation; it is meant to invoke fear. "Baby killer" is a term that successfully whipped a lunatic like Scott Roeder into a homicidal frenzy. It transforms a debate into a fight, a discussion into a brawl, a disagreement into a head-stomping melee that puts someone in the hospital.

It means something to use those words. It means the same thing to Laurie and me as it did to Dr. George Tiller: *you are a target*.

I don't mean to suggest that this vandal means to kill Laurie, any more than she (lipstick, remember?) truly believes that Laurie has committed murder herself. But isn't it something that this angry person didn't write "FUCK OFF"? Nor did she scribble "YOU SUCK" or "I HATE YOU." She chose her words very carefully. She wrote what she did to scare the shit out of someone who has put herself in the public eye to protect the rights of others—not unlike a certain dead doctor from Kansas.

Vote next Tuesday as if your life depends on it, because it does.

A postmortem on sanity (and my once-liberal home)
Radical Housewife blog, November 1, 2010

In the wake of the absolute insanity mentioned above, Daily Show *host Jon Stewart sponsored a Rally to Restore Sanity in Washington DC on October 30, 2010. Non-Easterners were encouraged to hold rallies in their own regions, and Minnesota complied. As the president of Minnesota NOW, I had spoken at more than a few events at the State Capitol, but never, ever had I encountered such a hostile audience at I did at this so-called sanity rally. I stand by my speech! It was funny, dammit!*

Sharron Angle is rightfully obscure these days, but in 2010 she was a U.S. Senate candidate and Tea Party heroine who really *did* compare rape to lemons and a resulting pregnancy to lemonade. *I know:* insane.

I was so excited to speak at the Rally to Restore Sanity that I sprang for a new T-shirt for the occasion. The message inside the Minnesota outline on my chest? I CAME TO GET DOWN! No one parties like a native blue-stater. Sanity, here we come!

At about one o'clock that afternoon, I stood at the podium and gave the following remarks, interspersed with necessary commentary.

"I speak to you today on behalf of the statewide membership of Minnesota NOW, an activist group that is strictly nonpartisan, though we do have an agenda. Since NOW has been in the game nationally since 1966, this shouldn't surprise anyone, but no less a political luminary than Sarah Palin lashed out at women's rights activists a couple months ago, labeling us with a very peculiar term: Cackle of Rads."

(This is where I paused for laughter that never came.)

"Cackle of Rads was Palin's strange Alaskan slang for women who, in her words, 'hijacked' feminism from . . . I don't know, a roving band of grizzly bears or something."

(Silence.)

"I know this rally isn't supposed to be partisan, and I agree with that noble aim. However, the truth is not partisan, and the truth is that Sarah Palin, is not, in fact, the designated mouthpiece for American women. Palin is also claiming to speak for the protective mothers in America by coming up with another gimmick just as weird to me as the Cackle of Rads: the Mama Grizzlies. According to Palin, the Mama Grizzly is an über-mom who will 'rise up' to protect her children the only way she knows how: by voting for a woman like Sharron Angle, who thinks that pregnant sexual assault victims need to shut up and use their rape lemons to make fetus lemonade. That's totally insane."

(I thought "fetus lemonade" was really fuckin' funny, but the crowd sure didn't.)

"We all know that Sarah Palin is a mother—it's a big part of her sales pitch. I'm a mother too. My son is ten, and my daughter is five. When I see the level of insanity that has infected our public discourse, the last symbol I, as a mother, want to identify with is a creature known for homicidal paranoia. I don't want to run back into my cave and hide, either! I want to do something to make the world a sane place for my children, your children, and the Palin children. In short, I'm not a mama grizzly—instead, I'm a mama cow."

(Crickets.)

"I'm going to tell you a story that was shared with me by one of my feminist friends, a woman named Barbra, who just happens to be a bovine midwife by trade. Barbra lives on a farm not far from Duluth with a herd of dairy cattle named after her own feminist heroes: Susan B. Anthony, Shirley Chisholm, Carol Mooo-seley Braun . . ."

(This is where I finally realized that I was absolutely, positively bombing and I needed to signal to my audience that I was aware of this fact.)

"WOW! TOUGH CROWD TODAY!"

"Anyway, up north near the farm, it's not unusual to be visited by coyotes or even wolves, all of which would be delighted to chew on a slab of fresh beef. Barbra tells me that when the herd senses danger, the healthy mothers gather the children and elders—that is, the most vulnerable in their community—into the center of a circle that they form with their bodies. Barbra says that this circle of care is instinctive to the mama cows, and it's something very remarkable and inspiring to watch, especially for those who consider the cow a stupid creature good for dinner, shoes, and not much else.

"Today, on a day when we celebrate sanity, I ask each of you to reconsider the language of grizzly bears, cackling rads (whatever the hell those are), teabaggers, head stompers, and disgusting lemonade makers, and really just slow yourself down. Be like a cow. Be calm. Eat, sleep, and take care of each other. Thank you."

(Polite clapping.)

My reception, while cold, was better than the reception for the next speaker, a woman from Students for a Democratic Society who had her mic unplugged and was yanked offstage. Apparently, calling the United States of America a supporter of terrorism (in Palestine and elsewhere) wasn't a very sane thing to do.

In hindsight, this should have alerted me to the fact that the political climate in my state was worse than I imagined.

I came to get down, unaware of how down things really were.

My street: A neighborhood makes a house a home

Minnesota Women's Press, November 1, 2010

At long last, a break from political posts! I am truly grateful for all of my neighbors in this corner of South Minneapolis—all of whom recognized themselves in this piece and made sure I knew it.

Not long ago, I picked up the detritus left in our recyclers' wake, a not uncommon occurrence. Beneath my oak tree, I found a small orange bottle, its label revealing that one neighbor took a strong antidepressant. My usual cleanup routine involves responsible re-sorting of recyclables, but this time I panicked and shoved the telltale bottle into my now-empty garbage bin.

Whenever it is appropriate, I am honest about my own challenges with anxiety and depression. I generally think more of those who attend to their mental health, not less. Despite my increased respect for this neighbor, I disposed of the bottle furtively, like a criminal in the shadows. I wouldn't want anyone to find my medication on the street—though it dawned on me later that this had almost certainly happened on a different garbage day.

Exposure is part of the neighborly experience. In the interest of saving energy, I air-dry my laundry, but unlike another neighbor, I don't hang out my bras or my husband's Fruit of the Looms. I feel smug until I realize that it's likely that everyone on the street, at one time or another, has seen me in my pajamas—or less.

A collection of neighbors is truly a variation on a family: a group of people, forced together by chance, who will witness you at your best and worst, whether you like it or not.

I remember a time when a different neighbor popped in to say hello, during that hazardous five-minute period just after lunch and just before cleanup, when a house with small children looks like Kansas after a cyclone. I might have made an excuse and kept my shame under wraps, had Elliott not already flung the door wide open and welcomed her in, his thrill at seeing her undiminished by the mess.

I like this neighbor very much, but she keeps a very tidy house. I saw her not so subtly survey the splayed-open cabinets, the stack of dishes waiting to be fed to the dishwasher, the coffee grounds sprinkled on the counter, the crumpled stack of newspapers, the unsorted pile of clutter that always accumulates by the back door (keys, loose Legos, sunglasses, Target receipts). We gabbed a bit before she scurried off to meet another neighbor for lunch, a mom whose compliant children have been witnessed not only holding, but also using, Swiffer mops. After she left, I collapsed on the couch next to the buckets of unfolded laundry and wondered why I hadn't chosen to live in a cabin in the woods, utterly alone.

I stopped wondering when I realized that if I were left to my own devices, I would need more than a prescription to cope with life's challenges.

The clean neighbor saved the day when a scheduling mix-up left my son locked out of our house. The earth-friendly launderer advocates powerfully on behalf of the public school that's served our neighborhood since her now-grown children were small. The Swiffer kids are always happy to feed our cat when we leave town to visit our other family—the one we were born into.

My husband and I bought a 1929 Tudor for its proximity to Minnehaha Creek and its space for our growing family, not because we knew the street was populated by interesting, funny, and thoughtful people, yet this latter feature has affected our lives most of all. Our neighborhood is what made this house our home.

I demand equal-pay reparations!
Radical Housewife blog, November 17, 2010

Back to politics! This post concerns one particular pay equity bill, but believe you me, I have been able to recycle my call for reparations on many, many occasions. So far I have yet to receive a nickel from any of the hypocritical women I've called out.

Money! It's what I want! Specifically, I want the money that should be summarily deducted from the Republican women in the United States Senate who voted to block a vote on the Paycheck Fairness Act.

Have you not heard of this bill? You must be a white, cis man, then. For everyone else outside of that small but powerful category, here's the summary in bumper sticker form: EQUAL PAY FOR EQUAL WORK! Did you know that in the United States the wage gap for white women is seventy-seven cents to every white man's dollar? That African-American women get sixty-two cents? That Hispanic women get fifty-three cents? The Paycheck Fairness Act is designed to help correct that. It would strengthen the existing Equal Pay Act of 1963 and would allow employees easier access to salary records without fear of retaliation. No-brainer, eh?

Olympia Snowe, Susan Collins, Lisa Murkowski, and Kay Bailey Hutchison hold the same positions as Al Franken, Henry Reid, and Mitch McConnell. The salary for the job of United States Senator is $174,000 a year. All the aforementioned ladies are white, and they are all Republicans who failed to break ranks to vote for this legislation. (Well, Murkowski didn't vote against it—she failed to show up for the vote. Same diff.) The dreaded filibuster killed it. That must mean that these four women do not agree that women employees need this kind of legal protection.

Grab your calculators! What *should* Collins, Snowe, Bailey Hutchison, and Murkowski be paid? And how much money do those four owe back to the federal government now that their hypocrisy has been exposed? I'll take an Ativan while I wait (the sheer stupidity of some people gives me anxiety attacks).

Ready? I was an English major, not a math major (I'm a *girl*, silly!), but my numbers tell me that each of these women should only be paid $132,240 per year. Let's subtract that from $174,000 and see what we get. Oh, mercy! These four, who do not believe that women have the right to equal pay, need to remit back to the federal government $41,760, each, for every year that they have served.

I'm starting a campaign to get my money back, because $41K times whatever might be just enough money to ensure that my public library, its hours slashed due to budget cuts, could reopen on Mondays. Luckily, most of its employees are women, and we know they work cheap! Start dialing, girls!

In the heart of a mother
Radical Housewife blog, November 29, 2010

This is the testimony of one of the bravest people I don't know—but probably see every day at the Lake Street Target, the Midtown YWCA, and/or Powderhorn Park. Years later, I remain astonished and humbled by it.

That it could happen in the poisonous political atmosphere of November 2010 was even more shocking and surprising. This mother made a deliberate choice not *to be a grizzly mama,* not *to stomp on someone's head, and* not *to engage in a downward spiral of hate and fear.*

Minneapolis is justifiably proud of its many hometown institutions, but none are more precious than our parks and lakes. Coming in close second to these natural wonders might be the annual MayDay Parade, brought to us since 1975 by the artists who make up In the Heart of the Beast Puppet and Mask Theatre. Back then, the company called itself the Powderhorn Puppet Theatre, in honor of the large park that gives the neighborhood its name. To most people in South Minneapolis, my home and hometown, Powderhorn Park is synonymous with this yearly celebration of community, an event so grassroots you can see dirt under the fingernails of everyone involved.

Powderhorn Park is an urban neighborhood, to be sure, not an idyll. Peace, love, and gigantic puppets rule one day out of the year, but the other 364 days are about just getting by.

Until the unthinkable happens.

Four boys, all between fourteen and sixteen years old, attacked a woman and her two children in the park last week, sexually assaulting the woman at gunpoint with her children nearby. Police following their tracks in the snow discovered the boys in a nearby garage in the act of assaulting two teenage girls.

What's your first instinct when you hear about these crimes? After you black out momentarily from rage, of course. Do you want blood? Explanations? Systems to blame, like the talk-radio men who wondered why this happened? (Their conclusion: these kids should have been locked up in juvie the first time they shoplifted candy. That woulda learned 'em!)

I couldn't stop thinking about what drives a fourteen-year-old child to commit such a horrific act of violence. My life in feminist activism has been about exposing the hypocrisy of a society that claims to worship both "family values" and "individual freedom," even if the latter implies the freedom to be poor, to be desperate, and to abuse one another.

But I write and think these things a mile south of the Powderhorn neighborhood. No one has attacked *me* lately. Sure, I shed tears of frustration reading an interview with Sister Helen Prejean in the August 2010 issue of *The Sun* ("To some extent violence is part of our nature," she said, "but compassion is too. Seeking justice for everybody is also part of human nature."). But while I was reading, I was on the treadmill at the YWCA, not lying in a hospital bed. What the hell do I know? Not much.

Yesterday afternoon, "the mother in the news" shared what she knows. Excerpts:

"The whole time I made a conscious choice to see the boys as human beings, not to see them as evil or bad . . . I see those boys as hurting, scared children who didn't get the kind of nurture, love, and care that they needed. I try to hold them now in compassion and hope that they might get the support they need to reconnect to their essential goodness. With the system of justice that we currently use, I'm hopeless that will happen."

This is exactly what Prejean told David Cook, her interviewer: "As a society, we have to examine our belief that severe punishment is the way to restore order. The main objective of prisons is to keep society safe, not to cause prisoners pain simply because they caused others pain." Similarly, the Powderhorn mother wrote:

"At one point the boys asked for our skis. I wish they could have taken them and used them and experienced the pure joy of gliding in the fresh snow, getting winded from exertion and breathing in cool, fresh air. Please send them all the love you can muster. I think they really need it."

To wish joy and love upon the one who has damaged your body and soul is an act of strength so confounding, so beyond comprehension, that it could only have come from a mother. Not a mama *grizzly*, mind you, a creature prone to violence and homicidal rage: *a mother*. A caregiver. A nurturer. A person who is connected, not isolated. A mother is what I am, but it's also what I hope to be.

Thank you, Powderhorn mother, Powderhorn Park, and all in my Minneapolis family.

Doing it anyway
Radical Housewife blog, December 6, 2010

This blog reads like a pep talk to my increasingly frustrated self, though, to be fair, most lefties were walking around dazed after the thrashing we got in the midterm elections. The Minnesota Legislature elected a Republican majority for the first time in nearly forty years, and they were gleefully planning all kinds of mayhem, including the long-threatened constitutional amendment to ban same-sex marriage. Our new governor was a Democrat, but his veto pen couldn't touch ballot measures. Ugh.

I'm sorry to say that not much has changed, neither in political parties nor in public schools.

I attended two very different activist gatherings last week. One consisted of parents and administrators at my kids' school, while the other brought together local feminists, a number of whom are involved in Democratic party politics. At both meetings, I heard the following:

"The left hand doesn't know what the right hand is doing."

"Is anyone looking at the big picture here?"

"We're talking to a brick wall half the time."

"Is this sabotage? Or just idiocy?"
"I'm exhausted."
"All of this work was for nothing?"
"We're not even talking about the same thing."
"What is wrong with people?"
"They want to wear us down so we will give up. And it's working."

Luckily each meeting came with some of my favorite treats in the world (coffee and mini-scones, wine and popcorn) to soothe my growing agitation. In the very cold light of Monday morning, though, it's obvious to me that we'll need more than snacks to get out of this.

Feminist Review assigned me to read Courtney E. Martin's book *Do It Anyway* at the perfect time to kick my tired, wintry butt into action. We all need to be told that even though improving our communities is hard, we have to do it anyway, especially when times are bleak. For example: instead of drowning in coffee this morning, I wrote a long letter to the Minneapolis Public Schools' Out 4 Good program, requesting that my son's middle school get some sorely needed anti-bullying support. Lately, when Elliott speaks out against sexist and homophobic teasing, he gets relentlessly teased back for his trouble. I see him tiring of being That Feminist Fifth Grader. And like the times I tell him to brush his teeth or finish his salad, when I tell him to "do it anyway!" his eyes glaze over . . .

The book would make a delightful holiday present for any activist burnout you know, be s/he feminist, PTA volunteer, phone banker, social worker, candidate, advocate, angry letter writer, all of the above, or even none of the above.

Pandora's Box by Nu Shooz
Feminist Review, December 15, 2010

Here is another totally random piece written for Feminist Review *that I am reprinting here to prove that I missed my calling as a record reviewer. Now I'm off to listen to "I Can't Wait" another hundred times.*

Conventional wisdom says that every young popster or rocker, no matter how devoted, will one day grow into a lover of smooth jazz. How else to explain Rod Stewart's resurgence as a tuxedo-clad, Bing-style crooner (aside from a mid-seventies deal with Beelzebub himself)? John Smith and Valerie Day, the duo behind '80s group Nu Shooz, are hardly stars of Stewart's caliber, but they did craft one of the finest American pop singles of all time, "I Can't Wait," and over two decades later, they've resurrected the song, and themselves, in predictably jazzy fashion.

Pandora's Box is the new self-released recording by Smith and Day's new project, the Nu Shooz Orchestra. The album includes "I Can't Wait: 20th Anniversary Edition" and ten more tracks of overbaked, hoochy-koochy coffeehouse pap that continues to smear John Coltrane by association.

But let's back up a couple decades to a great song from a band with a silly name. "I Can't Wait" is a single so phenomenal that I have yet to tire of it. In fact, I'm listening to it right now, though in MP3 form, which lacks the warm crackle of old twelve-inch vinyl. The track's bass line is addictively slinky, and powerful enough to support countless layers of snappy percussion, synths, twinkly guitars, a stealth horn section, and Day's coolly vibrato-free voice. The idea of a jazzy "I Can't Wait" has no appeal—in fact, it's antithetical to what makes the song work so well. Funk-influenced dance pop is propelled by deep grooves of the kind that powers "I Can't Wait," and that depth can only be created on a vintage Roland synthesizer. Individual notes will transpose to the stand-up bass, of course, but if I wanted to hear stand-up bass, I'd listen to Jimmy Garrison on *A Love Supreme*. I wouldn't listen to Nu Shooz, with or without its orchestra.

Therein lies the artist's curse of doing one thing extremely, even extraordinarily, well. Musicians are especially vulnerable to fans' fickleness: if I want to hear a pop song that sounds like "I Can't Wait," I can quite easily listen to "I Can't Wait" (and I did, three more times). The name Nu Shooz, however ridiculous, means classic '80s dance pop. The last thing this world needs is mediocrity, no matter what the genre.

Everyone needs to earn a living, so I don't fault Smith or Day for dipping into the seemingly bottomless wallets of our nation's latte sippers. The harsh reality is that if these tracks were released under a completely different name ("old sneakers"?), this album wouldn't even be reviewed, much less panned for not sounding like one snotty critic wanted it to. All is not lost, however! In my research for this review I discovered that no less a tastemaker than 50 Cent remixed the original "I Can't Wait" into his song "Buzzin'," and it's *really* good. I hope the residuals afford Smith and Day the chance to tune up the old Roland. The world and its shoes are waiting.

2011
Triggered

Obligatory trigger warning: this year we talk a lot about rape. And about trigger warnings, which we needed because of all of the constant, unrelenting, wall-to-wall discussion of rape! Sharron "fetus lemonade" Angle may have lost her Senate bid in 2010, but the fact that *anyone* took her bullshit seriously should have warned us that 2011 was going to get ugly—really ugly. I never dreamed that I would spend most of the year attempting to explain why I, as well as the leadership of Minnesota NOW, thought SlutWalk was actually a good thing. As I told the reporter from the *St. Paul Pioneer Press* who came calling, no one gave a shit when this march was called Take Back the Night, did they? I had to wade through an alarming amount of victim blaming to make my point, which made me trigger-happy indeed. One person became a target of my considerable rage, but believe me, he deserved it. And no, it wasn't any of the loonballs running to lose to Obama in 2012, though *they* would have deserved it, too.

Love in the time of contraception
Skirt! magazine, February 2011

As much as I complain about the inconvenience of contraception in this piece, I always, always *had access to it.* I never thought my feminist activism would have to backtrack to fight for contraceptive access . . . y'know, that stuff that makes it very unlikely that you'd need an abortion in the first place.

This essay, written for a laugh to keep from crying, appeared in Skirt!, a South Carolina–based women's magazine. It details one hetero woman's lifelong struggle to get it on without getting the clap, knocked up, or worse—mortally embarrassed. All of it absolutely, 100 percent true!

Sadly, a novelization of my sexual life story wouldn't be published by Harlequin—it would be a Tom Clancy-esque thriller, a tale of perseverance against an inexhaustible foe. My clear and present danger? The poisonous discharge of my sexual partners, or, as it's more commonly known, spunk.

Puberty arrived for yours truly in 1984, a time when AIDS hysteria was nearly as pitched as the threat of thermonuclear war. In the Reagan years, the possibility of AIDS transforming from a death sentence to a chronic illness was nearly as unimaginable as German reunification or George Michael's homosexuality. The message sent to horny teens everywhere was loud and clear: DON'T HAVE SEX BECAUSE YOU'LL DIE! Just say no, indeed.

Later, the warning was appended thusly: IF YOU'RE GOING TO HAVE SEX ANYWAY, EVEN THOUGH WE TOLD YOU NOT TO, USE A CONDOM, OTHERWISE YOU'LL DIE! These were very sexy times.

My generation of college students, especially those on campuses in decidedly non–Studio 54 settings, worried less about contracting HIV than catching chlamydia or, worse, an unplanned pregnancy. As a result, every campus bathroom held a small envelope packed with spermicide-coated condoms. Unfortunately, condoms were slippery, as dangerously unreliable as a nervous eighteen-year-old's erection. A regular complaint around the happy hour table was the young male's tendency to panic at the tear of the package, so frantic about keeping it up while the condom was adjusted that softness attacked. Beer, the main source of nutrients for the average college student, didn't help things.

Should we have postponed sex until marriage? It's true that many of my friends wed their college sweethearts, but no sane person buys a car without taking it out for a test drive.

After graduation, in a trusting relationship with a non-alcoholic, I filled my first prescription for the Pill. On Day 10, when one of my Starbucks customers complained that he had asked for a no-whip mocha, I crawled to the back room and wept. This is a big deal in the coffee world, where you're expected to be so blasted on caffeine that you can charge through eight hours without stopping. After work, I remained too skittish to desire sex at all, defeating the Pill's purpose entirely.

If modern science could defang AIDS, why couldn't it develop a reliable contraceptive free of side effects? Even a hopelessly retro mag like *Cosmopolitan* regularly bemoans this sorry state of affairs. Why the pills, the shots, the rings, the ooey-gooey sponge? (Sorry, *Seinfeld* fans: I tried the Today sponge and hated it. If unrolling a condom is a turnoff, imagine asking your boyfriend to help cram a foamy white blob up your vagina because you can't get the proper angle on it. Exactly.)

Why weren't there any of those sticky and embarrassing options being developed and marketed to men? Men can take a pill for a potent erection. Why not a pill for impotent sperm? Why is sexual health and safety the responsibility of straight women alone? (I'll give you a clue: it starts with a "p" and rhymes with "atriarchy." You're welcome.) If we all pulled a Lysistrata-style sexual strike, I'm sure that contraceptive R & D at GlaxoSmithKline would get busy (pun intended). Why not start teaching to this paradigm shift in public school?

Just kidding! Today's mandated message to horny teens has varied only slightly in the twenty-five years since my last health class. I believe the curriculum today goes like this: DON'T HAVE SEX BECAUSE YOU'LL DIE

... OF EMBARRASSMENT, BECAUSE THEN YOU CAN'T WEAR A PURITY RING ON YOUR FINGER, YOU DIRTY SLUT! This suspicion was confirmed by a friend with two boys enrolled in an exurban public school. When Kriss claimed that her sixteen-year-old endured a session with a guest speaker whose best advice was "no touchy," I thought she was kidding and said so.

"I'm serious," Kriss replied. "Then she told the kids that in case they got carried away, they needed to learn her special safe word." And that word is? "Turnip."

Nancy Reagan, come back! All is forgiven. You never exhorted anyone to "just say turnip."

I suspect that, like me, most straight girls bask in the rosy glow of nostalgia, not about their first sexual experience (since it almost always involves tears, pain, or, in my case, laughter), but about their first sexual experience sans contraception. Contraceptive-free sex with my husband was delightful and resulted in our son, born February 2000. We enjoyed it so much that when our sex drives resumed, around Christmas 2001, we realized that we'd have to start the contraceptive-go-round all over again.

My sister, with whom I never, ever discussed my sex life, off-handedly suggested that I consider a copper IUD. I imagined the old Dalkon Shield that, once placed inside the uterus, exploded like an Iraqi car bomb. "These new ones are totally different," she said. "No hormones, nothing funky. Safe as milk." As the clinic manager of a Planned Parenthood, she ought to know.

I made an appointment with a nurse practitioner named Judy, who explained that the old IUDs had come without warnings about STDs; since the seventies, it had been discovered that unchecked infections blew uteruses apart, not the flexible piece of copper boinging in Judy's latex-clad hand. Judy paused. "You are monogamous, aren't you?"

I nodded. *Non*ogamous was more like it, but I hoped the IUD would change that. I felt a mild cramp, no nastier than the squeeze of Aunt Flo. I heard the snap of latex gloves unpeeling as Judy announced: "All done." Then the bleeding commenced.

Just kidding, again! Yes, my periods lasted somewhat longer, requiring larger than usual stores of Tampax Slender Regulars, Always Ultra Thins, and black underwear—Jack Ryan dealt with red scares more serious than that. And, unlike the Cold War, they could end whenever I wanted them to: nine months after a second visit with Judy, I gave birth to my daughter. As I recuperated in the maternity ward, the nurse midwife on the late night shift dropped by. "I see you're nursing," she said, "but you'll need a backup. Have you thought about the contraception you'll be using when you get the"—she raised her eyebrows—"go-ahead?"

I nodded toward my husband, passed out in a plastic hospital recliner, his wadded-up hoodie substituting for a pillow. I made a scissoring motion with my fingers and whispered, "We already made the appointment."

What would Shirley do?
Radical Housewife blog, February 1, 2011

The midterm elections resulted in big victories for Republicans nationally and in Minnesota, which meant only one thing: more policing women's bodies! Not to be outdone, however, were the socially conservative Democrats who joined them. I lost my patience when the Democratic leadership started fundraising to fight these so-called "anti-woman extremists" while refusing to apply pressure to Dems voting in lockstep with them.

HR 3 passed the House but failed in the Senate. The Hyde Amendment still bans federal funding for abortion, and Collin Peterson still represents Minnesota's Seventh District, the jerk.

If you know me, you know that I come from a long line of old-fashioned Minnesota liberals who put the "farmer" and "labor" in the name of our state's Democratic-Farmer-Labor Party. My Grandma Rose revered FDR like a god. My own political shero, Shirley Chisholm, wasn't treated wonderfully by the party back in the day, but she remained convinced that reform from within was the only way to go. In her spirit (call it "What Would Shirley Do?"), I felt moved to respond to a new campaign of the Democratic Congressional Campaign Committee (DCCC).

Since all my readers are well-informed, I don't need to tell you that the newly introduced bill HR 3, the No Taxpayer Funding For Abortion Act, is a disaster for women's rights, essentially codifying the Hyde Amendment into federal law while gently peeling away what qualifies as "rape" for a woman needing such a funding exemption. You know: HR 3 is bad, bad, bad. So when you receive a message like this one from the DCCC, asking for you to sign a petition called "Rape is Rape: Denounce Republicans' Extremist Anti-Choice Legislation," you think it's something good to support. "Fightin' words!" you think. "It's about time"—especially since you haven't quite trusted the Democratic Party since the debacle of Stupak-Pitts. You're probably kinder to them than I am: I don't trust them at all since that mess.

For good reason, as it turns out: several Democrats are *cosponsors* of HR 3, including Minnesota's Collin Peterson. So why am I being asked to lash out at Republicans for this misogynist measure when there are *Democrats* sponsoring it? WHY?

I went to the DCCC's Facebook page to pose the question—politely, I thought: "Collin Peterson, a Democrat, is a cosponsor of this bill. Get his name off this bill, and I will give my name to your petition. Otherwise you are hypocrites."

Hey, the truth hurts. As I watched the flurry of messages on the page, I saw my comment get a thumbs-up. Nice. Others ignored my question, so I tried to post it again. This time I was blocked. For telling the truth? Did they think that the photo of a blonde kindergartener on my Facebook profile meant I was a Mama Grizzly plant? Seconds later, my comment was gone.

So now What Would Shirley Do? It's hard to say, especially since she didn't have Twitter at her disposal. I'll mull it over while I tweet the shit out of @DCCC.

What eleven-year-olds look like
Radical Housewife blog, March 10, 2011

In 2011, we did a lot of talking about rape: forcible rape, date rape, child rape, "rape" rape. Everyone talked about it like it was just another pro/con issue instead of a terrible crime. Even the New York Times *framed a story about the horrific gang rape of an eleven-year-old in a way that deflected blame from her attackers.*

I began this post with a photograph of my son at the Mall of America, where we took him for dinner and rides on his eleventh birthday, which we celebrated two weeks earlier. I thought it might be a helpful reminder for people unused to fifth graders.

I see my own eleven-year-old as an unusually beautiful specimen, but he is actually pretty typical of the species. While he is marketed to as a "tween," suggesting that he is on the brink of pubescence, he's more child than teen and nowhere near adult. For his birthday he requested and received a set of emo-skate-punk fashions from the Tony Hawk line at Kohl's, but wearing these did not suddenly transform him into a cast member of *Jackass*. One look at the roundness of his face tells you that this eleven-year-old is absolutely, unmistakably a child.

As a longtime feminist activist, I know about slut shaming and victim blaming. But as a mother of an eleven-year-old, I slumped over and wept when I heard about the *New York Times'* now infamous coverage of an eleven-year-old Texas gang-rape victim, including this quote: "Residents in the neighborhood . . . said [the victim] dressed older than her age, wearing makeup and fashions more appropriate to a woman in her 20s…"

Yes, author James C. McKinley, Jr., can hide behind the fact that the statements were made by people in the community itself, but he didn't bother to include a counterpoint from a sexual assault counselor, who may have reminded McKinley that a victim's clothing is irrelevant to the horrific crime perpetrated against her. Interestingly, McKinley placed this quote near the beginning of the story: "'It's just destroyed our community,' said Sheila Harrison, 48, a hospital worker who says she knows several of the defendants. 'These boys have to live with this the rest of their lives.'"

McKinley doesn't provide a voice that muses what the eleven-year-old *victim* will have to live with for the rest of her life. Why? I'm a writer, not a journalist, but even I know that it would only take one phone call to a domestic violence shelter or sexual assault hotline to find someone willing to speak up for this eleven-year-old child. Hell, McKinley could go to a large mall and find a mother of an eleven-year-old willing to go on record. This is what she'd probably say:

"My heart is breaking for that little girl. I hope that she gets the support she needs to recover from this terrible crime and that the perpetrators are brought to justice."

Then she'd hold her own eleven-year-old and cry.

Concern for the unborn, not so much for the born but homeless

Minnesota Public Radio News, March 25, 2011

A classic case of what "pro-life" means—and does not mean. The bill in question passed the GOP-led Minnesota House and Senate but was vetoed by Governor Mark Dayton in May 2011.

I don't fret over my children's learning waning over spring break—sometimes it seems Elliott and Miriam are too smart for their own good—but I do endeavor to keep them busy, especially with activities that don't require the Wii. Yet our spring break has provided us with an education all the same, though not on academic subjects. Instead my children learned a painful lesson about current Minnesota values.

Early on the first Sunday of break, our family found itself inside the quiet St. Paul skyway system, eagerly awaiting the nine o'clock opening of the Minnesota Children's Museum. Elliott and I left Miriam and their dad to wait in line while we wandered in search of an open coffee shop. Not far from the museum, another line was forming outside the skyway McDonald's. These adults were accompanied by rolling suitcases or plastic bags, not small children, and all bore weary expressions of bone-deep exhaustion that made my caffeine jones seem wimpy indeed. "Why are they carrying all that stuff?" Elliott asked. "Are they traveling?"

"Not exactly," I replied. I hoped I could delay a discussion of homelessness until I had a latte in my grasp, but my search ended abruptly as we encountered a skyway that was not only closed, but also the napping spot of a dirt-smudged man whose head was resting on a stuffed Target bag. Elliott stopped and asked what on earth the man was doing. "He's there," I said, "because it's too cold to sleep outside."

And so began a discussion of homelessness in Minnesota, tailored to the understanding of an eleven-year-old. I told him that, for a complex tangle of reasons, including entrenched poverty and a frayed social net, there were hundreds of people in the Twin Cities without homes. I didn't know until I did my own research that the actual number of homeless Minnesotans is closer to *nine thousand*, according to the Wilder Research Center. I mentioned that many of the homeless in our community were children, like him—but I didn't know that Wilder had found that children made up nearly *half* our state's homeless population.

Though Elliott is now a tween, already mimicking the studied carelessness of his adolescent idols, he still has a child's sense of injustice. "That is *so wrong*," he observed, once out of the sleeping man's earshot. I told him I agreed.

The next day, I received word from my colleagues in the reproductive rights community of a hearing on HF 936, the so-called Pain Capable Unborn Child Protection Act. I packed a bag of goodies and dragged my kids on another St. Paul field trip. They were the only children present at a hearing in which legislators argued over the bill's actual purpose: to define a person for reasons of protection under Minnesota law.

While Miriam chomped a stick of Extra bubblegum and read an Archie comic book, members of the House Civil Law committee bickered with the witnesses and each other over whether life begins at conception, whether the truth can be decided by majority vote, and whether Soul Asylum should be summoned to testify. I'm kidding about the last bit, though Rep. John Lesch did offer up one of the band's lyrics to make a point about opinion versus fact: "The right thing changes from state to state."

Elliott usually asks to play Angry Birds on my phone as soon as he's placed in a room full of grown-ups, but to my surprise he watched attentively while a representative of the Minnesota Citizens Concerned for Life testified that fetuses were "part of our human family" and that their vulnerability obligated the state to protect them. I clawed my chair in frustration as the committee chair, Torrey Westrom, insisted upon referring to a fetus that could not survive outside a woman's womb as an *infant*, a *baby*, or a *child*, whether at twenty weeks of gestation or two, as though the creature in question were interchangeable with my comics-reading daughter or my fascinated son. I leaned over to Elliott and whispered, "Do you think the people we saw in the skyway yesterday are part of our human family, too?"

He looked at me like I had just lost my mind. "Duh," he said. "Of course they are."

"So why aren't these important people talking about *them*, do you think?"

Elliott paused, cracked his gum, and offered, "Because they smell bad?" I nodded. "Because they are ugly and no one wants to look at them?" I nodded again. Elliott shook his head and muttered, "That is *so wrong*."

Lesson learned.

The trials of the introverted activist
Minnesota Women's Press, April 2011

I think my courage peaked sometime in 2010 and has been going downhill ever since. The panel I mention here was quite successful, but I haven't repeated it. Don't be offended when I don't come to your party/opening/fundraiser: it's not you, it's me.

The words rattled around my head so forcefully that my brain felt bruised: I can't do this, I can't do this, *I can't do this*!

Just months earlier, my cheeks burned with excitement, not fear, as I pounded away at my keyboard to enter a panel idea for Netroots Minnesota. "Feminist Activism in a Gone-Rogue Age," I called it, and as I typed I congratulated myself for my cleverness. Fast forward to the morning before my gone-rogue panel would begin—off the keyboard and into the world, I heard that voice again. *I can't do this!* The negative self-talk I experienced is fairly common among women, of course, conditioned as we are to doubt both our abilities and our potential. But this voice wasn't a product of patriarchy alone—it was a frank evaluation of my temperament. You see, I am an introvert.

I am an introvert, and I am an activist. At times these two selves integrate flawlessly. The writing career I enjoy today was sparked by friends who suggested that I start a blog on MySpace, which should give you an idea of how long I've been at this. At other times, my desire to network, strategize, and act runs afoul of my innate discomfort with unfamiliar groups of people. Try this experiment with your own introverted friend (you do have one; we make up as much as half the population): ask her if she's more comfortable writing a speech or delivering it. The former she could do with no problem. The latter? I bet she'll blush, stammer, and sneak toward the nearest exit, if she doesn't just laugh in your face.

For eighteen months I've worked on a political memoir that shares its name with that original MySpace blog: *The Radical Housewife*. Writing the book, all 350 pages of it, was a pleasure—in fact, I could have started another full-length manuscript the very day I finished. I didn't, though, because if I want to see *The Radical Housewife* published in my lifetime, I have to market it and myself to unfamiliar groups of people.

Cue that inner voice, with its odd combination of rationality and panic.

As I move toward my goal of publishing my book, I gird myself with how-to books, seminars, and consultations with publishing experts. One editor expressed sympathy for my plight but insisted I get over it. "No one writes to remain anonymous," she huffed. I admitted that she was right; I remain unusually delighted whenever I run a Google search on my name. I could have chosen anonymity on that MySpace blog, but I didn't. I could have just shown up for Netroots Minnesota and hoped that someone else had thought up a feminist panel, but I didn't.

I wish I could end this column with a shattering, life-changing insight for other introverts out there, activist or otherwise. If I had the solution for quieting that frightened inner voice, I'd write a book on *that*, and I'd sell it in an instant. Introversion is a part of me, as fixed a part of my makeup as my blue eyes. I admit to my fears in hopes that this small act of courage will build upon that previous one at Netroots Minnesota, which in turn built upon others—just as the feminist activism I do today is built upon the work of the foremothers who earned me the right to vote and the right to publish my writing under my own name.

Recently, while reading a book by an artist I admire a great deal, I stumbled upon the following quote: "Nothing in the world is more common than unsuccessful people with talent. Leave the house before you find something worth staying in for." The author of those words? The British graffiti artist Banksy—real name unknown. Maybe I *can* do this, after all.

Constitutional ban on same-sex marriage does no one's family any good

Minnesota Public Radio News, May 24, 2011

In this piece for MPR News, I express my views on the Republicans' marriage amendment in much calmer language that I used in front of my computer the day the bill passed. I ponder the hurt of "family values" pandering not only for the children of same-sex couples, but the children of straight couples who could one day identify as LGBT.

I'm a married, stay-at-home mom of two kids, a son and a daughter. I spend a great deal of time viewing the world through their eyes, negotiating their needs, hurts, joys, and the like. My parenting decisions are informed by my obligation to prepare them for the complexities of adulthood, in which obvious answers are few. I may be able to fix a skinned knee, but I can't make sense of heartbreak. I aim for an attitude of flexibility, in hopes that they will too.

For example, I play John Coltrane records in the house, but I don't take it personally that the kids prefer Ke$ha. Friends tease that my liberalism will one day boomerang on me, resulting in Elliott's transformation into a junior Alex P. Keaton, the Reaganite spawn of hippies on the sitcom *Family Ties*. They don't know that I've already decided to parent on the side of caution: in my house, conservatism is presented as a moral philosophy I don't happen to share, not a subject so taboo it gains allure by virtue of parental rejection (a win-win, I think).

Parenting with doubt is not easy, but I believe that it will reap significant benefits in the long run. My children's adulthoods are not fixed in my imagination, so they will never hear a "but I always thought you were going to law school!" sermon. My children sometimes examine the photograph of their parents' wedding in our Minneapolis backyard, but it doesn't lead into an automatic discussion of their own wedding days. Maybe they'll decide to marry, maybe they won't—or maybe the state they live in won't allow them to marry the partner of their choice.

I care about children, my own and those in our community, but I don't agree that limiting marriage to heterosexual unions like my own is necessary for "protecting the legitimate interests of children," in the words of Jennifer Roback Morse, a writer and researcher affiliated with the National Organization for Marriage. On April 29, Morse presented testimony before the Minnesota Senate Judiciary Committee in support of a constitutional amendment that would ban same-sex marriage in our state. In her testimony, Morse stated,

"Marriage exists to meet the social necessity of caring for helpless children, who are not and cannot be contracting parties. Children are protected parties."

As she opened her testimony, Morse identified herself as a parent of two, like me. I wonder if she ever considered the possibility that one or both of them could be gay? Nowhere in the transcript of her testimony does she mention how legal discrimination might affect the self-image of gay and lesbians themselves, preferring to focus her disapproval only on the children conceived by gay and lesbian parents, whom she rather coldly described as "partially purchased." This strikes me as an odd way to describe a family created out of love and significant emotional and financial commitment, which I would think Morse would find preferable to one formed in the aftermath of a drunken hookup.

Some LGBT citizens in Minnesota have children. Some LGBT citizens in Minnesota *are* children. As Senator Scott Dibble noted in emotional testimony before the full Minnesota Senate on May 11, "What family is this helping? Not a single family in Minnesota is helped by this effort." The bitterness of the language is already affecting two children I love dearly, sisters who will be in attendance at Miriam's sixth birthday party this weekend. Jennifer Roback Morse believes these two girls are doomed to ask "uncomfortable questions about their origins," but the only questions Mia and Margaret have today are about why Morse or anyone would describe their family as evidence of "the brutality of the marriage 'equality' regime." The only brutality I see would result from these children being caught in a culture war that the National Organization for Marriage has threatened to wage in our state, as it has elsewhere.

And the damage this fight would inflict on my children, should one or both be gay, is absolutely intolerable. Morse may be confident that her kids don't land anywhere on the LGBT spectrum, but I'm not. I parent on the side of caution and assume nothing. To do otherwise would be brutal, indeed.

I love Courtney
Radical Housewife blog, May 31, 2011

In which I announce one of the most exciting moments in my writing career: my long-form essay about Courtney Love's family was going to appear in Bitch magazine! Yippee! Forgive me for not reprinting it here—paying up the wazoo to license the song lyrics and book quotes in it would bankrupt me. Print copies are long gone, but digital editions of the Reverb Issue, #51, cost only four bucks through Bitch Media, a far better cause than Frances's trust fund.

Ah, the 1990s! I may have been a child in the seventies and endured adolescence in the eighties, but the nineties is when I really grew up. I spent the first twenty years of my life being what was expected of me: a fine student, an exemplary daughter, and a sidekick to my dominant friends. If an unsettling rage occasionally bubbled to the surface, it was my fault for not playing my role appropriately. Girls weren't angry—girls were *good*. I identified strongly with fucked-up boy-men like Holden Caulfield and Paul Westerberg, though my cisgendered heteronormative temperament prevented me from imagining myself as anything but a grunge god's loyal girlfriend. I had no seething female role models save Sylvia Plath, whose example was not one I cared to follow.

Enter Courtney!

Now, one could make a convincing argument that, like Plath, Courtney Love isn't a role model worth following. But in the early nineties, it seemed that the world might be ready to embrace a loud, smart, cranky, bitchy, flawed, contradictory, kick-ass feminist. Those were heady times! I loved (and still love) the riot grrrls with all my heart, but be honest: isn't Kathleen Hanna a little *too* perfect? She's the punk Anne Welles, while Courtney is Neely O'Hara, who, despite her many flaws, always says what she thinks and is the Doll in the Valley that you root for in the end. In the nineties, I finally learned to appreciate honesty over perfection. It doesn't make you popular—hell, it might not make you *happy*! But it's better than the alternative, to "fake it so real [you are] beyond fake," as Courtney warned. I remain flawed, but I'm no longer a liar to myself or to anyone else.

I'm very excited that years of following Courtney's career have led to my first piece for what is probably the smartest magazine in the country, *Bitch: Feminist Response to Pop Culture*. In "Nobody's Mother: Abandonment as Art in the Courtney Love Family Tree," I look at memoirs written by Courtney's mother, Linda Carroll, and grandmother, Paula Fox, to trace four generations of women who've been either unable or unwilling to care for their firstborns, all daughters.

It's not available online, so you'll have to run to your independent magazine purveyor for a copy. Which reminds me—does anyone have Courtney's mailing address?

Finger on the trigger warning
Radical Housewife blog, July 11, 2011

This post is very much a product of the fresh wave of consciousness raising about sexual assault in the aftermath of an Ontario cop's remarks that women should "avoid dressing like sluts" to prevent rape. The comments inspired the first ever SlutWalk in Toronto that April. In July, Minnesota NOW was already in talks with local advocates for survivors of sexual violence about how to replicate a walk in the Twin Cities.

As important as it is to have one's consciousness raised, it can be a painful process. Trauma gets compartmentalized until there aren't any compartments left.

The bumper sticker announces, "If you're not outraged, you're not paying attention." I'd like to amend that thought. For women, if we're not occasionally homicidal, we're not fucking human.

I am having a Valerie Solanas moment. Known to most as the paranoid schizophrenic who attempted to kill Andy Warhol, thus earning a biopic portrayal by Lili Taylor, Solanas is often trotted out as an example of misandry in the feminist movement by those who seek to undermine our credibility. Solanas wrote in 1968's *The SCUM Manifesto* that "civic-minded, responsible" women had an obligation to "destroy the male sex." Countless women who would like equal pay and safety everywhere they walk *still* refuse to identify as feminists, because if they did so, they'd be seen as "anti-male."

I love men. I married a man, probably the finest person of any gender I've ever known. My firstborn is a beautiful boy for whom I would do anything, including give up my life if necessary. That goes for my sweet nephew as well.

But God almighty, there are times when I hate *men* so deeply I shake. I hate them. To be a thinking woman in a rape culture is to know suffering so intense it is almost unendurable. It's not post-traumatic stress, it's *pre*-traumatic stress, formed the moment that a male doctor pulled me out of my unconscious mother's body (as was typical in 1971), took a look between my legs, and declared "It's a girl!"

I have never experienced sexual violence, but this can be attributed more to dumb luck than anything else—not the unfashionable clothes I wore, the confrontational stance I took in public, the self-defense class I aced, or the well-lit streets I have walked. I am *lucky*, not "better."

Women with their hearts open live in both fear and pain. Women I know have been raped in their homes, in their dorm rooms, and in their workplaces. They have been raped by their fathers, their brothers, their partners, and their bosses. They were raped as girls, and they were raped as women. The circumstances around the crimes were different, but the attackers had *what* in common?

If you said they were *men*, you're right.

If you're going to argue with me about women abusers and how terrible it is to wish anyone dead, you need to go elsewhere. Go to People.com and examine photos of the Duchess of Cambridge's hats. Order something from Etsy. Flame Mark Dayton on StarTribune.com, I don't care.

Allow me to experience and then move forward from this rage.

To our male allies: A challenge
Radical Housewife blog, July 18, 2011

Nathan, the troll who called me "racist" and "gynocentric" for my support of Hillary Clinton in 2008, was back! I knew his real name from careful googling done back then, but I never revealed it. Three years of spewing bile in relative anonymity, however, gave him the nerve to post his unvarnished opinion on what he thought of SlutWalk Minneapolis. I was so outraged that I published his real name (which is not Nathan, by the way) in my reaction post.

Two years ago, I participated in a panel on sexual violence during the University of Minnesota's Welcome Week. To their great credit, a large number of earnest eighteen-year-olds showed up to discuss an issue far less appealing than learning the forehand Frisbee throw. During both the morning and the afternoon sessions, I heard a question that I remember from my own college days, asked by the bravest straight male in the room: "This is really upsetting. Are women actually assuming I'm a perpetrator just because I have a penis?"

I'm sorry if it feels that way, I said. But don't blame women. Blame guys like Nathan.

Now I'm not saying that Nathan is a perp any more than those college guys were, but I do know that he has a mean streak a mile wide, and he vents said meanness on his blog. Normally, I'm of a mind to let creeps like him be. Why send him the web traffic? But today, the circumstances are different than when he called me a "matriarchic supremacist" back in 2008. I can handle personal trashing, but when I read his new post about SlutWalk Minneapolis (titled "If she dresses like a slut and acts like a slut, is she really a feminist?"), I felt a response was necessary.

Last week I wrote a post about frustration with rape culture that was borderline misandrous, and I was called out as such by a secret fan of mine who linked to it on a discussion forum. Since this poster also mentioned that I am "great" and "super smart," I know that he must have seen my point: that rape culture curdles the souls of even sensible women from time to time. And Nathan's piece on SlutWalk Minneapolis is as soul-curdling a bit of rape apologia as I have read in a long time. Set your TRIGGER WARNING alarm and read what he has to say:

"SlutWalk ideology is not about rape . . . it is about an attempt to abrogate the moral agency of women. It posits that women can behave as they wish with no consequences for their acts . . . [like] holding raw meat out in front of a starving dog . . . [caption below a photo of a woman, her bra visible, holding a 'no means no sign'] Does NO still mean NO if this gorgeous Asian slutwalker does everything to say 'f--- me'?"

I hear quite a bit from straight men saying that they aren't sure that feminism is for them while at the same time bemoaning the guilty-until-proven-innocent phenomenon mentioned above. Well, guess what? It's antifeminist jerks like Nathan who are making your lives difficult, fellas. What on earth could make anyone feel comfortable comparing a woman to a slab of "raw meat"? Sexism. It's not confined to small-time weirdos on the Internet, either. It's everywhere.

Help us end it, guys. We can't do it without your help. We need you to speak out against this warped view of the world. You are not dogs, and we are not meat. We are all human beings who deserve respect, safety, and freedom.

What's the saddest thing about a piece of writing like this? Nathan *knows* rape survivors. He's friends with them, he works with them, and he even has some in his own family. He doesn't realize this, though, because no survivor would ever share her truth with a guy like him. Yet he takes to his blog and condemns these very women for failing to apply "reasonable judgment and common sense." I wonder how that goes over with the women in his life who were molested by family members or raped by their boyfriends, let alone the ones who were victimized after a night on the town. They have my compassion and pity. Nathan? Not so much.

When privilege reminds you to STFU
Radical Housewife blog, September 20, 2011

Finally, a parenting post! Though I couldn't resist mentioning SlutWalk and several of the Republicans who were already running for the opportunity to lose to Obama in the 2012 election . . . forgive me.

I admit it: as a mom and a bit of a Facebook junkie, I enjoy the site *STFU (for Shut the Fuck Up) Parents*. Though I am darkening the door of forty, I am still extremely immature and enjoy a good laugh at someone else's expense whenever possible. Happily, I am not so oblivious that I don't recognize myself in some of the posts, especially the ones that are pointedly labeled "first world problems." Why, just last week I whined on my personal Facebook page, "Did I get dumber? Or did the school picture order form get exponentially more difficult?"

I got more replies to that post than I did to anything related to SlutWalk, let me assure you.* It seems I'm not the only one who finds the process annoying. Yesterday, though, I got a much-needed real world reality check. Yesterday, at the urging of a neighborhood supermom, I volunteered to assist in the photo-taking process at Miriam's school. I straightened collars, adjusted wobbly headbands, and urged kiddos to sit up straight and smile. I was taken aback, though, by how many children didn't have their annoying order forms in their hands. Some asked if they would still be able to get their pictures taken, and I assured them that everyone—yes, everyone—would have a chance to be yelled at by the already impatient photographer. Though the school office had put out the word that scholarships for photos would be available, there were far too many children who either hadn't gotten the message or hadn't snapped up available funds in time. I strongly suspect the latter.

I felt very, very dumb. Filling out that form gave me a headache, but not because a 5"×7" photo for the Wisconsin grandparents was beyond my family budget. And my daughter's school is among the more comfortable in our large urban district. STFU, indeed.

In the meantime, the fact that President Obama is talking about taxing America's wealthiest individuals and corporations has supply-siders crying into their silk hankies. Rep. Michelle Bachmann calls it "warfare," but here's a news flash: the rich declared war on the poor a couple of generations ago. While folks like the Koch brothers pour money into teabag campaigns like hers, *ordinary families can't afford to buy school pictures.*

It's infuriating. It makes me want to scream "STFU, ALREADY!" at the top of my lungs.

*Confidential to nonparent readers: thanks to the millions of school photo options now possible with digital technology, the order forms are as challenging to complete properly as 1040s.**

**Confidential to Rick Perry, Mitt Romney, et al.: 1040s are the forms we little people use to pay our *taxes*. You're welcome.

Criticism = good. Victim blaming = bad.
Radical Housewife blog, September 27, 2011

SlutWalk exposed as deep a generational schism in the feminist movement as the Hillary Clinton campaign had in 2008, but with much higher stakes. As I write in this blog post, survivors I knew were having a hell of a time negotiating any safe space in the ongoing debate over whether SlutWalk was feminist or terrible.

Does my headline make sense to you? Is it simple enough?

It better be, for I no longer have any interest whatsoever in defending the words "slut" or "SlutWalk." Really. I'm done. One more interview with the college kid who wrote me this morning, and that's it.

Right now I'm in triage mode. Sexual assault survivors I know are hurt. They feel attacked, and for good reason. They are triggered. *I* am triggered, observing them. Just because I haven't experienced rape today doesn't mean I won't tomorrow. No woman can say she's out from under the shadow of rape culture for as long as she lives.

According to conservative estimates, a person is sexually assaulted in the United States every two seconds. By the time I finish this post, there will be . . . Christ, who am I kidding? Untold numbers of people—sisters, mothers, daughters, brothers, and sons—will experience sexual violence at the rate I'm going.

Eldridge Cleaver said that if you're not part of the solution, you're part of the problem. I hate to get all binary, but that's what happens when I'm pissed off.

So which are *you*? A solution? A problem? If you're not sure, ask around. One of your friends is a rape survivor: ask her. Ask what she was wearing when she was assaulted. What she was doing. What she'd been drinking and how much. Ask how she'd feel if a discussion on the merits of SlutWalk degenerated into a referendum on how her recovery from her rape is going.

Go ahead, ask!

I'll wait.

In the meantime, I'll remind you that I'm not so far up on my high horse that I cannot accept criticism. Far from it—as a privileged white woman (PWW), learning from others is my job! I'm serious! PWW isn't a label I reject. How can I reject something that's true? I mean, have you *seen* me?

Have you heard back from your survivor friend yet? The clock is ticking, you know.

In her address to the participants of SlutWalk Philadelphia, Aishah Shahidah Simmons said, "As strange as it may seem today, I'm sure some, if not many people [once] took the position 'What do you mean 'Take back the night? You shouldn't be out at night!'"

Will SlutWalks last forever? I have no idea. Nor do I care! What matters is that SlutWalk is happening. Here. Now.

We won't always agree, and we shouldn't. A movement like that would be too boring for words—even words like "slut" and "SlutWalk."

Just leave the survivors the hell alone.

Please.

A rape protest whose talk draws attention to the walk
Minnesota Public Radio News, September 28, 2011

By now, my phone was ringing off the metaphorical hook with reporters who wanted me to comment on the generational rift over SlutWalk. The whole mess made me convinced that the Equal Rights Amendment should be renamed the Sluts' Rights Amendment—at least it would get some damned media coverage!

I have served as president of Minnesota NOW since May 2006, shortly after my daughter Miriam turned one. Today Miriam is a spunky first grader who knows that her mom goes to meetings to talk with grown-ups about something called "girl power." That's my kid-friendly shorthand for feminism, a concept so laden with historical baggage that even many adults are confused by it.

As a writer and as a self-identified third-wave feminist, I take words and ideas extremely seriously. Certain words are so loaded that they draw the air from a room: "feminism" is one in certain contexts. "Rape" is another.

Today the most loaded word in the feminist vocabulary is "slut." The term is at the forefront of a new grassroots movement to end stigmatization of rape and sexual assault survivors, kicked into gear last January when a Toronto police officer advised against "looking like a slut" as part of a smart rape-prevention strategy (the officer failed to define what clothing might qualify, a crucial omission considering that conservative estimates guess that one in six women will be raped in her lifetime. Not all of them dressed like Snooki at a nightclub, I'm sure). Local activists organized a protest march they dubbed SlutWalk, and more than three thousand Toronto residents participated. Since the original walk in April, dozens more have popped up in cities around the globe, including one that will be held on the Minneapolis riverfront on October 1 (Minnesota NOW is a cosponsor).

For every enthusiastic walker, though, there is an equally frustrated person, feminist or otherwise, bringing a different set of assumptions to the word "slut" and what it means in this context. Snarky comments from pseudonymous bloggers I anticipated; vitriolic reactions from women whom I considered feminist allies were a surprise. One in particular accused my friends and me of patriarchal collaboration—a high crime indeed.

Also a surprise was a phone call from a reporter with the St. Paul *Pioneer Press* asking to speak to me about the walk and the controversy surrounding it. In the five and a half years I've been Minnesota NOW's president, this is the first time a major media outlet has come calling. I've been active in independent and public media, but no one at the PiPress has given much thought to Minnesota NOW's lobbying of Senator Amy Klobuchar on behalf of the newly revitalized Equal Rights Amendment, and our stance on the threats to pay-equity legislation. I was called because of the word "slut." Why? It can't be because feminism is outdated or unnecessary. I suspect it's because the hard work of moving equality forward is neither dramatic nor exciting enough to warrant column space.

Sex sells, with or without consent. In a puritanical society as baffled by sexual behavior and expression as ours, it follows that any frank discussion of sexual violence would lead to confusion. Ours is a world in which a television program about preschool girls costumed as adult women can be a hit (*Toddlers & Tiaras*), yet these girls' teenage sisters aren't allowed science-based sexual information in their schools.

Perhaps the most damning evidence of our failure to confront reality is provided by the Rape, Abuse and Incest National Network: in the United States, a person is sexually assaulted every two minutes. I spoke with the *Pioneer Press* reporter for thirty minutes about SlutWalk, and during that time, fifteen people were sexually assaulted. These fifteen people are daughters, mothers, and sisters—and, lest we forget, some of them are sons, brothers, and fathers. Yet our discomfort with the topic, the air-draining energy we give to words like "rape" and "slut," disrupts frank public discussion over what responsibility we *all* bear to stop violence.

Minnesota NOW decided to participate in SlutWalk because we too are fed up with the constant refrain to women "To avoid rape, don't do X." We want the message changed to "Don't rape." Period. I challenge the opinion that SlutWalks draw negative attention, for I believe that negative attention is already here. It's called silence.

During the course of those thirty minutes, the reporter mentioned that a previous interviewee had said she would fear for her daughter's safety if she were to wear a SlutWalk T-shirt in public. I replied that everything I do for women's civil rights is done to ensure that my daughter's world is a little better than the one my feminist mentors left me. Why should I accept limitations for her? Shouldn't I demand that my culture accept her dignity, her humanity, and her bodily autonomy? In the end, the one quote he pulled was about feminists in provocative clothing.

Miriam, Mommy has work to do.

The power of exposure
Radical Housewife blog, October 12, 2011

In which readers learn what happened after Nathan discovered I had revealed his real name!

I know there are millions of posts that we blog addicts deem "must-reads," but yesterday's by s.e. smith on *Tiger Beatdown* is one that truly earns that title. In an essay called "On Blogging, Threats, and Silence," smith writes about her experiences with online threats, opening her piece with the very startling revelation, "I got my first rape threat as a blogger when I was on Blogspot, so new that I still had the default theme up . . . someone really had thought it was appropriate not just to write this email to a complete stranger, a totally unknown person, but to send it."

Smith tells her tale not just to reveal how very often this happens to women bloggers, but also to illuminate how often our concerns are minimized with the advice "Don't feed the trolls." As if the burden of dealing with nasty behavior is on us, not the perpetrator.

Regular readers of this blog know about my resident antagonist, Nathan. He's been on my case since a 2008 *Minnesota Women's Press* column in which I expressed support for Hillary Clinton in the Democratic primary. At the time, he blogged under a pseudonym. The depth of his venom so rattled me that I did a little digging and discovered that his was typical of a million pseudonymous blogs in which the author assumes that "anonymity" grants carte blanche to express opinions that would never be tolerated in polite company. Among Nathan's bugaboos were feminism, LGBT rights, and *any* support for Palestinian human rights, and in his blog he heaped scorn upon Twin Cities folks active in any of these civil rights movements.

But Nathan wasn't anonymous, really. It took only a handful of Google searches to discover his real name and that he was, in fact, a local activist with the Minnesota DFL Party.

The DFL? Minnesota's Democratic Party? Really? Why, yes! This is the party whose platform states opposition to "discrimination against any person on the basis of race, creed, religion, immigration status, sex, sexual or affectational orientation, HIV status, gender identity or expression, marital or homemaker status, disability or age."

Huh.

Do you think Nathan would allow his online persona to speak aloud at DFL meetings? Not likely. Do you think Nathan, like those who targeted s.e. smith, *Tiger Beatdown*, and other bloggers, took advantage of this perceived anonymity as well as bloggers' ongoing reluctance to talk about it?

This summer, I had enough. Inspired by news of the upcoming SlutWalk Minneapolis, Nathan wrote as disturbing a piece of rape apologia as I have ever read, and he made sure the post included the name of its director, my friend Kim, in an attempt to rattle her as I had once been rattled. I responded with a piece I called "To our male allies: A challenge," in which I identified Nathan by name. And take it from me, friends: nothing could have terrified him more.

He closed up his blog for a time. He officially resigned from the DFL Party. He begged me to redact his name, to stuff the genie back in the bottle. Today, his blog contains the longest rant against me yet, with specific threats of legal action against me and veiled threats of personal harm in calling me "Shannon Drury (YM"SH)." For those whose Hebrew is rusty, this is apparently a curse that calls for the destruction of a person and her memory. I'm not certain myself, so I think I'll ask the rabbi with whom I'm meeting next week (I'm not kidding—I really am).

In the words of s.e. smith, "I'm still not going to shut up, and not just because I am bullheaded and don't take kindly to being told to be silent or die . . . I don't shut up for all the people who have been silenced, who did throw in the towel because they just couldn't take it anymore."

I hope you, dear reader, will join me in accepting smith's call to keep talking about this on our blogs, our social media sites, and in our communities. Refuse to be silenced. Demand accountability. Speak out!

The awareness-industrial complex, or: Who hearts nutsacks?

Radical Housewife blog, November 29, 2011

Thankfully, these stupid bracelets are no longer a fad, but there are still far too many cleavage jokes made every time it's Breast Cancer Awareness Month. My campaign for nutsack awareness has yet to take off, however.

I hate cancer. I hate it *so*, so much. I hate it to the depths of my soul and back again. I have never been diagnosed with cancer, but it's taken plenty away from me all the same. The hole in me isn't from a surgeon's knife or a radiation beam, but from what my dear friend Liz took with her when she died of colon cancer in 2007.

Cancer is everywhere. Members of my family have it, friends have it, and neighbors have it. Just before Thanksgiving, I learned that *yet another* person I care about is under attack from the demon cancer. I hate it.

You know what else I hate? The trendy "I Heart Boobies" bracelets that pretend to support cancer awareness, like no one has ever heard of breast cancer ever.

A few months ago, a feminist lawyer of my acquaintance contacted me in my role as Minnesota NOW president to let me know about a suit being brought by a local girl against officials at her middle school, who disciplined her for wearing one of these god-awful things. This was a feminist/free speech/women's health issue, she suggested.

Bullshit, I said.

As the mother of a middle schooler, I have been familiar with these bracelets for some time. Perhaps the best way to explain my position on the matter is to dramatize what occurred when Elliott expressed interest in getting one for himself.

Mom: No way are you getting one of those. They're sexist.

Elliott: But Mom, they're for cancer.

Mom: Oh yeah? Did you know that men get a very serious form of cancer themselves? It's called testicular cancer.

Elliott: Uhh . . .

Mom: Are there kids at your school wearing bracelets that say "I heart nutsacks"?

Elliott: [Giggles uncontrollably.]

Mom: I didn't think so. These bracelets aren't about cancer; they're about making fun of women's bodies with cancer as a cover. Until men's bodies get in on the joke, no bracelets for you.

I planned to write a post about this lawyer's request back when she made it, back in the thick of the "Is it or isn't it feminist" debate swirling around SlutWalk. This lawyer, as it happened, hinted that SlutWalk might not have been *her* feminist cup of tea. I invited her to share the issue with a future meeting of Minnesota NOW officers, state board delegates, and members, all of whom could debate the issue more intelligently than me, a person who attempts to fill the Liz-shaped hole inside of her with white hot rage directed at any and all cancer "awareness" campaigns.

Really.

Because that's where we've arrived in the cancer "awareness" movement. We are *aware* of cancer every day. We run in races, we walk for three days, we wear rubber things on our wrists. We are granted freedom to make as many boob, ta-ta, knockers, bazooms, and tit jokes as we want to. We paint everything pink for "awareness," yet the dollars are not reaching the scientists in the labs who need them. More and more of the money stays with the pinked-out corporations and enormous foundations that exist to make you *feel* good, not *do* good. Think about it: since the Empire State Building started glowing pink during the month of October, have breast cancer rates gone down? NO. In the most egregious example of pinkwashing yet, Susan G. Komen For the Cure actually commissioned an "awareness" perfume that contained toluene, a neurotoxicant, and galaxolide, a hormone disruptor.

You read right: *Cancer awareness is giving us cancer.*

That's a feminist issue.

2012

A casualty of the War on Women

The constant vitriol of 2011 left everyone shaken, but I was on ever more unstable ground. The process of submitting stacks of *The Radical Housewife* proposals and enduring countless rejections was a little (!) tougher than I had thought it would be. It was even tougher receiving these rejections while being attacked online for the high crime of supporting rape and sexual assault survivors in SlutWalks around the globe. And even tougher when *another* friend of mine was diagnosed with cancer! In 2012 I started writing honestly about the toll all this took on my mental health.

Happily, I did find a supportive publisher in Terena Scott of Medusa's Muse Press, and in 2012 we began the harrowing process of editing my original manuscript—when I wasn't dressing in housewife drag and claiming victory in the ongoing War on Women, of course.

A human being, not a human doing
Minnesota Women's Press, January 2012

In 2011 I turned forty and experienced the accompanying midlife crisis. Instead of buying a red convertible I signed up for a mindfulness course that actually had me meditating every day—for about six months. Then I went back to drinking too much coffee and biting my nails. While I was still a practitioner, my teacher told me she read this column and found it amusing. Yes, "amusing." Buddhists are the weirdest people.

All my life, I've sought relief from a hurricane of thoughts and emotions churning throughout my body and mind. To me, "inner peace" is not woo-woo jargon meant to sell me incense or crystals; like other chronic anxiety sufferers, it's a state that I yearn for yet fear I will never reach.

I've experienced peace in fleeting moments—watching the sun set over Rose Lake, curling up under the covers with a Nancy Drew mystery, nursing a tired infant to sleep—and have been haunted by their transience. Eventually, the sun dipped over the horizon and the mosquitoes came out; the twentieth chapter ended; the baby woke up.

My search for lasting peace grew somewhat desperate last year as I approached my fortieth birthday. As a gift to myself, I signed up for a class in mindfulness-based stress reduction. A complementary medicine program designed to be useful for anxiety sufferers and anyone else seeking relief from physical or emotional pain, MBSR was developed by Jon Kabat-Zinn in the late 1970s and centers around cultivating awareness in the present moment. Not the past, which is over, and not the future, which we can neither control nor predict, but the *present* moment, the only moment we really have.

The course lasted eight weeks, and the first few were anything but calming. The full-body-scan technique, which the teacher warned could put some people to sleep, gave me a splitting headache. When I practiced the course's mindful (i.e., slow as molasses) yoga postures, I remembered why I always like to sneak out of my YWCA's vinyasa class five minutes early.

"Why?" my teacher asked.

"Because relaxation pose is boring," I said.

"Why?" she asked again.

"Because you're not *doing* anything," I growled, sounding more like my surly preteen than a mom in a midlife crisis.

"But you're a human *being*, not a human *doing*," my teacher said. I hadn't thought of that.

Finally we reached the cornerstone of the MBSR program: daily meditation. My brain raced like it was outrunning an SST: *What was that noise? Did my phone ring? I should check. It could be important. I bet Elliott forgot his lunch again. That kid! Why am I so rotten at this? I shouldn't be thinking about lunch. Is there peanut butter at home? I should stop by Target after class. But I'm wearing yoga pants. I look stupid in yoga pants. What if I ran into somebody? I bet I am the worst student this woman ever had.*

"I can't do this," I admitted. "I can't turn off my brain."

My teacher reminded me that no one's mind has an on/off switch. All she asked of my mindfulness study was that I pay attention to my breath in the present moment.

"Just breathe," she said. "The wonderful thing about the breath is that it grounds us, reminding us that in change lies opportunity. We always have a chance to start over with another new breath."

In other words, the sun will set, but it will rise. Nancy Drew solves *The Secret of the Old Clock*, but she moves on to *The Hidden Staircase*. The baby will wean herself and will grow and change, but that means she'll be able to do things she couldn't before, including saying "I love you."

Breath by breath, my present moments were richer than they'd ever been before. They were untainted by mistakes of the past and freed from the anxieties of future. Is this peace? Maybe. I know that my journey to *being* from *doing* is underway, one breath at a time.

The problem of feminist mental health
Radical Housewife blog, January 10, 2012

This blog post appears in slightly different form near the end of The Radical Housewife. *At the time I posted it, I didn't plan on talking about activist burnout in my book at all—why bum everyone out? I thought that my story was one of rising from the ashes of postpartum depression, not dipping back into it again. Oops.*

This post gained new life years later when it was discovered by Reddit misogynists calling themselves Men's Rights Activists. Their reaction proved the point that compassionate vulnerability is often, if not always, mistaken for insanity. Sigh . . .

In 1963, Betty Friedan dropped a bomb on American culture called *The Feminine Mystique*, a book that diagnosed untold millions of women with "the problem that has no name." The book kicked off the second wave of feminism, but if you're a regular reader here, you already know that.

What I want to talk about is another problem that, though it is named and we all know it exists, is rarely discussed openly in feminist circles: the stubborn problem of feminist mental health. Everyone we know is on an antidepressant or twelve, yet we talk more about abortion, sexual assault, gender identity, and other formerly taboo topics than we do our own addled minds.

Believe me, this is no royal "we" I'm using here. My own mental health, on unstable ground since my teens, has been in a slow decline for the better part of a year, due to factors both internal (genetic predisposition, hormone dysregulation) and external (professional disappointment, thorny family issues, a friend's terminal illness). Like many other smart, capable, honest women I know, this is how I faced it: by pretending nothing was wrong.

Some time ago, I expressed my disgust over one body part or another (belly? batwings? blotches? pick 'em), and a feminist friend stopped short. "You?" she asked. "*You* feel body shame?"

"Of course I do!" I replied.

"But," she spluttered, "*you are such a good feminist!*"

I laughed and told her I was a feminist *because* I have body shame, I know how much it sucks, and I want to stop it! Duh! I use this anecdote to illustrate a question I've been thinking about for a long time: are feminists depressed and anxious because they're feminists, or are they feminists because they're depressed and anxious? Are we the chickens, or are we the eggs?

From childhood on I felt uneasy with cultural norms—I was always the only kid in my social circle who loathed the ending of *Grease*. We sensitive types recognize injustice more quickly and are attuned to suffering more deeply, so it makes sense that we would seek to participate in movements that are dedicated to ending injustice and relieving suffering.

We are chickens. Depressives and anxiety fiends make *great* feminists.

The work of feminism, whether in action or in our own minds, is exhausting. Being aware of oppression is a painful state. In the phraseology of most popular philosophical text of the late twentieth century (that would be *The Matrix*, duh), we swallowed the red pills, not the blue ones. Additionally, feminism confronts the horrors of rape, sexual assault and abuse, domestic and dating violence, and other *really, really awful things* that over time become re-traumatizing. A lot of the things I hear and know are very upsetting, and there are times when I just can't fucking take anymore.

We are eggs. Feminism can make you *greatly* depressed and anxious.

Like all good (if not great!) feminists, however, I try not to paint everything into a binary box, so I am in no way suggesting that this is an either/or proposition: feminism and happiness are not mutually exclusive. Why, one arm of the vast right-wing conspiracy is dedicated solely to convincing women that we'd be better off in our pre-Friedan kitchens and baby nurseries, because all this agitating for equal rights is what's making us so cranky! Perhaps that is one reason that feminists like me have been cagey about admitting to emotional frailty. Despite the fact that 11 percent of Americans take antidepressant medication these days, talking frankly about mental health care feels about as safe as walking down a dark alley, drunk, in nothing but filmy lingerie.

Didja get the analogy there? In America today, the prevailing wisdom is that people with mental health challenges bear some of the blame for their condition. As in, "Yeah, no one deserves to be raped, but y'know, you really *shouldn't* have been in that alley, drunk, in your underwear." Anorexics are told to "eat a sandwich." The anxious are told to "practice yoga." Addicts are told to "quit, already." Depressives are told to *"suck it up, for God's sake; you're bringing me down."*

Ahem.

This is the part of the blog post in which you, dear reader, usually discover the Great Lesson in all this, but today I don't have one. In fact, I've been putting off writing this blog post for weeks, hoping for a bolt of clarity, either intellectual or emotional, that has yet to strike. I am eager to hear your thoughts on the matter, though, as they relate to both your own story and to the big-picture issue of keeping sane in a world that isn't.

In any case, I'm resolved in 2012 to speak more frankly about my own struggles. Will it be more or less difficult than my perennial resolutions to exercise daily and eat more green food (apple Laffy Taffy excepted)?

Watch this space to find out.

How the Kid Scout cookie crumbles

Radical Housewife blog, January 17, 2012

In 2012, a group calling themselves the "Honest Girl Scouts" made a video protesting a Colorado troop that was admitting a trans girl to their ranks. The video went viral, of course, because everyone wins when cookie buying suddenly becomes An Important Political Statement! The scouts in my neighborhood couldn't sell me Thin Mints fast enough.

By now, I'm sure all y'all have seen the video complaining that your Thin Mint dollars are being spent on including transgender girls in the organization.

Sprinkled throughout last week's Facebook timeline were sighs of relief, for our cookie addictions can now be reclassified as Important Political Statements. I love when things come together like that!

Anyway, everyone's still talking about what's under those green skirts. Used to be we just cared about the cookies, not the genitalia.

On a related note, my last post on the conundrum of feminist mental health garnered this comment, with some unexpected advice: "The more I move into separatism, the more I do whatever it takes to have less and less to do with men and male-identified women, the happier I become . . ."

Interesting!

Occasional bouts of misandrist rage, I understand. Patriarchy can turn any woman, whether cis- or trans-, into a lunatic. But separatism?

Admittedly, I always feel prickly whenever it is suggested that heterosexual feminists like me are Doing It Wrong. Personal rebuff aside, it implies that GOP presidential candidate Rick Santorum is correct in his belief that sexuality is a choice, which leads us all into a bullshit-filled rabbit hole. And I defy any radical separatist to come to my house to have a crack at the difficult daily work of raising a feminist son. I *might* even go out on a limb and suggest that it's *the* most important work of our movement—that is, if I were the sort of person prone to the kind of "nyah, nyah, my feminism is better than yours" that I try to avoid.

Really, I do.

You know who's an unequivocally *great* feminist, though? That boy of mine. He could out-feminist a wannabe like Sarah Palin in a heartbeat. And with his gorgeous hazel eyes, he'd look amazing in a green and white uniform.

Is separatism really the answer? Isn't it time we had Kid Scouts, open to anyone interested in hustling Thin Mints for merit badges? No, not Boy Scouts, Kid Scouts. Is there some way we could convince trans activists Kate Bornstein and Chaz Bono to spearhead a movement that untethers scouting from gender entirely?

And, for once, can we let cookies be cookies and kids be kids, regardless of flavor?

Why doesn't she leave? Only she knows
Radical Housewife blog, January 27, 2012

You guessed it—this blog post was written in response to a dustup involving several of my activist friends. I wish I could say that it was resolved to everyone's satisfaction, with the person out of the dangerous relationship and the former friends back on speaking terms, but I can't. Sometimes being compassionate is the hardest activist work of all.

I love my feminist sisters and brothers, but they aren't perfect. Feminists can be power trippers, backstabbers, and *my*-shit-don't-stinkers as much as any other segment of the human population.

With that said, there are certain ground rules that are accepted when one claims membership in The Feminist Club. They are so mind-numbingly obvious that I feel idiotic even replicating them, but here they are:

Feminists who've had abortions are not called "baby killers."

Feminists of color are not called racist slurs.

Feminists who are rape survivors are not called "sluts."

Feminists who are LGBTQ are not called any homophobic insults.

We gird ourselves daily against this disapprobation from the general population, so we should understand that when we are in a feminist space, we will be safe from this kind of garbage.

It follows, then, that this is also a Feminist Club Ground Rule:

Feminists in abusive relationships are not called "weak," or dissed publicly for what they are going through.

Yet it happens, and much more often than you'd think. WHY? Marie De Santos, director of the Women's Justice Center, an advocacy group in Sonoma County, California, asked about this in a piece called "Why Doesn't She Leave?" "Why do so many people still hold a view, as cloaked as it may be in paternal tones, that is more in sync with the perpetrator's stance than with the victim's?"

Why, indeed.

There was a time, I admit, when I did think that the first thing an abused woman should do was leave. She should walk out, call the cops, get one of those restraining-order thingies that I thought solved everything . . . but there was also a time when I didn't think that women could be raped by their boyfriends. I also spent a portion of my life believing in Santa Claus. What happened?

I listened, I learned, and I grew the fuck up.

Despite our gut feeling that a woman in an abusive relationship "needs" to leave, she might have good reasons for not going anywhere. Statistics tell us that the victim is actually in the *most* danger when she is in the process of leaving—and seventy-six percent of women killed by their abusers had been stalked prior to their murders.

On December 28, 2011, the author, entrepreneur, and blogger Penelope Trunk posted a photo of a bruise her husband had given her. Naturally, it went viral. Four days later, she responded, "I'm absolutely shocked by the collective hatred and disdain for women who are in violent relationships. . . . for some reason, people feel it is honorable to rip a woman to shreds if she is living with domestic violence." She also declared, in no uncertain terms, that she is staying with her husband.

If I were Penelope Trunk's friend, I'd let her know that she had my support whenever and wherever she needed it. If she showed interest, I'd help her create a detailed and thorough safety plan. Penelope isn't keeping her abuse a secret, obviously, but other women might want to, so I would be absolutely certain that I didn't expose my friend's situation without her permission. After all, the consequences of breaking the silence would be borne by my friend, not me. Reality check: thirty percent of women homicide victims were killed by their intimate partners.

If you aren't sure how to react to a person's story of domestic violence, don't judge. Listen. Answers will reveal themselves, one story at a time.

Pink'd

Radical Housewife blog, February 2, 1012

In early 2012, the Susan G. Komen Foundation announced that it was not renewing a $700,000 mammography grant to Planned Parenthood with a bunch of baloney excuses that had nothing to do with cancer prevention and everything to do with abortion politics. The ensuing controversy was a great opportunity for anti-pinkwashers to get their complaints about Komen to a wider audience.

I wasn't speaking rhetorically about the pain that cancer inflicts upon a family—in February 2012 my friend Pam was receiving hospice care for terminal brain cancer. I brought meals, walked the dog, and did whatever else I could to support her and her family. I did not bring over any goddamn ribbons, that's for sure.

I posted a blog last November that I called "The awareness-industrial complex," spurred in large part by my blistering rage against a world that lets us drown in cancer-support products but not actual cancer *cures*.

Sure, the pink crap hawked by the Susan G. Komen Foundation at a Walk/Run/Crawl/Kvetch For the Cure™ makes people feel good, but here's a news flash: maybe cancer shouldn't make people feel good. Cancer, to those whose lives are touched by it, feels very, very bad. Cancer, to those whose bodies are actually enduring it, feels more terrifying than anything imaginable.

What would a world in which cancer made people *angry* look like? For one thing, there would be none of this NFL-players-in-pink shoes bullshit. Don't get me wrong—Tom Brady looks cute in pink. But what he wears doesn't do a damn thing for a suffering patient. Not the way that a research program at Johns Hopkins would.

Honestly, the Komen vs. Planned Parenthood kerfuffle makes me happy. I'm disappointed that PP is losing over half a million dollars of Komen grant money, of course, but I'm pleased that PP supporters have kicked in nearly $400,000 since Komen's boner became public (feminists are the nicest people). Most importantly, however, the public is starting to question the motives of a foundation that has very deep ties to Republican lawmakers who oppose not only women's-health initiatives, but also the environmental regulation that could . . . wait for it . . . *prevent cancer*. Worst of all, it has long been known that Komen's founder Nancy Brinker, is a great friend of pharmaceutical companies that *depend upon cancer to make money*.

Watching the Komen brand suffer is schadenfreude at its finest. But any amount of suffering it endures is a trip to Disneyland compared to the pain of a cancer patient, her children, and her family.

Against Daddy Dearests, biological or mythological

Radical Housewife blog, February 13, 2012

As Minnesotans took up battle stations for and against the same-sex marriage ban on our fall ballot, we heard more and more about how essential it was for kids to have a father and a mother living together under the same roof, as if that automatically conferred a kind of bulletproof magic over their children. Family values! As a mother living under the same roof as her children and their father, I felt compelled to call bullshit.

On February 3, the *Washington Post* published a George F. Will column called "Lifting Up the Fatherless," in which we meet Robert Lewis "Sugar Bear" Jackson, a formerly incarcerated man who is turning his life around. Here is how Jackson is introduced: "Born to an unmarried, mentally ill prostitute, he acquired his interest in driving from his grandfather, who would drive around the block with Sugar Bear in his lap. Not until Sugar Bear was twenty-five did he learn that his grandfather was his father, too, having had a sexual relationship with Sugar Bear's mother."

Don't you love the nimble use of the euphemism "sexual relationship" to define incest, an act that rarely occurs between consenting adults? Especially not when one of them is already identified as having a mental illness? I suppose the word "rape" is too unsettling for Will, a guy who wears a bow tie.

Will writes that "Sugar Bear grew up mostly on the streets, episodically drifting into and out of the care, such as it was, of various female relatives." He doesn't state that Sugar Bear would have been better off in the care of his rapist father/grandfather instead of "female relatives," but I felt that the correlation was strong enough to say so on my Facebook page. A couple of readers thought I went a bit far in chastising Will, and perhaps they're right. I'm just very sensitive to the assumption that children suffer without a dude in their lives, for that assumption leads us to a January 7 article in the *Los Angeles Times* with the headline "Rick Santorum dwells on gay marriage: he suggests to a New Hampshire audience that an imprisoned father is preferable to a same-sex parent."

!!!

Because any time I get even the faintest whiff of the suggestion that my friends Morgan, Mia, and Margaret are somehow *not being loved adequately* because neither of their parents has a dick, I want to scream! *And explode into a fiery ball of exclamation points!!!!!!!*

Happily, a Facebook reader recognized that the fault lies neither with Will, the editor who crafted his column's headline, nor Santorum, for that matter. We remain such a grossly sexist society that whenever something goes wrong, we're quick to assume that a *man* ought to be able to fix it. In the case of Will's column, a closer reading reveals that the *man* in question is not Sugar Bear's bio-dad after all, but a man named Jesus and his alleged father, the Good Lord Himself™. As the smart reader wrote on my Facebook wall, "I object to the insinuation that biological or mythological fathers are the only options for good role models."

Right on! Sugar Bear was failed by much more than his father/grandfather/heavenly father. Social problems as tough as entrenched poverty and mental illness aren't going to be fixed with a dad-shaped Band-Aid.

Interested in the thoughts of an actual, honest-to-gosh cis-fella, I turned to the Radical Hubby. "Oh, whatever," he huffed. "People tell themselves that crap all the time. *I'm* a good father, so *I'm* the reason that my kids aren't in prison.* When the truth is we are all a mess of nature versus nurture versus all the other bullshit the world throws at us. Kids need people who love them. Period."

Yep.

*Matt *is* a wonderful parent, by the way. He's a great believer in quantity time as well as quality time. Still, when my son was old enough to realize that his best buddy had two moms, he whined: "*What?* Morgan has two moms but I only get *one?* That's not fair!" Ha!

Diary of a mad birth-control mom
Radical Housewife blog, March 7, 2012

In 2012, House Republicans sponsored a committee to discuss objections to federal contraceptive coverage. The committee included a total of zero women. Democrats invited a Georgetown Law student named Sandra Fluke, but she wasn't allowed to speak. Noted paragon of sexual morality Rush Limbaugh ridiculed her mercilessly, drawing so much ire that advertisers pulled their spots and El Rushbo was even moved to apologize. I wish this meant that everyone agreed that contraceptive coverage for all was a good thing, but after the dust settled, the same stupid old white men were in charge of everything.

One year ago, *Skirt!* magazine published an essay of mine entitled "Love in the Time of Contraception." In the piece, I laid bare (pun intended) many sordid details from my love life to make the point that there is no sexual blunder more embarrassing than ignorance . . . and that includes having to ask your boyfriend to retrieve a Today sponge gone rogue in your lady parts.

Rereading the essay, I find myself cringing once more at the stubborn persistence of America's puritanical values. I wish my European forebears had thought to resettle in the British colony settled by criminals, not uptight prudes. Fleeing famine and conscription leaves one with limited choices, I realize, but I have to believe that my great-great-greats would have preferred their descendants to spend Good Friday frolicking on a sandy beach instead of heading out to show solidarity for a *legal* but beleaguered and threatened facility that performs *legal* procedures and dispenses *legal* medications.

I've been involved in feminist activism for a long time, and I'm committed to it. I'm a realist, and I know that the anti-choicers won't go away. I didn't assume that one day I wouldn't have to show up. I assumed that one day I'd be out in St. Paul with my adult children, demonstrating our support for safe, legal abortion, on demand and without apology.

But here we are in 2012, and I cannot believe I just might have to fight for the right to *contraception!*

Remember contraception? The stuff that makes controversial procedures like abortions *unnecessary?* (Duhhh.)

Isn't it *our right as Americans* to be embarrassed by slimy sponges? To go soft at the crinkling sound of the condom wrapper? To take a pill that makes you a hysterical, bloated mess, so on edge that no one wants to have sex with you anyway (or is that just me?)?

But it's come to that. Now, millions of moms who wouldn't have dragged their kids to Planned Parenthood in the past are being jolted into action by hearing law student Sandra Fluke be slammed as a "slut" and a "prostitute" by Rush Limbaugh for the high crime of supporting contraceptive coverage in Obamacare.

Of course, noted slut (four wives) and prostitute (uses his big mouth to make money) Rush doesn't believe that there could be a voting bloc of Birth Control Moms. Sayeth he: "Isn't that kind of contradictory? A birth-control mom? How do you become a mom if you're into birth control?"

Well, duh. You use condoms so you don't become a nineteen-year-old parent with a boyfriend who is a manipulative asshole. Or you use sponges *and* condoms so you don't become a twenty-two-year-old parent with a boyfriend who is much nicer than the old one, but who still has a few mental health issues to clear up. Et cetera.

Get the idea? The clinic is called *Planned* Parenthood for a reason. Parenting is a job too important to leave either to chance or to anyone too young to vote.*

Are *you* a pissed-off Birth Control Mom? Look for a family-planning clinic in your neighborhood that could use your voice for reproductive freedom. Why not send them a bouquet of flowers (with your donation check, natch) to thank them for the fine work they're doing?

*Dear younger readers: please don't bother writing with the admonition that you are doing a better job than say, Bristol Palin, *Jersey Shore* star Snooki, or my own parental units, who spawned me at the tender age of twenty-one. I think we all can agree that it would be preferable for children to be raised by grown-ups who've been slutty, had their hearts broken a few times, visited New York City, etc., and have the acquired wisdom that such experience implies.

I want my money!
Radical Housewife blog, April 19, 2012

Hilary Rosen was a Democratic advisor who scoffed to the press that the wife of Republican presidential candidate Mitt Romney, Ann, a stay-at-home mom of five kids, "never worked a day in her life." I could easily have ripped into Rosen myself, but I thought the kerfuffle might provide a better opportunity for a look at the value of unpaid labor, which is expected of all women whether they work for pay or not.

The new Vikings stadium opens for business in August 2016, but my school still needs money for pencils and copier paper. Pay up, bitches!

So Hilary Rosen, Ann Romney, blah blah blah. You didn't get commentary from me on the matter because last week was the buildup to the 2012 Minnesota NOW conference, which involved a great deal of work . . . for which I was not paid.

At the conference I was approached by a political campaign that was interested talking with me about my writing. "Is this a volunteer opportunity or a job?" I asked.

You can guess the answer.

A friend of mine works more than forty hours weekly at the school our daughters attend. She monitors the cafeteria, goes on field trips, assists with special events, and fundraises like a maniac. I'm not exaggerating when I say that school would crumble without her. What's her job title, you ask?

Cochair of the PTA. Yearly salary: nothing.

On Facebook, a friend posted one of the bajillion links to the Rosen-Romney feud, and one of *her* friends claimed that her stay-at-home-mommy work is "priceless" and she would be "offended" if the government paid her.

This at-home mama's response? "I want my money, bitch!" And I wasn't kidding.

Jill Filipovic at *Feministe* wrote a few thousand words on the subject before getting to the real heart of the matter, which is, "Free female labor props up our economy and saves us all tax money. . . . [Women are] filling the gaps that state and federal funding leaves, so in the short term kids get necessary classroom assistance when lawmakers cut programs. As a nation, we can afford to not pay for necessary things because there are so many women who are doing those things for free."

Again, in all caps: "FREE FEMALE LABOR PROPS UP OUR ECONOMY."

Capitalism depends on our unpaid work. We are conditioned to do it at every turn. My job is so idealized by our culture that my colleagues in the business (women like the Facebook poster) feel *ashamed* to ask for what is their due. Ashamed! Can you believe it?

Second-wave feminism declared that women should have opportunities outside the home but forgot to add that men need to help shoulder the burdens inside the home. The revolution should have demanded as many stay-at-home dads as female CEOs, but it didn't. The goals of the movement became allied with making money, which is one reason why feminism gets accused of being antifamily. Family is so precious that it cannot be allied with something *dirty* like *making money*! It's the madonna/whore binary all over again.

No matter what women do, we're made to be either/or. To rob us of nuance is to rob us of autonomy, and *that's just how patriarchal capitalism likes it!*

If you think that all your decisions in life are your own, that you "choose your choice," then you fail to question the systems in place that perpetuate oppression—systems such as capitalism, patriarchy, racism, classism, you name it.

Here's an example.

Minneapolis Public Schools is in trouble. Every year, the budget cuts get deeper and deeper and the achievement gap between poor and not-poor students widens. Yet somehow, my daughter's school seems to persevere and will continue to do so as the ax drops in the future. Why? Because of people like that PTA cochair I know. One day I asked her, "Would you consider going on strike to highlight how much free work the district gets out of you?" She looked at me like I was nuts, and I knew why: a PTA strike in our school would only hurt *the children*, and women are conditioned to think of *the children* and not themselves. Minneapolis Public Schools counts on the free labor of middle- to upper-class women to prop up schools when their budgets are cut. Schools without the free labor force are left to fend for themselves, and their test scores show it. Class systems stay rigidly enforced.

If women went on strike and refused to volunteer, our school district would have to put much more, and I do mean *much more*, pressure on government officials to fund them adequately. If the women who prop up our school system went on strike, Minneapolis Mayor R. T. Rybak would be forced to put $150 million of city tax money toward hiring school staff, not toward a Vikings stadium whose profits will be funneled straight into the pockets of the 1 percent.

Just think about our poor, old, inadequate football stadium! I think it just needs an army of unpaid women to puff it back up again, don't you? Maybe we gals could install some of those fancy new corporate suites that the menfolk say they need to conduct the networking-business whatchamacallit.

The Official Mommy War Narrative™ would have this PTA cochair incredibly offended by my suggesting such radical ideas. We live under consumer capitalism, a system that encourages competition and discontent—if I'm right, you're wrong. Either/or. If I pick a philosophical fight with Hilary Rosen, Ann Romney, the PTA moms, Linda Hirshman, Phyllis Schlafly, Gloria Steinem, or Madonna, I'll be distracted. In my absence, Minneapolis will build a billion-dollar football stadium, and its achievement gap will remain one of the worst in the nation.

The (white, male) rich will get richer; the poor will get . . .

The post–Title IX girls

Minnesota Women's Press, May 2012

When I realized that my tenth-grade decision to drop math had been far more nurture than nature, I was painfully embarrassed. My daughter is learning the drums and how to program a Lego robot in addition to reading the Betsy-Tacy series; I hope her choices will be more informed.

These days, Samantha is considering a career in public policy and/or law. So much for med school!

When I was a little girl, I didn't fear numbers—on the contrary, I found their patterns and mysteries fascinating. My parents had no explanation for this, other than my great affection for the pinball sequence on *Sesame Street* that made counting to twelve so funky.

Why, then, did I quit math forever at the end of tenth grade? And I do mean forever: in depressingly gendered fashion, my husband takes care of the math (the checkbook balancing, the tax filing) that keeps our household functioning. "I'm an English major," I joke, for while I did like numbers, I loved words. When I raided the library, I reached for books by Maud Hart Lovelace (the "Betsy-Tacy" series), not Ada Lovelace, the woman considered to be history's first computer programmer.

Only since I became a parent to a daughter have I wondered how truly informed my decision to drop math was. Subtle pressures to leave the calculating to the boys were everywhere. My high school counselor, a man, showed no surprise when a bright female student wanted to quit a subject so essential to twenty-first-century career preparation.

When I was a high school student, Title IX was the law of the land in word but not deed. Those who knew about the 1972 law only remembered its application in the case of a female classmate who tried out for the hockey team. In the late eighties, we had only one hockey team, and its players were all boys—a clear violation of Title IX. Anguish reverberated throughout my suburb as appalled students and parents wondered why this pushy but admittedly talented girl couldn't just leave well enough alone.

Today, my school has a girls' hockey team that competes with dozens of others in a state tournament that in 2012 drew nearly twenty thousand fans! Is there a similar sea change happening for girls in math and science? Happily, I can look for answers no farther than across the alley. My friend Samantha, a sharp, funny sixth grader at our neighborhood middle school, is a kid who's happiest when she's absorbed in a great book—though she much prefers Katniss Everdeen to perfumed Betsy and shy Tacy. When I told her that I was writing a column about generational changes in educational opportunities for girls and women, she gave me an endearingly blank stare.

"Is it cool these days for girls to like math and science?" I asked.

"Um, yeah," she said, as if I had asked her if "these days" the sky was still blue. I told her that it hadn't been cool when I was in middle school. She remained unimpressed, so I asked her what she wanted to be when she grew up.

"I want to be a doctor of some kind," she replied. "I don't know which, though. My grandma keeps giving me advice."

Aha! I remembered that her grandmother was a nurse, not a doctor. "Did you know that in your grandma's day, girls who were interested in medicine were discouraged from becoming doctors? Nursing was all they could aspire to."

Samantha remained blank, but not in the way most preteens are when they interact with their unhip elders; she really couldn't fathom the scenario I described. After all, she'd just returned from a spring break trip to Costa Rica with her school's Girls in Engineering, Math, and Science program. This was no beach vacation—the girls conducted experiments at a field station deep in the rainforest. Samantha was experiencing math and science on a level much funkier than anything I could have seen either on my TV or in my high school classroom.

I felt a little envious—but more than a little happy. "Go into geriatric medicine," I told her. "In twenty-five years, I want you on my team."

Why we ladies see the need for a War on Women
Minnesota Public Radio News, May 14, 2012

By 2012, the widespread attacks on women's health care and sexual autonomy since the 2010 midterm elections had a name: the War on Women. Conservatives dismissed us as typically hysterical females, but when the Conference of Catholic Bishops has more sway with Congress on reproductive health policy than I do, that's a problem. When there's a national "debate" over what in the heck rape is, that's a problem. When there's confusion over how contraceptives actually work, that's a problem. Put together, it sure sounds like a declaration of war to me.

On April 28, 2012, there were nationwide rallies scheduled to protest this fear of a female planet. I was invited to speak at an event in St. Paul, and as a gag, I dressed up in my best thrift-store housewife drag and performed as Mrs. Matthew Black, which according to some Republicans was already my real name. I adapted the speech for an MPR News essay that had readers chuckling in their lattes.

My name is Mrs. Matthew Black. Some of you might remember me from when I used to be called Shannon Drury, but I didn't get married to have a name that was my own. I got married to fulfill my life's sole purpose—to be a proper lady.

And as a lady, I was thrilled to hear that there is a War on Women.

To my way of thinking, women started this country on the road to ruin ninety years ago, when they passed that amendment that gave every adult the right to vote. At first, it didn't seem like such a bad idea—everyone assumed that wives would vote the way their husbands told them to, which meant that every married man got two votes instead of one. That sounds like a good incentive to get more fellows to the altar, doesn't it?

Over time, though, it became clear that women were voting however the heck they wanted to, without the permission of their husbands, fathers, or male guardians. It's shocking.

But not as shocking as when people came up to me last year and said, "Mrs. Black, aren't you excited that a nice lady like Michele Bachmann is running for president?" I had to tell them that Michele Bachmann was no lady. If she were, we would be calling her Mrs. Marcus Bachmann, thank you very much, and she wouldn't run for president. Why, she shouldn't even be running for the House of Representatives! Frankly, the only house Mrs. Bachmann should serve in is her own. Poor Marcus has been doing his own laundry for years.

That's why I'm so happy that there is a War on Women. It tickled me to hear that a gentleman like Rick Santorum had been out there saying that contraception is "harmful to women." (Of course, he meant that it's harmful to *ladies*, not women, but even Mr. Santorum can make mistakes. I hear that his wife once attended law school, but I assume that by now he has forgiven her.) It takes a man to tell the truth about ladies' sex lives.

And the truth is, no lady should use contraception. Ever. If she did, it would suggest that she was having sexual intercourse because she *wanted* to. No lady *wants* to have sexual intercourse. Ladies submit to their husbands' advances because it is their duty to breed the next generation of male leaders and the women who are told to vote for them.

I'm glad that Governor Scott Walker repealed a pay-equity law in Wisconsin, and that one of his gentlemen friends, Wisconsin state Senator Glenn Grothman, came right out and said, "Money is more important for men." Of course it is. That's why housewives like me aren't allowed to open lines of credit on their own. We have to drag our husbands along to open the account for us and to ask that the girls behind the counter kindly not roll their eyes when we ask for our card to read "Mrs. Matthew Black."

I'm glad that Senator Grothman recognizes that money is strictly the purview of menfolk. My only quibble is that he told the press that he learned this bit of information from reading a book by that awful woman, Miss Ann Coulter. While she and I agree that the Nineteenth Amendment ought to be repealed, I just can't trust a woman of her age who has never been married. Even that vulgar trollop Miss Madonna Ciccone has been married twice. Miss Coulter, if you're reading, please unplug your computer, put on a decent outfit, and get to the singles' mixer at your nearest VFW. You're sure to meet a lovely widower whose socks need darning. Leave the writing to the gentlemen, please!

Oh dear, I see I've broken my own rule and spoken about my beliefs in public. That ought to tell you how important this War on Women is to me. I hope that you agree and that you'll join me in not going to the polls this November 6. Thank you.

You will never be "mom enough"
Radical Housewife blog, May 15, 2012

Remember when Time *magazine ran a cover photo of a white four-year-old nursing from the breast of his pretty mother? I know you do! What you may not recall is that the caption to the left of the photo demanded to know "ARE YOU MOM ENOUGH?" You know what they say—if you have to ask, the answer is probably no!*

This issue came out around the time that the country discovered the existence of Patricia Krentcil, the tanning-booth addict who was charged with child endangerment after her fair-skinned five-year-old arrived at school with burns on her body. You may not be "mom enough," but at least you're not that bad, right?

Tits out, ladies!

Unhook your bras and settle in for another battle in the 2012 Mommy Wars, kicked into gear ever since Hilary Rosen thoughtlessly insisted that Ann Romney "never worked a day in her life" and French academic Elisabeth Badinter published a book called *The Conflict: How Modern Motherhood Undermines the Status of Women*. Why, even the *New York Times* devoted an opinion page to a debate it called "Motherhood vs. Feminism." Yes: motherhood *versus* feminism, as if the two are mutually exclusive.

One of the NYT essays is titled "Let's Not Pass Judgment." Women shouldn't be fighting each other for our "choices"—we should be wagging our shame fingers at the systems that conspire against us, consumer culture and patriarchal capitalism in particular. Repeat after me: class wars, not Mommy Wars.

I've been thinking about this not-passing-of-judgment thing. A few weeks ago, a feminist site I enjoy posted a photo on Facebook of the now-infamous Tan Mom, wondering if all the harsh criticism of this woman's "choice" to fry her pale skin wasn't antithetical to the feminist ideal of "to each her own."

Hmm. *Hmmmmmmmm.*

Once again, we must return to the tricky notion of "choice." Patricia Krentcil, the Tan Mom, *chose* to change her appearance rather drastically. But did she, really? Let's ask our frenemy, good old consumer culture. Pale women are told to buy creams and tanning beds to look acceptable. Dark women are told to buy fading creams and treatments (such as Photoshop) to look acceptable. It doesn't take long for these messages to tip vulnerable people into obsession, if not outright mental illness.

Is Krentcil "mom enough"? A lot of people don't think so. For one thing, she is *awfully* ugly, unlike the lovely Jamie Lynne Grumet, she of the boob seen 'round the world on the cover of *Time*.

Breastfeeding is, of course, a very good thing. Unlike tanning, it has clear health benefits and does not cause cancer. The fact that Grumet nurses her four-year-old threatens me not a whit. Her defiant stance on the cover, however, coupled with the hysterical tone of the copy, adds more fuel to the already tired notion of breastfeeding as a lifestyle "choice," and *that's* when I get pissed.

I hate to break it to y'all, but nursing a baby is a biological function. Our bodies are designed to do it—but *please do not confuse this fact with a moral judgment upon you for not doing it*! PLEASE! If you feel threatened by what you perceive to be my judgment, you are going to waste your time battling little old *me*, not demanding change from the systems that conspire against a truly family-friendly society.

Suck on this: the United States is one of only four countries in the world that does not offer some kind of paid maternity leave. The other three are Papua New Guinea, Swaziland, and Lesotho. The latter country has an annual per-capita income of $1,600, so I can see why they can't afford it. The U.S.A., not so much.

Would you "choose" to nurse your child if you had the "choice" to take paid maternity leave? I bet you would. And no matter your skin color, your body size or shape, you'd look damned good doing it.

Under patriarchal capitalism, you are *not* mom enough, and you never will be. You have to hate yourself to buy what they're selling: tanning packages, magazines, economic systems that trickle down slower than a dried-up teat (and that's s-l-o-w).

So tuck in those tits and start shopping, gals!

A small victory against heteronormativity

Radical Housewife blog, May 24, 2012

These moments are the payoff for years of hard work, so like any proud parent, I gotta blab about 'em to the world!

Though I try to model critical thinking for my kids, like most parents I assume that they're not paying attention. This is especially true when they reach an age when pop culture becomes infinitely more alluring than their boring old mama.

Last week, my daughter Miriam turned seven. One of my favorite things to do with her is play Just Dance for Wii. On Just Dance 2, the game's interpretation of Avril Lavigne's "Girlfriend" is a duet with two girls dance-arguing with one another. It's one of Miriam's favorite songs, and she especially adores its cheerleadery chorus: "Hey! You! I don't like your girlfriend! I think you need a new one!"

In the game, the girls snarl at each other, throwing fake punches and baring their kitty-girl claws. It's all a very predictable interpretation of how girls act when they're fighting over a dumb boy, like Miriam's other obsessions, Betty and Veronica.

Now, I loved Betty and Veronica, too—in fact, the comic books that got Miriam hooked in the first place were my beloved old Double Digests, saved since I purchased them from the kind of dingy old corner stores that have long since turned into yuppie patisseries and wine bars.

But back to the Wii. At one point in the song, the dancer in the geek-girl drag assumes a pleading posture, as though she's begging the rocker chick for something. I thought I knew what she was begging for (a freckle-faced dork from Riverdale High?), but today Miriam corrected me.

"She *really* wants the rocker girl to be her new girlfriend," she announced.

You think so?

"Yeah. But the rocker girl doesn't wanna, so the other girl is saying *'Please, be my girlfriend, please!'*"

I looked twice, and Miriam was right—with no redheaded boy in sight, it *did* appear that the cute nerd was appealing to the rocker to join her for a romantic date at the Choklit Shoppe. I was doing a better job than I had thought!

A small victory for boring old mama.

Racism in the neighborhood
Minnesota Public Radio News, July 10, 2012

I started writing this piece in October 2011, just after the community event that I mention in the first paragraph. It languished as other things took precedence, including Pam, who was still receiving hospice care at her home directly across East Forty-ninth Street from where Michelle Norris once lived. Kelcy and Megan, the friends mentioned in the piece, are Pam's daughters.

Sadly, the shooting death of a child in predominantly African-American North Minneapolis provided a fresh hook for the piece.

Last fall, I attended an event sponsored by Building Bridges, a community organization that, according to its mission statement, "seeks to understand how race and racism impact our communities and to build the future of our neighborhoods together." The group's name reflects the yawning gap exposed when Southside neighbors clashed over a proposal to create an off-leash dog area in a park named for Dr. Martin Luther King, Jr. It's also a literal reference to the east-west divide created when Interstate 35W was built in the 1950s.

Held in Minneapolis's Field neighborhood, the event featured remarks from Minneapolis native Michele Norris, former cohost of NPR's *All Things Considered* and author of the 2010 memoir *The Grace of Silence*. Norris grew up in a two-story Tudor on a corner lot only three blocks away from where we feted her, and her book describes not only her Minneapolis childhood but also the painful legacy of racism in the silence and secrets carried by members of her family and, by extension, members of her hometown and nation.

Here in Field, our discussions over the book are personal, indeed—Norris spent her childhood on the same street where my children Elliott and Miriam are spending theirs. The corner house where Norris lived with her parents Belvin and Betty is where my kids and their friends alight from the bus every afternoon.

My kids were thrilled when they learned that "the lady on the radio" once lived on the block. But their joy turned to confusion when I shared that Norris's white neighbors put their homes up for sale as soon as the block's first black family moved in. Next door, Norris wrote, "the forlorn For Sale sign sat in front of the house for weeks. At one point, someone attached a flyer that read BEWARE NEGRO NEIGHBORS."

When he heard that, Elliott looked as stricken as if he'd bit into an apple and tasted a worm. To a young white child in the Midwest of the twenty-first century, racism is not unfamiliar, but it is too easily categorized as part of "the distant past" or "the South." His school did a terrific job teaching about the horrors of the Middle Passage as part of a unit on colonial history, and the work of Dr. King is recalled throughout the year, not just on the days near his birthday. But here? In this bucolic backyard where friends of many different colors like to play with one another?

His reaction was immediate: "That's *awful*," he said, adding quickly, "We can't tell Kelcy and Megan about this." Like the Norris sisters, these two friends are African-American.

"Why?" I asked.

He looked at me like I was insane. "It would *hurt* them," he said.

I couldn't blame Elliott for automatically defaulting to silence. As Norris writes, "The mere mention of the word race can make some people apoplectic or pious or frozen by anxiety, only to beat a hasty retreat to their comfort zone: grim taciturnity." At the Building Bridges event, Norris acknowledged that even she and her husband struggle with how much they care to expose their own kids to what she writes is "a 400-year-old cancerous social disease."

Though the discussion that evening was fascinating, heartfelt, and honest, I had to admit to myself later that I had attended in hopes that it would immediately thaw my own anxiety about discussing the thorny issues of race with my children and their friends. It's melting, but like most parents, I am impatient; I want to fix ugliness for them *now!*

On June 26, five-year-old Nizzel George was killed when gang members fired into the North Minneapolis home where he slept. We heard the story reported on the radio as we drove to summer swimming lessons. "Could that happen to me?" Elliott asked anxiously.

"No," I replied. Nizzel may have lived in the same city, but he inhabited a different world. The North Side might as well be on another planet, racked as it is by poverty, unemployment, violence, and the painful legacy of racial quarantining—the same separate-and-unequal attitudes that confronted the Norris family when they were among the first to integrate the South Side. How could I begin to untangle all this for a confused twelve-year-old, a kid who wanted answers *now?*

Our human response to discomfort is fight or flight, anger or withdrawal, seething or silence. Rarely do we allow ourselves the opportunity to grapple with nuance, yet this is where the real transformations occur. Building Bridges and *The Grace of Silence* are essential tools as we tread that middle path—and I'm happy to say that the book is now on my son's nightstand.

An exclusive interview with a contributor to *Atheist Voices of Minnesota*

Radical Housewife blog, September 5, 2012

Matt and I have been card-carrying members of the Minnesota Atheists for years, and when I heard they were compiling a book of personal narratives, I sent them an essay immediately. I am very proud of the piece, an nonbeliever's reflection on the grieving process, and I encourage you to grab a copy of the book wherever you shop for the printed word.

Readers, you are in for a treat. I've secured an interview with one of the contributors to the just-released anthology *Atheist Voices of Minnesota*. The contributor who chose to talk with me is the author of the essay that opens the collection, a piece that *Doubt: A History* author Jennifer Michael Hecht called "sensitive" and "compelling."

The Radical Housewife: Have you always been an atheist?

Shannon Drury: My go-to joke is that I was baptized Catholic but it didn't take. I was raised in a secular home by two products of the adage that the best way to raise an atheist adult is to send him or her to Catholic school—especially in the late fifties and early sixties, when nuns were still smacking naughty children with rulers. My mother told me she'd been singled out for particular abuse because she'd had the bad luck to be born redheaded *and* left-handed, both of which were considered early predictors of demonic possession. I bought my mom a Nunzilla wind-up toy back in the nineties that breathed fire as it stomped toward you. She said it was eerily accurate.

RH: Wait a minute. I know for a fact that you are a great fan of Pema Chödrön, the well-known Buddhist . . . wait for it . . . *nun*! How can that be?

SD: Hey, just because I don't think The Answer to Life, the Universe, and Everything is a god or gods doesn't mean I've abandoned the quest. I suspect that if you asked Pema Chödrön for The Answer, she might reply that it's neither the Buddha nor the number 42—it's love. Which is what my essay in the book is all about.

RH: Your essay, "An Atheist Grieves," made me cry.

SD: It made me cry, too.

RH: Was it hard to write? You're laying bare some pretty raw emotions: the death of your maternal grandfather, the death of your close friend, the deep anxiety felt by a parent who wants desperately to make sense of the world for her curious children.

SD: It's more difficult to read than it was to write, honestly. It kinda just poured out of me in a few particularly wrenching sessions at the laptop—after years of puzzling and puzzling over why the death of my friend Liz has been so goddamn (pun intended) hard to get over.

When my grandfather died in 1979, it made some sort of sense to me. He was old (though today sixty-five doesn't seem as ancient as it did when I was a third-grader), he had seen his children through to adulthood, including marriages and the births of their own kids. Though my parents weren't Catholic anymore at that point, they still relied on its framework to sort the whole thing out. Grandpa Cliff had a full funeral mass, and everyone said that he was "in a better place" and that kind of thing.

Liz and I were the same age. We met at Carleton College and both graduated with the class of 1994. She died just two months after her oldest daughter started kindergarten. Her youngest daughter was not even a year old when Liz got her cancer diagnosis, and she won't have any memories of her mom healthy—that is, if she remembers her mom at all. What the fuck is *that* all about? How do you sort *that* out?

RH: I have no idea.

SD: Most people have religious rituals to guide them through grief. I didn't. The original title of the essay was actually called "What an Atheist Grieves When an Atheist Grieves," because over time I realized that I wasn't simply mourning *her*; I was mourning a lot of other stuff, too.

RH: Like what?

SD: My illusions of immortality, for one thing, though everyone confronting the death of a peer feels that. I think I realized that my smarty-pants attitude about organized religion wasn't exactly keeping me warm at night, if you know what I mean. As I write in the piece, "My atheism requires maintaining a delicate and oftentimes painful balance between intellectual superiority and emotional terror."

RH: Intellectual superiority, eh? No wonder you don't talk about your atheism much. You could get yourself punched in the face for saying something like that.

SD: Oh c'mon. Do I *really* think that I am smarter than my beloved neighbors, dedicated parishioners of St. Joan of Arc? Of course not! But when you watch some dope on YouTube claiming that the Bible's word refutes evolution, the dinosaurs, miscegenation, climate change, homosexuality, and "women's lib," it's hard not to feel like unbelievers are awesome. And then there's the Taliban . . . ugh. I do feel sympathy for people of faith who have to contend with the lunatic fringe that makes them appear guilty by association.

I also tend to avoid embracing my atheism for fear of being stereotyped as yet another member of the secular, white, liberal elite. Secular, white, and liberal, yes. But elite? I'm a garbageman's daughter, for cryin' out loud!

RH: Admit it—you almost said "for Christ's sake" there.

SD: You know I did.

Anyway, the real reason I don't talk about my atheism much is that faith, and its lack, seems like a pretty private thing to me. It feels akin to discussing all the gory details of your sex life—though I suppose that's the very excuse that Elton John made, once upon a time.

RH: I think you're brilliant.

SD: Thanks. I feel the same way about you.

Lawn signs have their place, but shouldn't neighbors be talking, too?

Minnesota Public Radio News, September 12, 2012

Another absolutely, 100 percent true story courtesy of my messy garden, Madonna, the strange lady who lives across the street from me, and a guy who happened to be taking his baby niece for a walk.

"Well, I'll be damned," the stranger said, catching my eye as I lifted my head from my unkempt boulevard garden. He was pushing a baby stroller with one hand and pointing across the street with another. I pulled my headphones out of my ears with grass-stained fingers and asked him to repeat himself (when I'm on weeding duty, or any household chore for that matter, I like to blast Madonna as loud as my forty-year-old ears can take). I followed his finger to the sign across the street, the green and white lawn sign that read: "VOTE YES: Marriage One Man, One Woman." The stranger's nose crinkled in disgust. "What's that all about?" he asked.

"I really don't know," I answered, flummoxed by the irony of discussing a serious social issue while a sleazy club jam thumped away on my iPod.

In the literal sense, of course, I knew exactly what the sign was about. It was our block's first public announcement in support of the so-called Minnesota Marriage Protection Amendment, on the ballot this November. I didn't know the neighbor who staked it in her front yard, only having seen her in passing glimpses. An elderly white woman, she hadn't attended the National Night Out event I organized just a few weeks before, though my kids put a flyer in her mailbox. In fact, I hadn't seen her at a single block event in the nine years I'd lived on the street. I didn't know her any more than I knew the strange stroller-pusher engaging me in conversation.

She didn't know me, either, so she didn't know why I had a bright orange "VOTE NO: Don't Limit the Freedom to Marry" sign on my front lawn. Had she attended the National Night Out event, I would have happily explained to her my reasons for believing not only that the amendment was a terrible idea, but also that civil marriages conferring civil benefits ought not to discriminate on the basis of gender.

But this neighbor wouldn't have learned much from me. She could, however, have learned something from other neighbors in attendance on National Night Out—neighbors such as the gay couple across the alley and the lesbian couple several doors down. To assure herself that not all LGBT people in the area were in a mad dash to the altar, she could also have met the singleton known to mingle in Palm Springs at Dinah Shore Weekend.

And these were the folks who were out; untold others could be B (bisexual), T (transgender), or part of the rainbow of difference in countless other ways. On our block's annual event last August 7, there were elderly neighbors, toddler neighbors, surly teenage neighbors, neighbors of color, white neighbors, a neighbor in a wheelchair, a neighbor with multiple disabilities, gluten-free neighbors who avoided the brownies, vegetarian neighbors who avoided the hot dogs. . . . You get the idea.

What things could *I* have learned from the neighbor who stayed inside on that summer night? Her lawn sign told us that she supported the marriage amendment, but not much else. What experiences brought her to this block in South Minneapolis? Could she and I have found common ground over a shared but secret loathing of the marinated beet salad brought by the health-conscious neighbor who shamed us into eating it instead of a second helping of Cool Ranch Doritos?

The stranger asked me what I knew about the Vote Yes neighbor, and I laughed, because I didn't know *him*, either. He apologized, introduced himself, and explained that he was in Minneapolis visiting his baby niece (that was her in the stroller). He lived with his partner in Burnsville, where he said he hadn't seen a single pro-amendment sign. "Everyone there's been really accepting of us," he said.

"That's the funny thing," I said, mentioning her absence at National Night Out. "In fact," I added, "I can't remember the last time I saw her leave her house."

"What a shame," Keith said (since he wasn't a stranger anymore), and I agreed. "Neighbors ought to talk to one another," he said, "not lawn signs." His niece, annoyed at the interruption of her walk, began fussing. Keith wished me luck with my unruly bee balm and went on his way. I popped my earbuds back in, just in time to catch Madonna cooing, on a track from 1986, that "love makes the world go 'round."

Then, because I find that song annoying, I skipped to her new *MDNA* album, cranked up the volume, and got back to work.

Why I stopped
Radical Housewife blog, October 12, 2012

In which a formerly frantic political mommyblogger admits that she is tired of the painful side of following politics. The poisonous climate of the same-sex-marriage fight, combined with the everyday vitriol of a presidential election, was getting to me.

As I committed more of my time to editing my manuscript and prioritizing my mental health, the number of blog posts I wrote started growing even smaller.

I didn't watch last night's vice-presidential debate. I didn't watch the presidential debate last week, either, and I don't plan on watching the next two.

I don't feel guilty.

I like to think of myself as a model of civic engagement, but the truth is I'm burned out. I know who's getting my vote, and you know who's getting yours.

Skipping the debates doesn't make me ignorant about the issues at stake in the election. Quite the contrary! As every idiot with a Wi-Fi-enabled laptop and smartphone knows, we are never wanting for information. The *amount* of information, however, and its volume and tenor, can be crazy making.

When my kids near tantrum stage for not achieving the high scores of their dreams on any of our four Just Dance games, I say this: "If it's not fun anymore, stop." Sometimes this dose of reality works. Sometimes, of course, there is an explosion of tears and curses and AA batteries as the Wii-mote hits the wall.

The Mitt Romney and Paul Ryan philosophy of governing makes me ill. They are not fun, and I can no longer watch them.

Happily, they inspire jokes and memes that are *hysterical*. Thanks to social media, the debates can be GIFed into a form that does not make me want to scream and destroy my household possessions. That's fun we can believe in!

Speaking of social media, this Audre Lorde quote has been making the rounds among my connected friends and social justice allies lately, which proves that I'm not the only one experiencing severe political burnout: "Caring for myself is not self-indulgence; it is self-preservation, and that is an act of political warfare."

Dear readers, don't forget to take care of *yourselves*, too. Remember: if it's not fun anymore, stop.

But if it *is* fun, be sure to repost it on Facebook and Twitter so I know about it!

Voting "No" for the children we love

Radical Housewife blog, November 5, 2012

On Election Day, I made my final effort to convince any Minnesota readers that the same-sex marriage ban shouldn't pass. I cried while writing it, and I might start crying now.

I'm voting "No" on Minnesota's ballot question regarding a constitutional amendment to ban same-sex marriage, of course. For a while I was convinced that regular readers of my blog didn't need me to itemize the reasons, including but not limited to the appalling notion of discrimination being enshrined into state law. Yuck.

My heterosexual hubby and I had a depressing conversation about how the totally symbolic nature of the amendment fight (for Minnesota already has a state statute banning same-sex marriage) is draining untold millions of dollars from actual, honest-to-gawd, on-the-ground work that both sides could be doing to achieve a more just society. Catholics and other religious groups are *not* feeding the hungry or healing the sick; lefties like yours truly are *not* supporting progressive candidates or funding Lambda Legal, the group working on the LGBT rights movement's version of *Brown v. Board of Education*.

Instead, an estimated *fifteen million smackeroos* is going to ad agencies, television studios, lawn-sign assemblers, radio announcers, T-shirt printers, leaflet copiers, etc. I've mentioned that I'm burned out, yes? Cynical, exhausted, ornery, drained, annoyed, jaded, the works?

Last weekend my hardened heart opened up again, and I remembered why I got into this business in the first place: *because I love children and care desperately about their physical and mental well-being.*

To be specific, I love and care for a child that my regular readers know as Mia. This little girl is as dear to me as my own daughter. I met her only hours after she was born, and I'll never forget the joy of nuzzling her squishy pink nose and telling her how happy I was to be a part of her life. Nothing activates the protective instinct more than a vulnerable newborn, so tiny and dependent upon loving grown-ups to nurture and protect her.

Mia is a third-grader now, and her vulnerability is different: her parents revealed to me that she has been driven to tears by the barrage of advertising by those who call this a marriage "protection" amendment. Mia cried when she saw strangers on the television tell her that:

Her family structure is inappropriate at best and aberrant at worst.

Her parents are selfish egotists who shouldn't have had her in the first place.

Her family is a threat to society.

Imagine all of that crap entering your head when *you* were only nine years old. What would *you* do?

You'd probably cry.

This post has been pinging around in my head for two days, moving from brain to fingers to web page with great difficulty, for every time I imagine Mia crying, I start welling up. There are fat tear splotches on my keyboard right now, so please forgive any egregious spelling and grammar mistakes.

The vote on the amendment tomorrow won't change any laws. It *is* symbolic—but what a symbol it would be to a little girl like Mia, a kid being raised by two loving and committed parents who just happen to be women. What a symbol a resounding rejection of this amendment would be to the thousands of Minnesota children who wonder where they fit, not only on the rainbow of queer identity, but in the fabric of our community.

Is there another symbol that could so powerfully represent a cultural shift away from fear and toward love? I can't think of one.

A feminist survival kit
Minnesota Women's Press, November 2012

Good prevails! The same-sex marriage amendment was defeated, and a new Democratic majority was swept into the Minnesota Legislature. Todd Akin, who was favored to win his Senate race in Missouri before he mused that "legitimate rape" rarely causes pregnancy, went down in flames. Oh, and Obama won too! Yay! . . . but all of these victories took a huge psychic toll.

Any doubts that I was burning the fuck out should be erased by the time you read this column.

I love feminism, but it doesn't always love me.

In fact, the very movement that has given me so much (from the right to vote to the WNBA) has also provided me with more than my fair share of headaches and anxiety attacks. Feminism by definition requires an awareness of systemic injustice, which is not a great feeling. It is exhausting to have a constantly functioning injustice detector, even when one is in Target Center, rooting for a professional women's team that didn't exist a generation ago. Unfortunately, the Twin Cities media will ignore Minnesota Lynx star forward Maya Moore's flawless jump shot if Viking Adrian Peterson so much as bruises his pinky while mowing his lawn.

On second thought, that would never happen—Peterson makes too much money as a pro athlete to do his own yard work. Olympic gold medalist and world champion Moore probably has to yank her own dandelions.

See what I mean? No wonder feminists have a reputation for being surly and unpleasant! It doesn't help that I can't surf to Facebook without seeing some new knucklehead in power claiming to be an expert on "legitimate rape," among other things.

It is now my pleasure (hell, my obligation—see tip #3) to provide you with the essentials to feminist survival in the twenty-first century:

1. Humor. At the end of an exhausting day, I usually turn to my husband and say, "Let's watch something really stupid on TV." People tell me that I should be watching intelligent, complex dramas like *Breaking Bad* or *Mad Men*, but I prefer *Jersey Shore* star Snooki's unabashed lunacy any day. Even better is the over-the-top theatrics of the queens on *RuPaul's Drag Race*, the greatest show on television. I'd advise you to stream it right now at Logo TV online if my next tip weren't for you to find...

2. Quiet. Last fall I took a Mindfulness-based stress reduction course. While I wish I could say that I've kept up my mediation practice regularly (hit or miss is more like it), the class opened my eyes to the sheer volume of garbage I was consuming in the name of "information." As my Internet speed improves, the cacophony amplifies and multiplies until it threatens to drown everything else in my head. I'm learning that I can write an angry blog post about Todd Akin *tomorrow*. Today, however, I can turn the computer off.

3. Honesty. Feminist women may be better equipped to combat gender programming, but we are by no means immune to the impulse to take care of everyone else's needs before our own. Burnout is painful but entirely preventable if we have the courage to make our frustrations known.

4. Therapy. I don't mean retail therapy, chocolate therapy, or wine therapy—I mean old-fashioned, honest-to-goodness, talk therapy with a licensed mental health professional. A quick glance at this paper's Women's Directory will reveal numerous feminist therapists who offer sliding-scale fees, so do not let that fear deter you. I think that everyone, feminist or not, deserves a good therapist upon whom to unload, a person who is not obligated to agree that everything is your boss's, spouse's, or mother's fault. A great therapist is someone who challenges you to learn more about yourself as you untangle the

knots in your heart and mind—and feminists are quite knotty people (if you don't believe me, see tip #1).

A quick tweet about this column generated many other suggestions, including but not limited to: patience, stubbornness, Aretha Franklin albums, and a properly fitted bra. I'm out of space, but not ideas—the feminist survival kit, like feminism itself, is definitely a work in progress.

What a "family man" looks like
Radical Housewife blog, December 12, 2012

Look, I love the Gray Lady, but she can be as biased in her reporting as anyone else. Remember when she subtly slut-shamed an eleven-year-old rape victim in 2011? She blew it again in her coverage of Jovan Belcher, a linebacker for the Kansas City Chiefs who murdered his girlfriend Kasandra Perkins before killing himself. Why does a football player get a pass that your average, everyday murderer doesn't?

Dear *New York Times*,

I would like to introduce you to a family man who loves football. His name is Matt, and he is my husband and my kids' father.

[I posted a photo of Matt and Miriam in full Vikings regalia, Matt in a Fran Tarkenton jersey and Miriam in one of those ridiculous Valkyrie hats with long yellow braids. I can't stand football myself, but marriage is all about compromise.]

New York Times, I know that you will hide behind the fact that your source, Ruben Marshall, is the one who called a man who had just committed a domestic homicide "a good man. A good, loving father, a family man." You will say that you are merely repeating the, er, "facts" of the case.

Hmm.

If we move forward with the idea that you presented the story of a murder-suicide in all its complexity, then why didn't you interview Becky Gonzalez? You could have asked what *she* thought about the man who killed her daughter, Kasandra Perkins. Though Jovan Belcher was the father of Gonzalez's three-month-old granddaughter, Zoey, I *highly doubt* that she would call Belcher a family man. She might call him a sick fuck. A perpetrator of domestic violence and terror. A murderer.

But you didn't ask her, did you?

I quote my friend, the fab freelance feminist Erin Matson, who tweeted, "Imagine your sister, mom, or friend being murdered by her boyfriend with their child in the next room and the newspaper story ending by calling him 'a family man.'"

Once again, *New York Times*, I must ask that you look into the eyes of my cute daughter. Perhaps your perception of any act of violence against her would be colored (pun very much intended) by the fact that she is young, a blue-eyed blonde, and very much a football *fan*, not a football girlfriend.

Football girlfriends must subsume their cuteness and vulnerability to the service of their lovers. Football players are *heroes*, am I right? Which is part of why you used heroic apologetics to describe the football player's sudden and shocking death as if it were a bizarrely random tragedy, rather than what it really was: part and parcel of the seemingly intractable culture of violence that happens every day, to daughters, mothers, and wives from all walks of life.

New York Times, you know that journalism does not occur in a vacuum. Each writer and editor brings his (yes, *his*) perspective to his writing. When you trot out "family man" tropes like these about men like Jovan Belcher, you trivialize the seriousness of domestic violence—and worst of all, you erase the stories and voices of women like Kasandra Perkins. You contribute to the problem.

As a small act of repentance for your part in this culture of silence, I suggest that you interview Perkins's family and friends for their perspectives, then gather your editorial board to issue a strong statement in support of reauthorizing the 1994 Violence Against Women Act. VAWA has stalled in Congress due to political dithering that reflects the cultural myth that domestic violence is something weird, something "other," and something not worthy of our Congress's time and energy, when the truth is that domestic violence affects twenty-four people in the United States every minute.

And if you need a family man to profile for an upcoming issue of the Sunday magazine, my husband's schedule is wide open.

xoxo,
The Radical Housewife

Fear

Radical Housewife blog December 18, 2012

2012, already a year filled with pain and sorrow, ended with unimaginable tragedy: twenty children and six adults were murdered at Sandy Hook Elementary school in Newtown, Connecticut, by a disturbed young man with a semiautomatic rifle. After the shooting, I couldn't stop crying and holding my children tight. It was all I could do to let them back into the world again.

Once upon a time, I thought that the opposite of love was hate. Now that I've grown (much) older, I believe that the opposite of love is fear.

Fear prevents us from asking for help when we need it, sometimes desperately. Fear prevents us from offering help to others when we know, from the gut, that it is desperately needed.

Fear stops us from accessing our own humanity.

Fear sells weapons.

Fear enforces stereotypes.

Fear tightens, restricts, and confines. Fear obscures our interconnectedness.

Fear hurts.

Fear feeds on fear. Fear snowballs, compounds, and multiplies. Fear makes you type dumb things on Facebook that you would never say to a person's face, things like "unfriend me now if you don't do this or that."

Fear creates an insatiable need to create and assign labels, from "outcast" to "weirdo" to "Trench Coat Mafia" to "mentally ill" to "autistic" to "threat to society" to "gun-worshipping NRA lunatic."

Fear stigmatizes. Fear isolates.

Fear kills.

Knowing that, what can we do? Here's a thought from Pema Chödrön, who has made the study of fear her life's work.

"When you open yourself to the continually changing, impermanent, dynamic nature of your own being and of reality, you increase your capacity to love and care about other people and your capacity to not be afraid. You're able to keep your eyes open, your heart open, and your mind open. And you notice when you get caught up in prejudice, bias, and aggression. You develop an enthusiasm for no longer watering those negative seeds, from now until the day you die. And, you begin to think of your life as offering endless opportunities to start to do things differently."

I'm starting to do things differently already—but it's not easy, and I am afraid. Are you?

2013

Am I a good mother yet?

In the aftermath of the shootings in Newtown, I started 2013 with the fervent wish that finally, *finally*, there would be common-sense gun legislation in this country. After all, a semiautomatic rifle is hardly what the framers of the Constitution had in mind when they drafted the Second Amendment. Surely the *murder of children* in their school would be the turning point in the fight against gun violence. *Am I right?*

I was wrong.

I had to start following the advice of Audre Lorde instead of just quoting her all the damn time. Posting to my blog became less important than working on my manuscript, my family, and my sanity (not necessarily in that order).

I still found time to obsess over my failings as a parent, plug the Equal Rights Amendment, and declare my loyalty to Madonna, the Queen of Pop.

The big abortion-rights question

Radical Housewife blog, January 22, 2013

A photo blog without photos! Hopefully my descriptions do it justice. This post was timed for the fortieth anniversary of the Roe v. Wade *decision.*

While we're reminiscing about Roe today, let's take a moment to remember what I looked like on Good Friday 2005, just one of the many days on which I have honored my commitment to speak out for reproductive rights:

[I looked seven months pregnant with Miriam, my second child!]

Back then, my son was a five-year-old preschooler, obsessed with Thomas the Tank Engine and the Hardy Boys. Today my son is almost thirteen, a fan of Katniss Everdeen and dubstep music that makes my head hurt. He has always been a curious kid, and now that he is older he is very interested in what I call The Big Questions: life, death, and the tools we use to make sense of what lies in between.

Not long ago he asked me how I felt about abortion. "I think whether or not to have an abortion is a woman's business and no one else's," I replied.

"But don't you think it's killing a baby?"

Bam! The Really Big Question!

Of course this discussion had to happen in the car, so I wasn't able to whip out the smartphone to add visuals to our conversation. It took much longer while driving to explain that *this*:

[a fertilized egg]

... or even *this*:

[a nine-week zygote, complete with tail]

... is not the same thing as *this*:

[a smiling, chubby baby]

... which is what his sister looked like six months *outside* my body.

"Some people think that a two-celled zygote is a human life," I told Elliott. "Some people think that a four-week zygote is, too. I saw you on a sonogram only nine weeks after your conception, and I saw your little heart fluttering."

"You did?" He was impressed. I had been, too, back in the summer of 1999, and I wrote about the experience in the manuscript for my book *The Radical Housewife*. The book uses language a little fancy for the average thirteen-year-old, even one as brilliant and handsome as my son, so I tried to craft my feelings about abortion, and life, in terms he could understand.

"A woman must have the right to decide what happens to her body," I told him. "How *I* feel about pregnancy, or how *you* feel, or how the lady next door feels, or the president feels or the pope feels can never be more important than the feelings of the woman going through it. No one can decide but her."

The backseat was quiet for a moment—a rare thing. Then he said,

"I get it."

With barriers to equality falling, it's time to ratify the ERA

Minnesota Public Radio News, January 29, 2013

My genteel readership at MPR News needed to know that all was not perfectly Minnesota Nice just because the same-sex marriage ban had been defeated. Oh, hell no! I felt compelled to remind everyone that all that drama could have been avoided had the ERA been ratified.

On Thursday, January 24, leaders of the U.S. military announced the end of the ban on women serving in combat roles in our nation's armed forces.

The loud "BAM!" you heard as Defense Secretary Leon Panetta delivered this announcement was neither an official twenty-one-gun salute nor the thumping of thousands of women's helmets as they celebrated the opportunity to be recognized for work they have already done in Iraq and are doing in Afghanistan—it was the sound of yet another barrier falling in the long path to ratify the Equal Rights Amendment.

A brief ERA primer: the original amendment was written by Alice Paul, the toughest of the activists now known as American feminism's first wave. Paul's street protests would be called Occupy Women's Suffrage today, but the passage of the Nineteenth Amendment didn't satisfy her. She penned a companion amendment that read, "Equality of rights under the law shall not be abridged by the United States or by any State on account of sex." This Equal Rights Amendment gained little traction during Paul's day, but in American feminism's second wave, it was given new life. With bipartisan support, the ERA was passed by Congress in 1972 and sent to the states for ratification. First Ladies Pat Nixon, Betty Ford, and Rosalynn Carter all lobbied for it. Passage seemed inevitable until Phyllis Schlafly stepped in to the fray.

Schlafly, whose Eagle Forum organization bills itself as "leaders of the pro-family movement since 1972," portrayed the Equal Rights Amendment as a tool of radical feminists bent on dismantling every aspect of American life. Her tactics were incredibly effective, and the ERA fell three states short of its ratification deadline in 1982.

How did she do it? By preying on the public's fear of the following bugaboos:

Unisex bathrooms: If you are a parent of small children, you know that these already exist. Called "family bathrooms," they recognize that children and parents do not always socialize in public in neatly matched gender pairs. Even restaurants as shockingly outré as Noodles & Company have done away with gendered stick people on their single restroom doors, allowing anyone who requires a toilet to use one. Radical.

Same-sex marriages: Currently, nine states have legalized same-sex marriage. California's marriage laws are still in limbo, pending appeal to the U.S. Supreme Court. Even if you feel that same-sex marriage is an affront to your religious beliefs, you must admit that Massachusetts hasn't exactly fallen into the Atlantic since it was legalized there in 2003. In fact, the formerly cursed Boston Red Sox won the World Series in 2004 and 2007! (Note to Governor Dayton and the Minnesota Legislature: the Twins haven't won a Series since 1991. Hint, hint.)

Women in combat: Panetta's announcement is a formal recognition of what has been going on for years now. Women are already on the front lines, albeit unofficially, in "support" roles. Women's presence in combat situations is a necessary reality in a military strained to the limit by a decade spent fighting two seemingly intractable wars. What these women haven't had until now are the recognition, leadership advancement, and benefits that having officially recognized combat experience confers. Women, especially military women, are a lot tougher than Mrs. Schlafly ever imagined.

Husbands not supporting their wives financially: Yes, they really worried about this.

America in 2013 looks a lot different than it did in 1972—and it would be nearly unrecognizable to Alice Paul—but the need for gender equality in our nation's guiding document remains constant. Let's take this fresh opportunity to right a historic wrong and restart the ratification process for the ERA.

A fan of feminist men
Minnesota Women's Press, February 2013

My February column was a sloppy Valentine to my husband and a big, fat middle finger to the truly horrible Suzanne Venker. As Madeline Albright often says, "There is a special place in hell for women who don't help other women." This atheist agrees!

Dear feminist men,

I love you. Really, I do. I know that there are some who say you don't exist (conservative gender essentialists like Phyllis Schlafly), and there are some who claim you can't exist (radical feminist separatists, Mrs. Schlafly's worst nightmare), but I see you. I believe in you. In fact, I live with a very special member of your tribe—my life partner of over fifteen years, Matt.

When I met your feminist brother, I knew that he was someone special. Here was a record-store hipster who, to my great surprise, enjoyed both the macho punks Black Flag and the exquisite operatic soprano Rosa Ponselle. He didn't compartmentalize people, either, by their gender, sexuality, or musical taste. I was his equal.

Our decision to marry was a mutual one, not a formal request made by one to another. When I declined an engagement ring, he wasn't miffed; when I opposed on principle a white dress, he understood completely. Comfortable with himself and our relationship, he didn't require constant cultural reaffirmation of his masculinity. He said that if I wanted to change my name after our wedding, I could, but the decision to do so was mine, not his (I didn't).

Now don't misunderstand me, heterosexual feminist men of the world: I am sure that there are many of you who have generously shared both diamond rings and your last names with your legally married beloveds. But my guess is you asked if she wanted them first. You're very aware of the romantic possibilities of consensus.

Last December, the writer Suzanne Venker (niece of the aforementioned Mrs. Schlafly) kicked up a media firestorm when she opined that second- and third-wave feminism's "war on men" was the reason that so many heterosexual women were miserable. In a piece for Fox News, she advised these women that "surrendering to [their] femininity" was the remedy. "It's okay if your guy's in charge," she wrote. "It's okay if you don't drive the car. In fact, it's rather liberating."

Feminist men, I know you are laughing right now, as you should. When I shared Venker's assertions with Matt, my feminist husband, he just stared at me, mystified. "Why should I care who drives the damn car?" he asked. "What does that have to do with real life?"

This, feminist men, is what you are here to teach us. When you resist the pressure to control everything in your grasp, you allow real life to unfold in all its complexity and sloppiness. And marriage is probably the sloppiest, most confusing, and difficult institution there is.

Feminist men, you know as well as I do that a truly equal partnership under capitalist patriarchy is a daily challenge. Like Matt, most of you outearn your female spouse by a significant margin, making her decisions regarding family life and the care of young children look less like "surrendering to femininity" than grappling with economic practicality. Yet you never use this as an excuse to absolve yourself of the responsibility of parenthood, for feminism helped you understand that kissing boo-boos and reading bedtime stories is your job, too. In this way, you model to your children that kindness and compassion are what liberate us, not power and control.

Thank you, feminist men, from the bottom of my heart. This ongoing revolution can't happen without you. I'll be so proud when my son Elliott, as yet still a feminist boy, matures and joins your ranks.

Your fan,
Shannon

One from the heart
Radical Housewife blog, March 6, 2013
In which a feminist mom blogger realizes that there are much worse things than being without a "brand."

I have started and stopped this post more than a dozen times. Here's the conversation I hear as I type, delete, type, hit save draft . . .

Head: It's time to write a blog post.

Heart: Yeah, probably, but I don't wanna.

Head: You have stuff to say, publications to plug, yadda yadda.

Heart: Ugh, I would rather sit under a blanket and watch *Scandal*, the best show on television.

Head: You streamed every episode available. There won't be a new one until March 21. WRITE THAT POST.

Heart: Dammit.

In last month's issue of the *Minnesota Women's Press*, themed "Matters of the Heart," I wrote a fan letter to feminist men. It was pretty good, I think—at least good enough to motivate several hetero women to ask where I had found my awesome feminist husband (behind the counter at Cheapo Records, of course). But I didn't do the usual thing and hawk it here on my blog, for an uncomfortable reason.

My big, fat, feminist heart is in pieces.

On January 30, my friend Pam passed away from brain cancer. She died with her family at her side, at home, in typically stubborn fashion—her doctors gave her just weeks to live, but she pushed that out to fourteen months. If you knew Pam, you knew she was not about to leave her two daughters *that* quickly. No way.

Usually, I respond to upheaval by writing. I wrote volumes when my dear friend Liz passed away in 2007, also of cancer, also at home, also leaving behind two young daughters. At the time, I kept my blog on MySpace, a charmingly mindless place to vent about the ugliness and unfairness of life. As a plus, there was an embedded music player that could depress everyone with a cheery tune like Paul Westerberg's "Let the Bad Times Roll."

In the years (yes, years) that I've been working on *The Radical Housewife*, the book, I've used the services of a number of industry professionals who advised me that my blog should be a place where I "build my platform," such as it is. I must be vigorous about promoting myself and my work at the Women's Press, at MPR, and at any analog or digital publication that would have me—never mind that this is contrary to every introverted cell in my body. I find that this push towards "branding" has strangled my natural impulse to write directly from my heart, whether it's broken or whole.

And more and more often, I see bloggers clashing with one another (and with their readers, sometimes) over anything and everything. Yahoo CEO Marissa Mayer and Facebook COO Sheryl Sandberg seem to have reinvigorated the Mommy Wars for 2013, and every feminist writer I know has taken a side. Page views and well-placed editorials are the reward for the winner, dontcha know! The Feminist Breeder was so fed up with backlash and trolls that she put up a paywall on her site.

Kinda makes you wish we were all gluing up zines at Kinko's, doesn't it? Goddammit, whatever happened to GIRL POWER? Forgive us, Bratmobile and Sporty Spice! We need you!

Ultimately, waxing nostalgic for long-lost "good old days" is as unhelpful as wishing very *very* VERY hard that people wouldn't die. You can give it a go—just don't expect results.

The heart is a fragile thing.

Gender essentialism and the feminist housewife

Radical Housewife blog, March 20, 2013

Every so often the New York–based mainstream media decides to dredge up the same Mommy Wars bullshit in pursuit of page views. I, of course, can't help but respond.

Hi there! My name is Shannon, and I am a feminist housewife.

[a selfie of me in my kitchen]

Behind my arm is—no joke—a loaf of homemade gluten-free bread. I am a housewife, and a damn good one!

Do you like my apron? It's from the H.O.T.D.I.S.H. Militia, a group that sells tasty casseroles to raise funds for abortion clinics—the acronym stands for Hand Over The Decision; It Should (be) Hers. I support affordable access to the full spectrum of women's reproductive health services, including abortion on demand, without apology. That's feminist, baby!

Combine my job with my passion, *et voilà*: you get me, a feminist housewife!

I didn't aspire to be a feminist housewife when I grew up. As a child, I wanted to write books. As a child, I assumed that writing books would *magically make money appear.*

Ha, ha.

Six-year-old Shannon can be blamed for her ignorance, but what excuse does Kelly Makino have? We meet Kelly in *New York* magazine's March 17, 2013, cover story, "The Retro Wife."

From the article: "The maternal instinct is a real thing, Kelly argues: Girls play with dolls from childhood, so 'women are raised from the get-go to raise children successfully. When we are moms, we have a better toolbox.' Women, she believes, are conditioned to be more patient with children, to be better multitaskers, to be more tolerant of the quotidian grind of playdates and temper tantrums; 'women,' she says, 'keep it together better than guys do.'"

Oh Mrs. Makino! You retrograde goofball, you. In case you missed this lecture in Women's Studies 101, let me break it down for you. Choosing your choice is feminist, sure! But *gender essentialism is not feminist.*

I can't pick on only Kelly, though, for the author of the piece, Lisa Miller, makes some mind-boggling observations of her own: "I believe that I have a special gift for arranging playdates, pediatrician appointments, and piano lessons...."

And that special gift is . . . ? Between her legs, maybe?

Makino tells Miller's magical vagina, "I feel like in today's society, women who don't work are bucking the convention we were raised with. . . . Why can't we just be girls? Why do we have to be boys and girls at the same time?"

Again, I must ask: what makes a girl a *girl*? Is it a baby? An apron? A kick-ass gluten-free bread recipe? A Pintcrest account?

What makes a boy a *boy*? A *wife*?

I made a choice to be my kids' caregiver, but that choice wasn't made in a vacuum. My hubby and I had to weigh some very harsh realities. Who made more money? Who would probably *always* make more money? Who could count on consistent work for the next two decades? If you guessed the boy, you're right! You win a wife.*

Understanding how patriarchal capitalism works is feminist. *Gender essentialism is not feminist.*

For the record, I am terrible at arranging playdates. My vagina has nothing to do with it: I am not only forgetful; I also hate using the telephone. I'd rather bake you a rice-tapioca-soy-flour bread loaf. If you want our kids to hang out, you will need my e-mail—or better yet, Matt's!

All of this is very funny in the echo chamber of the Internet. I really don't care whether Kelly Makino, Lisa Miller, or, hell, even Sheryl Sandberg is a housewife or not. I *do* care when one pretty, white New Yorker's lifestyle is trotted out as "proof" that women are this or that and feminism is a failure, blah blah blah, because you know that articles like these delight conservatives eager to push back on women's rights, especially reproductive rights. Senator

Rand Paul, a 2016 presidential contender, has already said he'd support a fetal personhood bill that would outlaw abortion and many forms of contraception. Without control over their fertility, women would be stuck in the kitchen making hotdish (and this is the important part) *whether they want to or not.*

It's a future too horrible to contemplate.

Maybe I'll cook a pie. That would make me feel better.

*Offer not valid for women

POP goes the feminist parent
Minnesota Women's Press, April 2013

At last, the payoff for countless hours watching YouTube videos and dancing around the house to Madonna's still-fabulous first album.

Once upon a time in the early eighties, a concerned parent called our home with an unusual question. The parent's daughter wanted to give my sister an album by a promising new pop singer for her birthday, but the parent had qualms about the singer's habit of baring her midriff at every opportunity.

My sister and I found this hilarious, of course: we knew Madonna was a pop star, not a role model! We just wanted to dance to "Lucky Star" and "Holiday." Weren't parents *silly*? As a pop music fan, a feminist, and now a parent of two pop-culture consumers myself, I wish I'd given that parent a break. I know I could use one.

In college, I completed the bulk of my media studies minor dissecting Madonna's live performances and videos, wedding two of my deepest loves: pop music and feminist cultural critique. I believe that our puritanical, sex-negative culture prevents all people from accessing their full humanity. Yet all this carefully practiced theory flew out the window when my children discovered their generation's single-monikered popstresses: Rihanna, Ke$ha, Beyoncé, et al. Now belly buttons are the least of my problems.

My mother allowed the Madonna birthday gift because she believed that banning any music or art would make it irresistible, but she never had to grapple with the information overload of the Internet age. I would much rather explain the lyrics of "Like a Virgin" than much of the tawdry information available with one click of Google—including why Rihanna still dates a man who beat her so badly that she needed hospitalization.

On the other hand, when I was once asked what in the heck Madonna was talking about on that song, I fumbled, "oh, it means she feels very . . . er, young." Ugh.

Intellectually, I know that force-feeding my daughter a diet of Joni Mitchell in a Lady Gaga world would be a useless exercise, and not just because I agree with my mom's philosophy. Confession time: as much as I've been told that Ani DiFranco is good for the feminist soul, I find her music boring. I love hearing women sing over 808 drums and thumping bass lines, so Madonna's "Express Yourself" is my feminist anthem, not "32 Flavors."

Interestingly, another birthday party renewed the tension between pop as youthful liberation and as a source of parental frustration, but this time with my sister and I in the parents' roles.

Rihanna's "We Found Love," a song as good as or better than anything Madonna has recorded, appeared on a mix CD my sister gave to guests at her own daughter's sixth birthday party. She should have asked for my permission, though, because the song is like a Rihanna gateway drug. My daughter Miriam wanted to listen to it again, and *again*, and AGAIN. Finally, she asked to see the video for the song on YouTube. We made it barely past the second chorus. Exposed navels I think a seven-year-old can handle, but simulated sex, dating violence, and butt tattoos? No way.

I admit that while writing this column I probably listened to "We Found Love" a hundred times—it really is that good. Would I have insisted that my sister *not* put it on the party mix, just to avoid having to explain why I slammed the laptop shut? I remain convinced that the liberating joy of a good pop song is worth the difficult conversation.

Still, it would be a lot easier if the kids and I were folkies. Did Ani DiFranco ever vomit ribbons in one of her videos? I didn't think so.

Corporate food sensitivity
Radical Housewife blog, April 12, 2013
Shout-out to the left-wing sanctimommies! We're all doing it wrong.

If you're a certain kind of hippy-dippy, über-crunchy, lefty pinko mom of particular socioeconomic status, you probably ingest (and perhaps most importantly, serve to your children) some kind of organic food product.

You don't go the full Paltrow, of course, but you *try*, and you try because you *care*: about your family's health, about Big Ag, about the environment, about everything. This is why liberals are called bleeding hearts—we *care*. We are sensitive not only to the lactose in cow's milk, but also to the myriad injustices of the world. We don't just care; we *ache*, dammit! We *so* want to do the Right Thing, especially at the breakfast table.

We also read Salon.com in large numbers. I know I'm not the only mom who gagged on her chocolate soymilk and coffee yesterday morning when she read this headline from the site: "Organic Eden Foods' Quiet Right-Wing Agenda."

!!!

Irin Carmon writes that Eden Foods is on the list of companies suing the Obama Administration to opt out of the contraceptive-coverage requirements in the Affordable Care Act—quite surprising for a biz that started as a hippy-dippy, über-crunchy co-op forty-five years ago in Ann Arbor, Michigan. I mean, it's no shocker that an Oklahoma-based craft-supply store like Hobby Lobby might raise a fuss about such things, but would you ever imagine phrases like *these*, taken directly from their legal complaint . . .

"The Affordable Care Act . . . attacks and desecrates a foremost tenet of the Catholic Church."

"The Affordable Care Act's contraception, abortion, and abortifacient mandate violates the rights of Plaintiffs."

"Plaintiff has never offered insurance which included coverage for contraception and abortifacients."

"Plaintiffs believe and teach that 'any action which either before, at the moment of, or after sexual intercourse, is specifically intended to prevent procreation, whether as an end or as a means'—including contraception, abortifacients, and abortion—is immoral and unnatural."

. . . coming from *a hippy-dippy, über-crunchy organic-foods company?* That started in the late sixties in a college town? One imagines that their original clientele had more problems with the immorality of deodorant than with non-procreative sex.

Just who does Eden Foods CEO Michael Potter think his customer base is? Let me give him a hint: it looks less like the Duggars and more like a certain skinny Oscar winner. And Gwyneth, for all her annoying organic, macrobiotic, gluten-free GOOPiness, is a loud and proud supporter of Planned Parenthood.

Happily, I do not drink Edensoy in my coffee, preferring the creamy deliciousness of Silk Light Chocolate Soymilk every morning. Instructed not to buy it from Whole Foods, I get it from the co-op we joined a year ago or, when I'm in a hurry, from my local Cub Foods, which has a fully unionized workforce. *I care.*

Just to be on the safe side, though, I thought I'd take a second look at the Silk carton in my fridge . . .

!!!

I thought it was organic. It's not, goddammit.

I guess I'll be taking my (shade-grown, fair-trade) coffee black from now on.

sniff

Parenting as Plan A
Radical Housewife blog, May 1, 2013

As my son and daughter grow older and surlier, I am even more convinced that parenting needs to be Plan A. If it's not, anyone who wants Plan B should be able to get it.

Yesterday the FDA approved plans to sell emergency contraception over the counter to anyone over the age of fifteen. This is a good thing, but it is not in compliance with a federal ruling that ordered Plan B be available to *anyone* in a CVS who wants to buy it. To quote the American Congress of Obstetricians and Gynecologists, "The medical evidence demonstrates that EC is safe and effective in preventing pregnancy for all reproductive-age females." *All* females. *All.*

When I was a teen, before I had my state-issued driver's license, I relied on my high school ID card to get discounts at the Southdale movie theater. I may have looked like a fierce baby punk on the outside, but inside I was a trembling, anxious, fearful mess. My contraception was my mother's insistence that, should I require it, she would be only too happy to help me procure some. This embarrassed me into celibacy until I left for college (though my scowl may have been a contributing factor).

Yesterday's announcement is a small step forward for white suburban teens like I was. We cannot forget, however, that the arbitrary identification requirement is a serious barrier for people who don't have the privilege to choose to look surly. With this policy in place, twelve-year-olds and undocumented women can purchase Tylenol and Robitussin, both extremely toxic in large doses, but they cannot buy Plan B. Why?

Conservatives who protest the availability of condoms in high school health clinics are suddenly horrified that Plan B doesn't protect against sexually transmitted infections. The drum of "parents' rights" is beaten long and loud. Safe, FDA-approved medications are "dangerous." Human sexuality is scary and wrong. There is no right to premarital, non-procreative sex. Since no one fears eternal damnation these days, fear of pregnancy needs to keep kids out of each other's pants.

This has not been one of my happiest parenting weeks. I received some very disappointing news about my son's grades, which led Matt and me to have *that talk* with him. While he curled into a surly ball in the corner of the couch, a very familiar scowl on his face, I could almost hear the thought *"This sucks"* rattling around his teenage brain. While my mouth was blabbering all the Very Important Lessons that my son needed to learn about his school responsibilities, inside my head I was thinking the same goddamn thing: *"This sucks!"*

So much about parenting sucks. It sucks to be the bad guy all the time, it sucks to clean up all the messes, both emotional and literal, and it sucks to send the person you love the most in the world to the place you hated the most in the world (middle school). It also sucks that there is tremendous social pressure to say "Why, no, parenting does *not* suck at any time ever; in fact, it is the best thing that ever happened to me."

Which it is, of course, but it's not a gig for the faint of heart or the unprepared. It really needs to be your Plan A.

If all sex can't be planned, at least parenthood ought to be. A person's ability to decide her future, whether it's Plan A, B, or C, ought not to depend whether she has an ID card in her pocket.

Scowl.

When food means "I love you"
Minnesota Women's Press, June 2013

My grandmother lived with scarcity and feared starvation; my mother lived with abundance and feared obesity. Me? I fear other mom bloggers will discover that I am still giving my children nonorganic soymilk. What food anxieties will plague my daughter?

My daughter recently presented me with a second-grade St. Patrick's Day–themed art project that read, "My mom is worth more than gold to me because she cooks me food." As a feminist writer who has considered the complex emotional connections women make with food, their families, and their lives, I laughed, wiped away a tear, and wondered if I had enough flour to bake her a cake.

In 2009 I wrote an essay for the Women's Press about modern housewifery ("Feminist Housewives Reclaim the Kitchen") that referenced my Grandma Rose, whose butter-based cuisine, not her words, expressed her affection for her large family. I never heard her say "I love you," but I tasted it in every decadent, from-scratch chocolate-chip cookie.

Now that I am older, with a family of my own, I suspect she could have saved herself a lot of hard work (and hardened arteries) by speaking her love instead of baking it.

Of course, to a girl growing up on a North Dakota farm in the early twentieth century, discussing emotion was as foreign as a European dish called "pizza." Becoming a terrific cook was not a gesture of generosity or kindness, but a matter of survival, especially when the Great Depression hit. I remember too well the disappointment on her face whenever I ate only the white meat off the hunks of chicken on my dinner plate. She didn't lament the rejected dark meat and marrow because she feared I didn't love her; rather, she mourned the meal that could be made out of what I considered scraps.

We live to eat, we eat to live; we eat to love, we love to eat. Women are doubly cursed by these cultural imperatives: we are expected not only to produce fine meals of exceptional taste and abundance, but also to avoid eating more than two bites, for fear of gaining an ounce. My grandmother was quite plump until various age-related afflictions ended her tenure as family chef; by the time she died, she was slight enough to wear clothes from the girls' department. I lie somewhere in the literally mushy middle, striving for emotional and nutritional balance and learning from my grandmother's example.

I know well that Rose never chose the job of housewife—it was thrust upon her by culture and circumstances. These days, many women are choosing to be home, and it's that choice that has informed the blossoming of parenting as "lifestyle," especially where food is concerned.

I follow a number of so-called mom blogs, and to read, them, you'd think that not even abortion is as loaded a topic as whether children ought to eat yogurt that contains high-fructose corn syrup. Even though we twenty-first century moms aren't shy about telling our little darlings we love them, our culture compels us to express our care and concern through cookery. I use the word "cookery" deliberately, for to love a child in the modern era, only homemade, organic, non-GMO treats will do. It's worth noting that this kind of nurturing requires a great deal of time and even more money. As a mom of six, my grandma Rose never had enough of either. I bet she was thrilled when cheap supermarket bread meant she didn't have to toil by a hot oven all day, corn syrup be damned.

In the end, I didn't bake Miriam a cake to thank her for her artwork. I gave her an enormous hug, and I told her this: "I love you so much."

Her response? "Mom, what's for dinner?"

Reframing the feminine
Minnesota Women's Press, August 2013

Another reflection on the generational tensions between mothers and daughters, this time through the lens of fashion, not food.

I still don't have any pink Chucks, but I do have a pair of gray and pink Saucony Jazz sneakers that are absolutely stunning. I bet Julia Serano would look great in 'em.

When I was a kid, my parents dressed me in what I called "number shirts"—generic, teamless jerseys that were popular among children in the mid-seventies. I had a few Holly Hobbie dresses, but the majority of the snapshots in the family album show my pals and me frolicking in our fives, twelves, and seventeens. I thought I'd wear numbers forever.

Imagine my confusion years later when the realities of puberty and the Reagan era collided in a fateful trip to the Southdale Dayton's. My mother steered me toward the juniors department, where she yanked Guess tops off the racks. "These shoulder pads will make you look fantastic," she announced happily.

They didn't. My mother howled with frustration every time she fished a pair of puffy ovals out of the trash. I didn't want to disappoint her (or my junior high friends, a heavily padded bunch), but the sudden insistence on feminine performance didn't sit well with me. I was a girl, but I didn't want to be girly, for girly style was not only fussy and impractical; it was also weak. It was wimpy. It was *dumb*.

Instead, I adopted the grungy style of my favorite band, the Replacements: worn Levi's, thrift store T-shirts and flannels, and Chuck Taylor sneakers. I finally felt comfortable—and more than a little superior to my high-maintenance sisters.

Two events conspired to knock me off my high horse: having kids of my own and reading a book by Julia Serano called *Whipping Girl: A Transsexual Woman on Sexism and the Scapegoating of Femininity*. Published in 2007, it is a fascinating unpacking of cultural misogyny everywhere, including among feminists. As she writes, "While most reasonable people see women and men as equals, few (if any) dare to claim that femininity is masculinity's equal." Until I read Serano, I didn't realize how much I believed in the inherent superiority of antifeminine fashion. I was a feminist who wouldn't judge a woman for her life experiences, but would make a snide crack about her high heels. And I thought shoulder pads were embarrassing!

Additionally, having children gave me the gentleness and compassion that my teenage self lacked. Is it possible that my mom panicked when she realized that the eighties weren't safe for androgynous children? In those days, middle schoolers thought AIDS was transmitted via mosquito bites and toilet seats. Tomboys existed, but they endured constant, relentless harassment. My mother's terror must have been profound, thus the mad rush to pad and ruffle me. If I knew of a product that would armor my children against social condemnation, I would put it on my Visa card in a hurry.

In the end, personal style is a partnership between what makes sense to your culture (national, social, racial, etc.) and to your body. Fashion, clothing, and costume work together to create the identity that is understood to be *you*, both as recognized by others and by your own eyes in the changing-room mirror. If I dropped my Chuck Taylors in favor of shoulder pads, my kids wouldn't recognize me, no matter how "fantastic" I looked. They probably wouldn't know me in a number shirt, either. I have settled into a style that is mine—neither good nor bad, but mine.

In *Whipping Girl*, Serano declares: "A feminist movement that encompasses both those who are female and those who are feminine has the potential to become a majority, one with the strength in numbers to finally challenge and overturn both traditional and oppositional sexism."

Wouldn't you know it? Chucks are now available in pink.

Good mothers, bad mothers

Radical Housewife blog, September 24, 2013

I became virtually acquainted with Avital Norman Nathman, aka The Mamafesto, through the feminist-mom blogosphere. When she announced her plan to create an anthology about the intense pressure to be the perfect mother to everyone all of the time, I knew I wanted to be part of it. Avi accepted my essay, Seal Press accepted her proposal, and the book was headed for publication when this was posted.

This fall, my son, an eighth grader, enrolled in an advanced math course for gifted kids at the University of Minnesota.

I am a good mother.

He has spent more than a few nights cussing me out for "forcing" him to do something that is so hard.

I am a bad mother.

One reason this math is so hard is that, for the previous thirteen years of his life, the math has been so goddamn *easy*. For once he is receiving instruction appropriate for his intellect.

I am a good mother.

His intellect may be highly developed, but many of his other skills are not. He did most of his first assignment in ballpoint pen because it did not occur to him to walk downstairs to get a pencil. Unfortunately, many of the problems written in pen were wrong. Did I neglect to teach him that you can't erase ink?

I am a bad mother.

When he forgot his math book and supplies at home, I brought them to school for him.

I am a good mother.

When I dropped them off, I chewed him out royally—this was the fourth time in two weeks that the math stuff had been left one place or another. He sobbed that he was a stupid idiot and I obviously hated him and believed he would be a loser all his life and he might as well quit the human race.

I am a bad mother.

Well? Which is it?

If you're like me, you ask yourself this question a thousand times an hour, a million times a day—despite knowing that it is unanswerable. When I thrash myself against the good/bad binary, I am wasting energy that would be better used to care for myself and the kids who are counting me.

So why do it? Whose interest does it serve? Offhand, I could name a few: the Bugaboo stroller company, Phyllis Schlafly, *Us Weekly* magazine, patriarchal capitalism—y'know, the usual axis of evil.

Avital Norman Nathman knows that the myth of the good mother won't be shattered by her anthology being released by Seal Press next January—but as I tell my math student, sometimes it's worth it to put yourself out there and *try* instead of just shaking your fist at the universe. Or something to that effect.

I'm proud to announce that Nathman's project, *The Good Mother Myth: Redefining Motherhood to Fit Reality*, features an essay I wrote last summer that is some of the most vulnerable stuff I've ever had the nerve to share with the reading public. I'm scared that you'll hate it and think I'm a loser and a stupid idiot and that I might as well quit the human race, because only bad mothers admit to frailty . . . or was it good mothers?

I hope I have it figured out in time for publication.

2014

Intersectionality for white people

I spent 2013 feeling pretty sad. Editing my book was no fun, and that was a Madonna-themed dance party compared to mourning my friend Pam.

But! By the time 2014 was out, I had achieved a lifelong dream: an honest-to-gosh published book with my name on it. The seven-year-old who wanted to be an author when she grew up is still in shock.

Note, too, that my writing output is definitely waning: 2014 will have less than half the posts of 2010. My acts of political warfare are happening off-screen and on a smaller scale. I am trying very hard to take care of myself, a difficult thing when offering a book to the public, an act almost as vulnerable as bringing a child into this messed-up world. Almost.

Unfortunately, I didn't take that same care while attempting to negotiate the back stairs in the dark on the evening of August 17, 2014. (Pro tip: never try to break a fall with your hands, especially if you're over forty. Fall on your padded ass instead.) I fractured my right wrist so badly that it required surgery. The ER doc doubted that I could heal in time for my book's release party, but my surgeon was more optimistic. In the end, I was able to sign books without too much trouble. Terena, my publisher, bought me a stamp that read "Shannon Drury is signing books with a broken wrist. Someday this will be collectible."

A very white-lady holiday
Radical Housewife blog, January 8, 2014

The amplified voices of people of color on Twitter have made a lot of white progressives very uncomfortable. Here I offer some advice to fellow white ladies who react with knee-jerk defensiveness. I also take another dig at poor Ani DiFranco.

The holidays kept me, your ever-lovin' Radical Housewife, too busy to blog (that spiked eggnog can't drink itself, ya know). In the rare moments that I could escape my family, I was on Twitter, learning all the latest new hashtags.

Like: #twitterfeminism! According to Meghan Murphy of the site *Feminist Current*, feminist action that occurs on Twitter isn't "real" feminism, in part because her feelings have been hurt sometimes.

Then there's: #stopblamingwhitewomenweneedunity. According to Adele Wilde-Blavatsky on Huffington Post, this hashtag is necessary because *her* feelings were hurt sometimes, too! And something to do with Beyoncé, I think. The hashtag was so blindingly dumb that I couldn't concentrate on anything else.

Next up: #RighteousRetreat! According to Ani DiFranco, hosting a songwriting retreat at a Louisiana plantation that whitewashed (pun intended) its slave history was not a big deal—in fact, in her cancellation announcement, she wrote, "I believe that people must go to [slave plantations turned into fancy resorts!] with awareness and with compassionate energy and meditate on what has happened and absorb some of the reverberating pain with their attention and their awareness." She later apologized, then apologized *again* for giving the world's lamest non-apology.

Best of all: #NotAllGreenPeople and #stopblamingKermitweneedunity. Huh? According to white lady Anne Chastain, it is possible to rise above racial disharmony just by wishing it so! As she wrote on Twitter, "I'm not white, black or Hispanic, I tell my kindergarteners. I'm beyond all that. I'm green: one w/nature." These hashtags were created to mock Chastain, who likened the negative response online to "lynching." Really.

I drank my eggnog in tears. I just hate it when dumb, white-lady feminists ruin things for me, another white-lady feminist!

Yep, I'm white. Just look at me! I'm descended from Northern Europeans and I live in Minnesota: the only color I get is boiled-lobster crimson when I've been out in the sun too long. Like the white ladies mentioned above, I've benefited from white privilege in a hundred million ways. I'm not very happy about it, but there it is. I do whatever I can to unpack my privilege, be aware of it, learn from it, and give my children the information that they need to do the same (because, as you have seen from their photographs, they're white, too).

I'm a cisgendered, middle-class, hetero, white, feminist lady. Does it hurt when call-out culture calls *me* out? *Oh my gawd, yes*. Of course it hurts. It hurts so much that, against my better judgment, I want to get out my Diversity Bingo card and wave it around (if you're a white liberal like me, you have one, even though it embarrasses you to admit it). I see words like "racist" or "heteronormative" or "trans-exclusionary" and want to hit the caps lock IMMEDIATELY AND TWEET "OH NO, THAT MIGHT BE *SOME* WHITE FEMINISTS, BUT IT SURE AS HELL ISN'T *ME*; NOPE, YOU'RE TOTALLY WRONG, THERE IS NO WAY THAT I COULD EVER, NO NO NO NO NO NO."

Which doesn't help at all and is over 140 characters besides.

So what can white-lady feminists do instead? I always like to give my readers advice, so here it comes: I suggest we grab a cup of eggnog (confidential to the green woman: Silk makes a vegan version I highly recommend), step away from the tweet button, and take it all in. Read, listen, and think. Stash the Diversity Bingo card in the drawer with the holiday gifts that don't fit. Pay attention. Go to the store and buy more eggnog, because in January it's on sale. Read, listen, and think. It's not that hard.

And *behave yourselves*, dammit! If any of you ruin Easter, I will hunt you down and break the ears off your chocolate fertility symbols!

My cage of you
Minnesota Women's Press, February 2014

Uh-oh. Here's where shit gets really real, people. I felt so low at this point in my life that I thought I had nothing to lose by being as honest as possible about my most humiliating insecurities.

Ironically, I received an incredible outpouring of letters from readers and messages from friends, all of whom said they felt the same way!

There are more than a few kinds of cages: some are made of brick and mortar, and some made of concrete and barbed wire. Mine is physically invisible but constricting nonetheless, for in this tiny, proscribed world, I can't act, think, or speak without you.

Yes, *you*.

I have to know: Am I appealing to you? Do you think I'm doing the right thing? Do you think I'm good enough?

Do you *like* me?

The framework you provided was initially a source of relief for me, an anxious and shy child mystified by many common social interactions. Pleasing grown-ups came easily to me, and when I saw how it smoothed the ragged edges of my unpredictable world, it became addictive. No alcoholic or smoker has clung to their habit since toddlerhood, but I have. It's been a fixation since long before I ever lifted a crayoned picture to Mrs. Leighton, my kindergarten teacher, and waited for the bun at the back of her head to bob forward and her pink lipsticked mouth to form the words I longed to hear: "Good job, Shannon."

Her validation felt marvelous. It manifested as a warmth in my heart that radiated out to all corners of my body. It was so delicious that I dedicated my life to feeling it again. And again. And again.

This is not to blame Mrs. Leighton, or anyone else who fed my ego in those early years: my parents, relatives, teachers, neighbors, and anyone else who looked at me and patted me on the head. I was a good child, an easy child, a compliant child. My head was patted so often that a groove could have been worn into my Dorothy Hamill haircut. Before I could even spell the word "approval" properly, I knew what it was—and that I needed to have it.

Remember though, that it's not just any approval that I need: it's *yours*.

Without your approval, I am bereft. When I have it, I am momentarily delighted, yet always aware of how deeply in its thrall I remain and how much it is my master. Unlike kindergarteners who accepted Mrs. Leighton's praise for their work and aspired to greater crayon masterpieces in first and second grade, I interpreted her words as an interpretation of my *self*. Five-year-old Shannon was good, not the artwork. Even at that young age, I gave her the power to define me. Today, I do the same thing to you.

You, dear reader, wield extraordinary power, though most of you don't know it. Hell, most of you reading this don't even know *me*. (Would you like to? Please say yes.)

Requiring your constant acceptance is exhausting, and it makes me hate you. (I didn't mean that. Forgive me.)

How can I convince you to set me free? (I'll do anything.)

Reach into your pocket for the key that will unlock the cage that has trapped me. (Please.)

But before you do, give me a little feedback about this column. Did it delight you? Excite you? Flatter you?

I'm not going anywhere. I'll wait to hear from you.

What makes a "good" Aspie mother?
Radical Housewife blog, February 10, 2014

At long last, The Good Mother Myth *was in stores! I took advantage of a fellow contributor's online controversy to plug the book and share my thoughts on what it's like to come to terms with a child's special needs.*

Last week, Gina Crosley-Corcoran, the blogger also known as The Feminist Breeder, wrote on her Facebook fan page that her oldest son was diagnosed with Asperger's Syndrome. When I saw her post, I responded as I always do to parents sharing this news for the first time: "Welcome to the club!"

In my essay in *The Good Mother Myth*, I write this about my son's diagnosis: "I hardly mourned when my son was diagnosed with Asperger's Syndrome when he was seven. After all, as countless psychologists reminded me, this was likely the same neurological quirk that had made Bill Gates the wealthiest man in the world."

The words here are elegant and composed, but in 2007 I was a wreck. In truth, I had been a wreck ever since my perfectly adorable infant opened his mouth in February 2000 and SCREAMED. He wouldn't stop for months.

So I *did* mourn: I mourned the stubbornly persistent beliefs that parenting was supposed to look like it did on TV, that my child and I would be so naturally in sync that I would know his every need, and that my child would be warmly accepted into the fabric of modern society by virtue of his very existence.

Instead, I had a kid who was regularly singled out by frustrated relatives, as well as preschool, kindergarten, and grade school teachers, for not being their version of "normal." His preschool classmate told me, upon learning whose mother I was, "I don't like Elliott. He screams a lot."

I have to pause here and collect myself, because I am tearing up. I haven't thought about that preschool experience in years, yet the memory still makes me clench my teeth so hard I can feel my crowns loosen.

It is painful to imagine a world that might not love your child as much as you love him. This is true for any parent of any kid, with or without special needs. A childhood diagnosis, however, kicks this panic up a thousand notches, for moms especially.

Why moms? Because we parent under the excruciating glare of The Good Mother Myth.

Gina herself has an essay in this anthology—a poignant look at the abuse and neglect she suffered in her childhood and her determination to break the cycle with her own kids. I write in my own essay about how much I fear passing on my family's tendency toward anxiety.

You didn't ask, but I'll tell you anyway: I believe that autism is genetic. My wholly unscientific theory is that in the latter part of the twentieth century, nerds and geeks who might otherwise have been isolated from one another were suddenly let loose on the campuses of research universities and liberal arts colleges, where they met, fell in love, and decided to breed (this theory holds true for my friends in same-sex couples, who selected donors that shared their interests, like, y'know, science and engineering).

Gina is very popular in the blogosphere and in social media, so naturally the post about her son drew a lot of traffic. What drew even more traffic was a series of follow-up comments and posts between Gina and autistic self-advocates who objected to what they perceived as Gina's desire to "cure" her son of his condition. I won't take a side in the debate, which as of this writing has devolved into a very bitter affair that includes name-calling, accusations of lying and harassment, the works. Nothing good comes of that, online or elsewhere.

Here's what I do know: there is genuine and deep pain on all sides. Autistic adults hurt because they feel humiliated and denigrated when the complexity of their lives is reduced to the image of a missing puzzle piece and ridiculous stunts like turning the Empire State Building blue. I can't speak for Gina, but holy crap, did I feel hurt and vulnerable when people tried to tell me the "best" way to support my son's diagnosis. For a few years there, I walked around like an open wound. Every suggestion stabbed my heart to a very familiar refrain:

"*You are not a good mother.*"

There is good news! My son is the coolest boy in the universe, and I would not change a damn thing about him. Not a damn thing! I *want* to give him the tools he needs to be a happy, socially successful adult, so I offer him help with skills that don't come naturally—like reciprocal conversation, sensory processing, and nonverbal communication—but I wouldn't change him. He knows he has Asperger's, and he's not ashamed of it. In fact, he wrote a short essay for his school newspaper about his life as an Aspie. I love him so much that I want to be not only a *good* mother, but also the *best* mother that he needs.

I don't always succeed, but I'm trying the best I possibly can.

I'm a white feminist writing something inflammatory
Radical Housewife blog, February 26, 2014

As I predicted, my spring holidays were in danger of being ruined by more irritating white feminists who claimed that they and they alone knew the secret to what was truly and officially Feminist™. To me, a white feminist on the sidelines, it looked less like a battle for ideological purity than a contest to rack up page views and Twitter followers. I thought I'd join right in!

Good day, Internet!

I am a cis white feminist. This is my blog.

Look! I am writing something enraging that I know will piss you off.

If I know it will piss you off, why am I writing it? Because it will "start a debate"? Because it's "my perspective on a complicated topic"? Because I believe that it's "true"?

Who cares? Instead of replying, I'll post a cute picture of my daughter.

(I am tempted to say something provocative about her, too, like how much smarter and prettier and well-behaved she is compared to your helicopter-parented kid, but that would be off topic. Another day, perhaps.)

Hey! Now I am writing something even more obnoxious than the previous thing!

Didn't see *that* coming, did ya?

Go give it a hashtag. I'll wait.

While I wait, I'll keep myself busy appropriating Flavia Dzodan's phrase "my feminism will be intersectional or it will be bullshit" to express an opinion that is less feminist than it is self-aggrandizing.

After all, I feel *great* about myself for writing something so deliberately outrageous that my page views have gone through the roof. Numbers validate me!

Oh, dear. You didn't like what I said. You called it "problematic."

This hurts my feelings.

I justify myself by calling you a bully, and why not? You hurt my feelings!

I don't like it when people hurt my feelings, so . . . I dig in deeper and refuse to accept anyone else's point of view!

Why should I? The inflammatory blog post has gone viral—viral, dammit!

Besides, it's a well-known fact that obstinacy confers accuracy.

And guess what? Refusing to budge on my initial statement actually makes it truer!

Don't ask me to prove it.

You leave me a comment. I leave a reply that's longer and meaner and ends with "This is my blog. If you don't like it, you can leave."

Also: "When you say something that hurts my feelings, the patriarchy wins." Put *that* in your vegan, half-caf, soy latte and suck it!

I hope we've learned something today. I know *I* have.

And that's what counts.

Ten things I don't want my insurance money to pay for

Radical Housewife blog, March 25, 2014

I ran out of patience with the "debate" over whether a company has the right to deny contraceptive coverage to its employee health plans. Hobby Lobby may have prevailed in the end, but I am hopeful that there's a badass company willing to take a bold stand against our nation's reckless suntanners!

Note that my blog style is changing, influenced by the rise of Buzzfeed listicles and Twitter character counts. I am less likely to offer you a well-reasoned argument than to put on the caps lock AND SCREAM IN YOUR FACE.

1. Your insulin

After all, it was *your* choice to eat a jelly donut every morning. Now it's *my* choice not to stabilize your blood sugar.

2. Your statin drugs

See above. When you weren't eating donuts, you were eating bacon! Sometimes you had both at one sitting! *Your* choice, not mine.

3. Your heart stents

See above, fatty! You shoulda been eating bran flakes.

4. Your kid's stimulants

I think little Tommy's just got an attitude problem. Discipline is what he needs, not money from my pocket.

5. Your mole removal

You got to go to the beach every year for spring break? Well, *I* had to go to a museum. Who's pissed off now?

6. Your painkillers

I hear that street heroin is easily and cheaply available on the street. As a capitalist, I believe that the free market is preferable to the artificial price controls of the pharmaceutical and insurance industries. Go chase that dragon on your own!

7. Your infertility treatments

God made you barren for a reason.

8. Your C-section

God gave you a stretchy vagina for a reason.

9. Your Viagra

God gave you a limp dick for a reason.

10. Your sad, pathetic life

Enough of this "civil society" crap. My money is *mine*, and I want to spend it on plastic flowers, yarn and glitter glue at Hobby Lobby! God bless America!

What about the sisterhood?
Minnesota Women's Press, May 2014

If there's anything that feminists enjoy doing, it's mulling over how and why our sisterhood isn't as strong as we had hoped or thought it was. What relationship can survive that kind of scrutiny? I used my relationship with my very different biological sister to unpack the constant bickering among my online sistren.

Whenever a disagreement occurs among feminists, in both the virtual and corporeal communities, a familiar refrain is often heard: "What about the sisterhood?" I usually reply, "What about it?" The relationship I have with my biological sister is among the most complicated in my life; why should the sisterhood of feminists be any different?

When my sister and I disagree, we experience much more than a difference of opinion; we relive every bump in our relationship since our parents brought her to meet me in the summer of 1974. If she finds my new jeans unflattering, it must mean that she still resents me for sneaking cherry Zotz from her Halloween candy stash. If I react slowly to news about her job, it means I don't take her any more seriously than I did when she was the annoying toddler gnawing on my Fisher Price Little People sets.

Sisters are thinner-skinned than other peers. Everything matters. Unlike friends, sisters demand, often forcefully, to be heard, respected, and understood. Though the word "sister" implies similarity, the fact remains that sisters can be as different from each other as any two people on earth.

My sister and I look so much alike that often people can't tell who's younger and who's older. They assume that my elegant and fashionable sister, who looks like she stepped out of *InStyle* magazine, must be more mature than the woman who's wearing scuffed Doc Martens well into her forties. As a born introvert, the idea of joining a group called Women in Networking makes me break out in a rash, but my gregarious sister has built a thriving real estate business on the connections she's made there. Growing up in the same house didn't guarantee we were simpatico.

At one time in my life, I assumed that because a person identified as feminist, it meant that we shared the same goals. We were all part of a sisterhood, right? If my sister and I shared a house, my feminist sisters and I shared a high-rise that gave us all the same shelter. Didn't it?

My liberal arts college was where I first met feminists, sisters, with whom I disagreed, often vehemently. I could have run off to my room and slammed the door, of course (my standard response to my biological sister's provocations), but instead, I sharpened my wits, unpacked my beliefs, and most importantly, started listening to the lived experiences of people who lived in different corners of our feminist house. As a freshman I might have insisted that every sexual assault be immediately reported to campus and local police, but I didn't feel the same once I graduated. I'm a better feminist and sister for opening my heart and mind.

Today, members of the sisterhood on social media challenge me daily, even to examine what is meant when we use the word "sisterhood" to define a group of people who may or may not identify as female! To me, that's more than okay—that's adding rooms onto a larger, more stable house.

When I realized how different my sister and I really were, I had to relax many of my expectations about our relationship, but I didn't love her any less. I learned that sisterhood is strengthened when it has the opportunity to prove its resilience.

So what about the sisterhood? It's doing just fine. Really.

Explaining rape culture to a man named Kyle
Radical Housewife blog, May 14, 2014

It amazed me throughout my blogging career that some of my old posts would get rediscovered, possibly based on some weird Google algorithm when the words "housewife" and "slut" were entered. I'm sure my political stances aren't what a guy named Kyle expected when he found me! In any case, my 2011 post asking men to be allies in the fight against rape culture moved him to share his thoughts on the matter. All the quotes attributed to Kyle are 100 percent his—I have no need to make up men who are totally unaware of their own privilege. They're everywhere!

Dear Kyle,

Thank you for your interest in my blog. I don't know what brought you here, particularly to an entry that I posted in 2011, but it's obvious you are exactly the sort of man that feminists like me are trying to reach when we talk about rape culture.

"This is one thing about feminism that rubs me the wrong way," you wrote. "What do you all mean when you say that you want the right to walk down the street and exist and not have to fear assault? I really don't understand that. What are you saying? Do you not feel safe when you walk down the street?"

From your defensive, almost unbelievably naïve viewpoint, I assume that you are the sort of person who has led a pretty charmed life. I don't know for sure, but I'd bet my Replacements reunion tour tickets that you are a cisgendered straight white male who is about to run to Google to research what the hell "cisgendered" means. You haven't met many people likely to challenge you on your rosy view of the world, but when you do, you say what you wrote in your comment to me:

"That sucks, but what exactly do you want me to do about it?"

This is such a common reaction that it has its own meme. Several, actually. Most are white men smiling and saying, "I have the privilege of being totally unaware of my own privilege."

You continue: "What do you want? More police on the street? Ankle tracking bracelets on all men? Is this even that big of a problem? Is there really an epidemic of rape going on, or are you all just sensationalizing a story and getting worked up into an irrational fear of the outside world?"

Kyle, this is the part of your comment that really breaks my heart. I'm totally serious. You can sit at a computer screen, with *the whole wide world* at your fingertips, and still believe that rape and sexual assault might not be "even that big of a problem." But let me be clear: my heart does not break for *you*, Kyle, but for the women in your life.

Because, Kyle, you know women who have experienced rape and sexual assault. A 2010 study by the Centers for Disease Control and Prevention found that one in five American women is raped in her lifetime. This number isn't from a feminist nonprofit with an interest in rounding up; it's from the government branch that studies dangers to public health.

Think about the last time you gathered with your family, Kyle. Maybe it was for Easter, a Passover Seder, or just a birthday party. Were there five women in the room? Grandma, aunts, cousins, nieces? Maybe you were there with your wife and daughters. One in five of those women is keeping a secret from you.

Why? Because you are an insensitive creep who would dare to suggest that rape is not "even that big of a problem." It's not a problem to *you*, Kyle, because the stigmatization of survivors prevents them from telling you that they are part of your family, part of your community, and part of your world. That's what we mean by "rape culture." If your daughter were robbed, no one would tell her that the theft was her fault, but the same would not be said if she were raped, especially if she were raped by someone she knows, which happens in sixty percent of cases.

You end your comment with this statement, the caps yours:

"If you want to feel safe, then YOU NEED TO STOP FEELING AFRAID."

This is rape culture, Kyle. A statement like this makes sexual assault an issue to be resolved by victims, not perpetrators. How backwards is that?

You say you don't rape. That's great. Now allow me to quote myself from the 2011 post, the point of which you totally missed in your clumsy attempt to absolve yourself of any blame for sexism in America: "Help us end [rape culture], guys. We can't do it without your help. We need you to speak out against this warped view of the world. You are not dogs, and we are not meat. We are all human beings who deserve respect, safety, and freedom."

I hope that you're listening, Kyle, and that you'll allow compassion for the survivors in your life to soften your angry, defensive heart.

Sincerely,
The Radical Housewife

Why write online?
Radical Housewife blog, July 21, 2014

Oops. . . . I did it again! I wrote about people online. My life fascinates me so much that sometimes I forget that there are other people in it.

I received my first blank book as a Christmas present in 1982. Before that, I scribbled my thoughts and various Archie fanfics (though in those days we didn't call them fanfics; we called them silly stories about comic book characters) in notebooks and scratch pads around the house. My mother believed me when I said I wanted to be a Writer When I Grew Up, so she thought I finally needed something Fancy to Write In.

And write in it I did. I was a faithful correspondent in that book for months, pushing myself to write something every day, including what I had for dinner (Green Mill pizza), what I watched on TV (*Powerhouse*), and whose family got a mysterious machine called a VCR that showed movies you actually wanted to watch (Rachel's, the lucky girl). Then I realized that my fifth-grade existence was actually pretty boring, and I gave it up.

In eighth grade I was given a new book, perhaps to sort out my complicated feelings about my parents' yearlong separation, but family problems barely made its pages, devoted as they were to my single-minded pursuit of the cute boy who sat in front of me in math class. Oh, sweet heavens, he was adorable. Even the sudden death of a classmate got only a page of reflection before devolving into a navel-gazing meditation on how important it was to make that cute boy like me before I, like the girl in my homeroom, got run over by a car on my way home from school.

After reading Natalie Goldberg's *Writing Down the Bones* in high school (another gift from my mother, who *still* believed me when I said I wanted to be a Writer When I Grew Up), I ditched the B. Dalton brand blank books and returned to notebooks. Goldberg swore by the unassuming nature of the lowly school notebook, believing that fancy books deterred creativity instead of inspiring it. I kept a journal only sporadically, however, since I was more interested in writing teenage angst fiction based on the skaters and McPunks who hung out at the Uptown McDonald's.

After graduation, I decided to take up the journaling habit again, this time in a series of beat-up notebooks covered in random riot grrrl stickers. I wrote constantly. I wrote at home, in coffee shops, at bars. I wrote so much that I gave myself cramps in my hands. In 1997, I fell head over heels for the cute boy at the record store—but this time, I was so busy being loved in return that I didn't have to pine about it. Requited love is a great productivity killer. I stopped journaling for a very long time.

Until I started a blog.

Of course I wasn't nearly as candid in my blog as I was with my blank books or journals, but I was still pretty honest when I wrote about my children, my family of origin, my best friend, and the parents at my kids' school.

Surprise! The only people who weren't pissed off were my kids, because they were too young to have MySpace accounts. Everyone else was furious.

I ponder these questions because I had a friendship end recently, and I somewhat naïvely commented on it online. I received a swift and brutal response from the person I wrote about that hit me so hard that I felt dizzy and unsettled for days. Again, I had to wonder why I ever thought to make the jump from easily hidden packs of paper to digital diaries that are open to the whole goddamn world. Why?

Why do I write a blog? These days I could say that I do it to push the soon-to-be-published book that shares the blog's name. But we're going to go deeper and *really wonder why*.

To make friends? To make enemies? To make manifest the promised Writer When I Grew Up? To feed my penchant for narcissistic navel-gazing? To make sense of what poet Mary Oliver called my "one wild and precious life"? To embarrass myself? To make myself happy?

All of the above?

By entering, you win
Minnesota Women's Press, August 2014

I freaked out when my Women's Press editor told me I would have a column in the state fair–themed issue. I love, love, love the Minnesota State Fair! Somehow my gluten-free chocolate chip cookies have not won a ribbon yet, but I'm not giving up—entering is fun, and practicing is delicious.

When I was a young state fair–goer, I treated the Creative Activities building with the kind of reverence some people show the Louvre, for inside those walls were works of art—in fabric and thread, flour and yeast, and cucumber and brine. The glass wall of jams and jellies shimmered in a spectacle of light and color as profound as any cathedral window. I loved these artifacts of Minnesota culture, and I found the array of names on colored ribbons as remote and mysterious as any Dutch master. Truly only a rarified class of domestic artist could earn a place in Creative Activities.

Then a Facebook friend posted a photo of her own cross-stitch piece enshrined in that hallowed location. I was thrilled, yet shocked: how could a normal human like Sarah *win a blue ribbon*? "By entering, dummy," I heard myself say out loud as I paged through the state fair website. "By entering."

Last summer, I downloaded the Creative Activities Premium Book, all fifty-plus pages of it, and studied it as closely as Dostoyevsky novel. I found a category that I hadn't heard of before: a gluten-free (GF) baking contest sponsored by the Northland Celiac Support Group. I took up GF baking a few years ago, ever since my husband was diagnosed with multiple food allergies and we realized that paying for commercial GF loaves would soon empty our kids' college funds. With a few cookbooks and a lot of trial and error, I had a repertoire of recipes that even my picky children would eat.

So I entered.

The jitters I felt when I filled out the official entry forms were like a day at the spa compared to the anxiety that nearly overwhelmed me the Sunday morning I delivered baked goods to the judges at the fair. Since GF foods are notoriously difficult to store, I woke up at dawn to bake my yeast bread and corn muffins fresh. I baked twelve muffins and agonized over which four were worthy of the judges. I ran the oven at 450 degrees on a hot August morning, dabbing my face with a dish towel to avoid sweating on my rice-, tapioca-, potato- and corn- based creations. "Mmm, freshly baked," noted the judge to whom I delivered the goods, while she bagged and tagged them and sent them on their way.

Despite the miserably hot weather, I felt light and happy, as though I had done something magical. And in a way I had, for at that moment I transformed from an observer of the beautiful mess that is the Minnesota State Fair to an active participant (snarfing mini doughnuts by the bucketful, while enjoyable, isn't quite the same). By entering, I felt like I'd already won.

It's possible that I love Creative Activities and the State Fair even more now that entering a contest has brought the whole process down to earth from its entirely too lofty pedestal. Creative Activities hosts phenomenal artists, to be sure, but those artists are just regular old Minnesota mini-doughnut snarfers just like you and me.

I suppose I should end this column with a Zen-like reflection that the action is more important than the outcome, which it is, but then I couldn't tell you that I WON A BLUE RIBBON. My yeast bread won first prize, and my corn muffins won second. This year I plan to enter a batch of GF chocolate chip cookies that are nearly as addictive as the Minnesota State Fair. Even if I leave without a ribbon, I've already won.

I would go to jail to protect my daughter, but I won't have to

Radical Housewife blog, September 24, 2014

Emily Bazelon's article "A Mother in Jail for Helping Her Daughter Have an Abortion" appeared in the New York Times *on September 22, 2014, and the feminist Internet could talk of nothing else for weeks. Whalen, faced with limited options when her teenage daughter asked for help ending a pregnancy, ordered Plan B online. She later pled guilty to dispensing medication without a prescription and performing an abortion without a license. Does that sound "pro-choice" to you?*

It was actually very interesting to research just what steps I would take to secure my daughter an abortion. Try it yourself! Would your journey be more like mine or Jennifer Whalen's?

Jennifer Whalen, a Pennsylvania mother of three, is currently serving a prison sentence for the "crime" of obtaining misoprostol and mifeprestone for her sixteen-year-old daughter, who used the drug to induce a miscarriage in the first trimester of an unplanned pregnancy.

In more SEO-worthy terms, this woman is in jail for helping her daughter have an abortion.

Like Whalen, I have a daughter. If she needed me to help her end an unwanted pregnancy, I would do it. Here are the steps we would take:

1. We would make an appointment at the Planned Parenthood clinic that is less than five miles from our home.

Jennifer Whalen's nearest abortion clinic was seventy-five miles away.

2. As required by Minnesota law, my husband and I would provide written documentation that we had been told of our daughter's decision to terminate her pregnancy at least forty-eight hours before the procedure.

Whalen "knew [her daughter's father] would be upset," so she didn't tell him about the pregnancy.

3. Twenty-four hours before the procedure, my daughter would be required to listen to a five-minute phone call about fetal development, the medical risks of abortion, and the medical risks of continuing the pregnancy to term. This is part of Minnesota's "Woman's Right to Know" Act, which was passed in 2003 under the assumption that all sexually active women are stupid.

I don't know if Pennsylvania has a bullshit law like this, but it wouldn't surprise me one bit.

4. At no point would I be concerned about the time this would take, because all the work I do for pay is done at home.

As a personal-care aide at an assisted-living center for the elderly, Whalen worried that taking time off for travel and waiting periods would endanger her job.

5. If I were unable to drive my daughter to the clinic on appointment day, we would take a bus to the light-rail line that stops just two blocks away.

At the time of her daughter's pregnancy, the Whalen family also had only one car, which both parents juggled to get to work. When my family's second car crapped out in 2010, we realized that abundant local transit options made purchasing a replacement unnecessary.

6. The fee for my daughter's first-trimester abortion would be covered by the health insurance provided by my husband's employer, a Fortune 500 company.

Emily Bazelon's *New York Times* article about the family states that the pregnant daughter was uninsured. I'm guessing that Jennifer and her other two daughters weren't insured, either.

7. If there were complications, I could take my daughter to the hospital without fear of being reported to child protective services.

Guess how the state of Pennsylvania learned about what Whalen did?

As I work on the promotional and marketing materials for my book *The Radical Housewife*, I find myself looking back to the very first days of my feminist reawakening, to the time when the birth of my children made real for me all the feminist talking points I'd only read about or listened to on my old *Free to Be . . . You and Me* record. Having a kid not only puts your heart outside your body; it puts your guts and soul out there too. It forces you to confront painful realities, one of which is the cold, hard fact that when I put myself in Jennifer Whalen's shoes, I can see myself doing the same thing for my daughter but never, *ever* experiencing the same consequences.

That's wrong. That's why I can't sit idly in my safe socioeconomic bubble and be content with the status quo.

This story illustrates perfectly why many abortion rights activists are no longer using the term "pro-choice." What good does being "pro-choice" do to help women whose choices have been taken from them?

I stand for reproductive justice and for the release of Jennifer Whalen.

The politics of unfairness
Minnesota Women's Press, October 2014

Another veiled reference to the friendship that ended online. Awareness of my own privilege led me to feminist activism in the first place, but it didn't protect me from being called out when I deserved it.

I am a white, cisgendered, heterosexual, able-bodied (if anxiety-addled) fortysomething member of the Midwestern American middle class.

That's not all I am, but it's as good a place as any to start, especially in an issue devoted to finding the political in the personal and vice versa.

You see, among my list of selves (see above) is a person who desperately wishes to understand and support the struggles of others. This self is motivated by a combination of compassion and guilt, for I recognize that my unique mix of privilege (see above) is not something I earned nor particularly deserve: two cisgendered, heterosexual, white, middle-class people living in America during the Nixon administration created me. I am a product of luck.

Have you ever tried explaining luck to a small child? They hate when the quarter you flipped didn't land on heads. They detest cakewalks that award plates of brownies to anyone but them. They hear from grown-ups every day that they need to be "fair," yet they are also expected to calmly accept bad luck.

As my own children grew older, they found my explanations even more frustrating. It seemed unfair that Laura's family had to move from their log cabin in *Little House on the Prairie*, but wasn't it more unfair that Pa thought he had a right to build on Osage land? Their confused looks told me that they didn't expect to learn about Native American genocide at bedtime. Why should they? They're lucky!

But I told them to have courage, not to give up; I reassured them with hugs that I needed as much as they did. I asked that they keep their hearts open, wide open, even though their privilege allowed them the opportunity to lock them up tight.

I am a lot of things (see above), but I am not a liar. I can't lie to my kids, even if it means staining Laura Ingalls Wilder's reputation. Today my kids want to know who's being more fair around the world: the Israelis or the Palestinians? Ukrainians or Russians? Guatemalan children or the U.S. Border Patrol? I can't lie, so I say the three words that they hate the most: "I don't know."

In the spirit of truth telling, I offer an admission: my unexpectedly tender heart was bruised recently by a friend whose luck is far different from mine. The personal is political, politics are personal, and the two of us clashed in the middle. The charge that I was a failure as an ally devastated me. I wanted to lock my heart up; I wanted to tweet "THAT'S NOT FAIR" a thousand times.

After some thought, I wrote this instead: "I'm sorry I hurt you."

My new book *The Radical Housewife* details the personal journey that sparked my political activism, as well as the politics that inform my personal life, not only as the selves above but also as a parent, spouse, and human being. By putting myself under a microscope, I hope to illuminate truths that will resonate with others, no matter where they land personally or politically. But the world doesn't owe me acceptance. The book could flop, and that would be perfectly fair.

It's difficult to live with an open heart, especially in a world that is absolutely, emphatically unfair. I strive to transform my luck into something healing, whether it is talking with my children, writing, retweeting, or making a PayPal donation. Sometimes I mess up. Sometimes I make mistakes. Sometimes I get called out for my privilege.

That's fair.

2014 in bests and worsts

Radical Housewife blog, December 31, 2014

In which I attempt to summarize one of the strangest but most rewarding years of my life.

2014 is over, long live 2014! Was it the *best* year I ever had? It wasn't the *worst*, but a lot of really crappy things happened.

In the best-year file is the culmination of a lifelong dream and five years of hard work: the publication of my first book. Too bad it had to happen when I was laid up with two additional, accidental firsts: my first broken bone and my first surgery.

Those were such painful worsts that I had to wonder if the universe had a message for me. I mean, neither Ariel Gore nor Cheryl Strayed broke their dominant wrists seven weeks before a book signing! Maybe this was evidence that I needed to use the laptop not for writing but for reposting videos of my daughter playing drums with the girls from rock camp.

Yes, Miriam really is the best! As a frustrated drummer myself, it is a thrill every day to hear her practice and to remember how much fun she had being part of a band. Gina Schock and Georgia Hubley should watch their backs.

But as much as I love my daughter, her band wasn't the best concert I saw this year. My sister and I got to relive our youth with the Replacements' hometown reunion show in September.

Paul Westerberg looks tiny [in the photo I posted] because I was not going to twiddle with the settings on my phone's camera while I was watching a performance by the band I've loved dearly for close to thirty years. The Replacements are the best band in the world.*

One of the worst things in life is definitely air travel, but the end result can be spectacular. In October, with a cast still on my wrist, I traveled with my family to Arizona.

The Grand Canyon is probably the best place on earth to have a nice hike and contemplate your tininess, your absolute meaninglessness in the presence of millions of years of geologic time. You think to yourself, "Is it really the worst thing ever to have just fourteen reviews of the book up on Amazon? Will it matter a hundred, or even a dozen years from now?"

That's the tricky thing about achieving a lifelong goal—the day after, you still have to get up and brush your own teeth. Everything around you looks the same; the world didn't shift off its axis like you thought it would. If you let that get inside your head, it can be the worst.

I should know.

2014 is over; long live 2014—the best *and* the worst.

*Anyone who complains about the lack of Bob Stinson, Chris Mars, or Slim Dunlap is the worst. Let it go.

2015

Getting older, not wiser

The book *The Radical Housewife* was on my shelf, which signaled a shift in my thinking about the necessity of The Radical Housewife, the blog. By now, Twitter had deposed personal blogs as the go-to source for freewheeling social commentary, and many of my feminist-mom colleagues were closing their sites for good. I didn't feel sad about this: in truth, I was as ready for a shift in my writing priorities as the world was ready for this fresh form of expression. I started publishing more personal essays—about grief, doubt, and unexpected viral infections—with nary a political argument in sight.

But darn it if my first Women's Press column of the year didn't celebrate the power of hashtag activism!

#YesAllWomen: A teachable moment

Minnesota Women's Press, January 2015

Feminist middle schoolers give me hope for humanity! Yes, they do!

Last spring my fourteen-year-old son, Elliott, returned from middle school in a foul mood; apparently a group of girls at his middle school were (and I am quoting him directly here) "causing a fuss about #YesAllWomen."

I knew about the hashtag, of course, because much of my feminist activism these days comes from and is inspired by Twitter, the social media platform that has transformed the way news is both reported and understood. Twitter, with its intricate system of retweets, subject hashtags, and trending topics, has the potential to amplify voices that decades ago wouldn't have warranted a mention in the last page of the *New York Times*.

My son required background on the topic, so here's how I filled him in: on May 23, 2014, a twenty-two-year-old gunman killed six people and injured thirteen in a violent spree fueled by his hatred of the college women whom he claimed rejected his romantic advances. Outrage at the killer's misogyny led a defensive few to tweet #NotAllMen. Twitter user @gildedspine, a self-identified "Muslim magical girl," not a member of the mainstream media, created the hashtag #YesAllWomen for others to discuss the violence that not all men perpetrate but that, yes, all women fear.

Elliott stared at me blankly. I expected as much; it's difficult for average adults, much less young teens, to wrap their heads around the ubiquity of gender-based violence. I asked him to elaborate on what was actually occurring, and he replied that girls were "posting" their favorite #YesAllWomen messages the old-fashioned way: on the walls of the school with pens, paper, and pieces of Scotch tape.

Feminist middle schoolers gave me hope for humanity, I told him, but he remained unhappy. "Because *I* don't do any of that stuff," he said. I told him I knew that. "But all those posts made me feel like *they* think I'm like that, but I'm not."

Instantly I knew that my son was the one fussing, not the girls. A mathematically inclined kid from the day he stacked his first Lego tower, Elliott fares best in situations that are orderly and precise; hashtag activism is anything but.

We must have debated the subject for at least thirty minutes before I asked, "Elliott, have you ever made fun of someone just because she was a girl? Assumed she was ignorant or incapable because of her gender?"

"No," he said immediately.

"Have you ever teased a girl about her clothes or her body?"

"Gross," he said.

"Have you ever called a girl a slut?"

For a moment, he looked like he might vomit. "No *way*," he gasped.

"Have you ever hurt a girl? Physically or mentally?" It made me sick to ask, but the conversation required it. "Have you, Elliott?"

"NO!" he shouted, so loudly that my ears rang.

"Then you don't need to worry," I announced, "because the girls at school aren't talking to you. You're one of the good guys! But what you need to understand," I added, before his sigh of relief got too deep, "is that there will be times when feminism makes you uncomfortable. If you want to *stay* one of the good guys, your job is to listen, learn, and let that weirdness happen. Then, if you still want to be part of the conversation, just ask what you can do to help. Can you do that?"

He paled slightly, gulped down a big breath, and . . . nodded yes. He got it, finally. I hugged him tightly and thanked him for being my kid.

Hashtag: #FeministParentingVictory.

Why this middle-class white mom is boycotting the Mall of America

Twin Cities Daily Planet, April 6, 2015

Minnesotans like to believe that we are protected from racial ugliness by virtue of being in the frozen north, but the truth is that we have some of the worst income and educational disparities in the country. Black Lives Matter Minneapolis (BLMM), formed in the unrest surrounding the death of Michael Brown in Ferguson, Missouri, in 2014, called attention to this ugliness with an action at the Mall of America just before Christmas. Hysterical mall officials coordinated with local police to respond to this peaceful protest with hundreds of riot cops and dozens of arrests. Several months later, the city of Bloomington filed charges against eleven of the activists and took the truly bizarre step of suing them for $40,000 in lost revenue.

I didn't attend the initial action, because of an important family Christmas tradition: getting sick. Matt and Miriam both had fevers that day, so I watched the events unfold on social media. To read some of the vitriol against BLMM, you'd think that the ability to buy shit at Bath & Body Works was more important than the civil rights of an entire population. Ugh.

My politely worded opinion on the newly filed criminal charges was delivered not on social media but on an indie news site.

As a white, middle-class mom of two with a certain amount of disposable income, I can safely say that I'm the Mall of America's target market.

I buy Converse at Foot Locker, jeans and hoodies at Old Navy, and birthday presents at American Girl and the Lego Store. I fork over my Visa card when my kids and their friends want to ride the Pepsi Orange Streak or Jimmy Neutron's Atomic Collider at Nickelodeon Universe. The multiplex on the fourth floor is where I enjoy Pixar films and endure movies based on comic-book characters. When Elliott wants a Blizzard but Miriam wants a Philly cheesesteak, I give them the cash they need to navigate the food court, then I order myself lattes at Starbucks as my reward for a job well done.

At least, I *used* to do these things. I haven't set foot in the Mall of America since twenty-five people were arrested by mall police in the infamous December demonstration by Black Lives Matter Minneapolis. This is the longest stretch without a megamall visit since I became a mother fifteen years ago. My boycott was informal, but since the city of Bloomington has decided to file criminal charges against eleven of the protesters, including an unprecedented demand for $40,000 in restitution fees, I have joined BLMM's nationwide call to boycott the Mall of America until these ridiculous charges are dropped.

I may pretend that I'm the trendy shop-local type who wouldn't dream of stepping foot in a 2.8-million-square-foot shrine to capitalism, but at my core I'm just another boring mom looking for a reliable way to entertain her kids. The megamall is an affordable getaway for us, a Cinnabon-scented playground where we can while away our minimal cares.

And my cares are quite minimal, indeed: If I turn my pale-complexioned son loose there, my greatest fear is that he will blow his entire allowance at the iCandy Sugar Shoppe. I need not fear that he will be singled out for harassment by mall security and Bloomington police. Racial profiling at the megamall was an issue long before Michael Brown was shot to death in Ferguson last August; the mall might not have been happy about a demonstration occurring on one of the busiest shopping weekends of the year, but it could have welcomed the activists and shown the world that commerce and cooperation need not be mutually exclusive.

Instead, Mall of America leadership overreacted, as did the city of Bloomington, looking like a group of spoiled brats who demanded a Death Star Lego set for Christmas but got stuck with another stupid X-Wing fighter. "But I *told* you what I wanted from you, Mom!" sobs the frustrated child, who stomps and cries and looks for someone, *anyone,* to blame for this indignity.

I'm not a kid; I'm an adult. I know that the letter of the law states that the Mall of America is private property. I also know that the letter of the law states every citizen's right to equal protection, whether they shop at Nordstrom or not, but all you need is an open heart and an open mind to know that that isn't reality in America today.

If the Mall of America has enough pull with Bloomington to have these charges filed, it can also ensure that they are dropped. Dare I suggest that the mall invite Black Lives Matter activists back for a public forum, perhaps in the Rotunda where the initial protests began?

I would be there, with a Starbucks coffee in my hand, an Old Navy hoodie on my back, and a Visa card burning a hole in my wallet.

What do *all* women want?
Minnesota Women's Press, May 2015
The eternal question! And the eternal answer: intersectionality! . . . right?

As a parent of a certain age, I haven't had the stamina to watch award-worthy films since the twentieth century, so when *The Lego Movie* was snubbed for Best Animated Feature, I knew I would probably skip watching the Academy Awards last February.

But as a feminist keeping up with the twenty-first century, I witnessed my Twitter timeline explode with the news that Patricia Arquette, an award winner for her role in *Boyhood,* used her thirty seconds in the worldwide spotlight to call for "pay equity once and for all." Wow! When was the last time you heard someone talk about pay equity on television? *Network* television?

Behind the scenes, as she faced the press with the Oscar in her hand, Arquette expanded on her remarks, saying, "It's time for all the women in America, and all the men that love women, and all the gay people, and all the people of color that we've all fought for to fight for us now."

Uh-oh.

I was immediately reminded of Gloria Steinem's January 8, 2008, *New York Times* op-ed that declared "Women Are Never Front Runners." It was a lament against Barack Obama's ascendancy that included the observation, "gender is probably the most restricting force in American life." This may have made sense to Steinem's (male) editors, but it didn't resonate with anyone of *any* color or gender who has ever tried to support a family with wages from Wal-Mart. I would venture to guess that this op-ed introduced more people to the concept of "intersectionality" than an army of tenured women's studies professors.

Intersectionality is the understanding that various forms of oppression, such as racism, sexism, classism, and homophobia, do not exist independently of one another. The idea demands recognition of what should be terribly obvious: that many of the gay people and people of color that Arquette mentioned in her speech are women, too. When these intersections are erased, so are lives, histories, and truths that are essential to a healthy, vibrant movement.

Erasure occurs when the figure cited about the gender pay gap is 78 cents to every man's dollar, because that figure is what *white* women earn. The latest research from the American Association of University Women reveals that black women make 64 cents and Hispanic women make 54 cents. Feminists fought hard for the English language to acknowledge that not all humans are male (when was the last time you heard the term "fireman"?), so why do we fight women of color who balk at defining women as a similar monolith?

Writing in response to the controversy for the website *The Broad Side*, Veronica Arreola stated plainly that "white feminists need to remember that intersectionalism is a requirement, it is not optional." I learned that lesson myself in 2008 when I wondered why Steinem, one of my heroes, was getting bashed all over the web. "She meant well," I said, but when I stopped defending and started listening, I realized how much harm was being done with noble intentions.

Casting a harsh light on the comments of an excited Hollywood star might seem the worst kind of nitpicky, and many accused critical feminists of "eating their own," but I would rather spread Patricia Arquette on toast than disengage from the tough work of dismantling oppression in all its forms.

As Tegan and Sara (twin sisters who happen to be "gay people"—imagine that!) sing on *The Lego Movie* soundtrack: "Everything is awesome! Everything is cool when you're part of a team!" As the feminist movement evolves, the feminist team expands.

That is awesome.

Yes, a child might belong at a Minneapolis protest
Minneapolis StarTribune, May 15, 2015

The Black Lives Matter movement brought all kinds of people out to protest actions, including kids. And why not? Racial profiling affected them too. Youth sure didn't protect Tamir Rice, the twelve-year-old boy fatally shot by Cleveland police in 2014.

When I read that a child had been maced by Minneapolis police at a protest, I was angry. I got angrier when I read the comment sections around the web that blamed the boy's mother, not the cop! The local paper of record printed my furious response, and yes, I read the comments. More on that later . . .

I can't remember when I heard a sound more harrowing than the piercing scream of a ten-year-old boy reacting to pepper spray in his eyes.

The boy, named Taye, was participating in a street action by a group called Black Liberation Project when he was maced by a member of the Minneapolis Police Department.

Video shot by a bystander shows a shaky jumble of bodies, cars, voices, and, about two minutes in, the terrifying screams of a child in pain. As a parent of two children myself, I had to stop watching; Taye's panicked, high-pitched howling was too much to bear.

Even nonparents must be horrified by the sound of young boy enduring a form of violence that brings fully grown people to their knees. So why is Susan Montgomery, Taye's mother, being smeared all over the web for what happened to her son? Why is the president-elect of the police union, Lt. Bob Kroll, implying to the media that Taye had no right to be there?

Montgomery brought her child to a protest that occurred in downtown Minneapolis, at night, where "f*** the police" was chanted and a flag was burned. This might not be my idea of a fun night out, but I am not the mother of an African-American male: I do not fear that my fifteen-year-old son could be shot dead for playing with his Nerf weapons at a nearby park. My reckless, foolhardy, and white teenager is not subject to the same harsh profiling and discrimination that Taye will endure.

Millions of people around the world heard Eric Garner's last words: "I can't breathe." Now we can hear Taye screaming in pain and confusion. No less a body than the United Nations Council on Human Rights has slammed the United States for its record on police brutality, but somehow Susan Montgomery is the problem? That she is being vilified for allowing her child to participate in a public protest is one more sign that our country and community need to reorganize their priorities.

My son's life is not at stake, but Susan Montgomery's son's life is. If I were in her shoes, I would consider active participation in Black Lives Matter to be as essential to his education as learning about right triangles, invertebrates, and the capitol of Bulgaria.

In fact, if I were raising an African-American child in twenty-first-century America, I would want that child to know that he has a voice and that he can use it. I would encourage his activism, not squelch it. I can think of no better way to connect deeply and emotionally with a child than to teach him, in both words and action, that *he matters*.

Put that way, Susan Montgomery is a fine mother, indeed.

It's the mother's fault
Radical Housewife blog, May 21, 2015
In which I read the comments so that my readers don't have to.

I wrote a commentary piece for the *Star Tribune* in a rage on May 14 in response to news that a ten-year-old child at an evening protest in Minneapolis was maced by police and that the person blamed for this event was *not*, in fact, the officer with the mace can, but the boy's mother.

It's always the mother's fault, isn't it? Think about it:

Sybrina Fulton killed Trayvon Martin—not George Zimmerman.

Samaria Rice killed Tamir Rice—not Officer Timothy Loehmann.

Lesley McSpadden killed Michael Brown—not Officer Darren Wilson.

If these women were 100 Percent Perfect, All-American, Good Mothers™, their children would be alive. Because in this country, bad things only happen to bad people.

(Or to brown and black people, which to many are the same thing.)

As of this writing there are 192 online comments posted, and most are awful, like this one: "This woman is a far left loon… look at the stats Susie and quit acting like you are some enlightened person overwhelmed by white guilt… [Black Lives Matter] are the black version of the KKK."

Some are hilarious, like this one: "Just google Shannon Drury and you will find her website complete with a picture of her with Franken and Hillary . . radical left has no shame."

Some are bewildering, like this one: "Trust me, your son's life is in far more danger . . .25,000 Caucasian males commit suicide every year in America."

But one made *all* the crappy ones worthwhile: "Thank you so very much for these kind words Shannon. It is so empowering that others are inspired by my son."

When I told my daughter that Taye's mom had written in with a comment, she was very happy for me. "That is so cool," my ten-year-old protest veteran said, and she hugged me.

I may not be 100 Percent Perfect but, damn, that sure made me feel like a Good Mother™.

Stuck in the middle with shingles
The Mid, June 8, 2015

The Mid, now a part of the Scary Mommy *blog network, is a site for Gen Xers like me who wish that their biggest challenge was passing their geometry exam so they could be allowed to go to the latest John Hughes movie at the mall. My sad tale of having an old-lady problem at a "young" age fit the demographic perfectly.*

Tell me the truth: is forty-three young or old? There's a burning slash of blisters on my lower back that really wants to know.

When my own mother was forty-three, I was a know-it-all college student, and to my jaded eyes, she was hopelessly, desperately *old*. After all, she chain-smoked Merit menthols, watched *Hill Street Blues*, and listened to Eric Clapton records on a Pioneer stereo system as big as a Japanese car. But my friends begged to differ. "She's so *young*," they'd sigh, for their folks were mostly pushing sixty, too square to smoke anything, and still suspicious of Clapton for being in a band called Cream.

Now I am forty-three, with two know-it-all children of my own. I flatter myself that, with the assistance of Miss Clairol and the stubborn patch of blackheads on my nose, I appear younger. I dress younger, having stuck to the same Converse and hoodie uniform since the days I rolled my eyes at my geezer mom. I certainly *act* younger: I like to cuss, and I still laugh when my kids fart.

Today I was diagnosed with a condition that I thought only afflicted the terribly old. It's on my forty-three-years-young back, and it hurts like a motherfucker.

I remember from my childhood an announcement, in hushed and sympathetic tones, that my poor grandmother was suffering from a flare-up of a horrible skin condition named after the stuff that kept our house from leaking during a rainstorm: shingles. I imagined Grandma Rose's skin scaling off into pieces that layered on top of one another until her back resembled a pitched roof.

When I'm at the pharmacy and the battery on my Samsung Galaxy is dead, I kill time in the unavoidable line by reading the ever-present pamphlet by the counter that explains all about shingles prevention. Page after page shows senior citizens in emotional states ranging from concern to outright panic as they considered whether they ought to talk to their doctors about this matter, as Merck Pharmaceuticals, publisher of said pamphlet and producer of a shingles vaccine, *very* strongly suggests. Like poor bladder control and osteoporosis, I thought, this shingles thing was only a problem for *old* people.

Or I used to think this, until I asked my husband to check out the hot rash I had found on the left side of my back. "Oh my God!" he shrieked, in typically supportive fashion.

"Whoa, Mom," my teenage son said, after demanding to know what the fuss was about. "That looks disgusting. Are you dying?"

"Gross," my tween daughter squealed.

Since my family had failed to support me, I turned to Google, good old nonjudgmental Google, entering the search terms "hot rash back lumpy." The amateur diagnosis? Shingles.

Shingles?

I AM TOO YOUNG FOR SHINGLES!

Yet when the nurse practitioner at the Minute Clinic took a peek, the first word out of her mouth was "herpes."

Herpes?

I AM TOO OLD FOR HERPES!

"Herpes zoster," she corrected. "The medical name for shingles."

Dammit.

I called the old lady. "Mom," I said, "how old were you when you first got shingles?"

"Shingles?" she asked, bewildered. At sixty-five, after two kids, four grandkids, and too many cartons of cigarettes to count, this is more or less her natural state. "You must be mistaken, Shannon. *I've* never had shingles. Your grandmother, on the other hand . . ."

I gritted my teeth during the entire drive to my pharmacy, where the Merck pamphlet mocked me from its stack near the blood-pressure machine (mine was 166/72. Is that good for an old person? Or bad for a young person?). The pharmacist apologized for having to fill my prescription with a name brand, not the generic, as the latter was out of stock. "What, did everyone get shingles all at the same time?" I cracked. I hoped to prove that being able to joke about my sorry condition proved that I was still *young*.

The pharmacist shook his pale, hairless head and whispered, "We're sold out of generic valacyclovir because so many people came in for, well . . . you know . . . *outbreaks*." His tone was low, almost conspiratorial, as if he were welcoming me into his circle—and not just of confidence.

I like this pharmacist. I've trusted him with my prescriptions for years. He's as helpful as can be, but the man is sixty if he's a day. He's *old*. With apologies to Groucho Marx (a man so old he's dead), I don't want to be in any club that has him as a member. And what made him think that I wasn't a libidinous tart who had caught a sexually transmitted infection at a very hip, very happening swingers' party? Even trollops wear hoodies when they need to pick up their prescriptions!

"It's pretty painful, isn't it?" he said, noting my watering eyes. I nodded. I asked if he had a preference among the various products that claimed to soothe aggravated skin. "I like the Aveeno oatmeal bath, and you can never go wrong with calamine lotion," he said.

I bought them both, with a six-pack of Ensure just to be safe.

Better known than unknown
Mamalode, June 11, 2015

My first two pieces for the excellent personal-essay website Mamalode *appeared within two weeks of each other. Make of that what you will. This piece, based on actual events that occurred when a freak tornado hit Minneapolis in August 2009, explores one anxious mom's relationship with warning systems—and reality.*

Mothers assume we are well-equipped to manage the balance between risk and reward, between health and hazard, but one rainy August afternoon, I tipped the scales so far that they broke. To protect my son from dust mites, I nearly drove him into a funnel cloud.

By two o'clock that day, it had already been storming for hours, but the ominously dark sky and waterlogged streets didn't frighten me nearly as much as the prospect of missing my son's weekly allergy appointment. Reactions to dust, mold, pollen, and our elderly cat left him with cement in his sinuses that could only be alleviated by immunotherapy and scrupulous cleaning, and since I sucked at the latter, I had to get him to his weekly shot, weather be damned.

I craned my head to look for oncoming traffic on Park Avenue, and to my surprise I saw an enormous elm tree lying flat across a wet lawn, beside a tangle of knotted roots and concrete chunks scattered across the boulevard. *That's odd*, I thought. *Is my iPod habit so bad that I can't hear lightning strikes anymore?* I kept the car chugging down south to the interstate, where traffic slowed to a crawl to avoid standing water, a not uncommon phenomenon during heavy rain. My son, daughter, and I arrived at the suburban clinic just before the door locked out any allergic stragglers who failed to arrive before the unusually early closing time. I was triumphant.

Elliott endured his shots bravely, and while we enjoyed a post-injection lollipop, the receptionist took a phone call. I heard her utter, in hushed, respectful tones, a word dreaded by all crisis-averse Minnesotans: *tornado*. When she completed the call, I asked her what she meant. I had been planning on taking the kids to Value Village to waste a rainy afternoon thrifting, but severe weather would change that. She replied that her friend had told her about a tornado watch in the eastern suburbs, but nothing on the south side of the metropolitan area. I thanked her and urged my children out of the office, towards the building's glass-walled entrance lobby.

"WOW," Elliott gasped at the violent slashes pounding against the windows. "COOL!" He rushed for the door, but I yanked him backwards by the hood of his jacket. We weren't going anywhere, I announced, until that rain backed off.

"What if it *never* lets up?" Elliott asks.

"It will," I said.

"Mom," he asked, his small face pinching, "what happens if there's a tornado?"

"There won't be," I said. "Our city has a lot of experience with tornadoes, so we have a very good warning system. If there's a tornado anywhere in our area, a siren would go off. Do you hear a siren?" We paused, tilting our heads as though the motion would increase our eardrums' sensitivity. "I don't."

"But Mom," he said, "what if it's too fast? What if the tornado just pops up out of nowhere?"

"It won't," I said. My brief experience with urban tornadoes had taught me that they don't appear in the pouring rain; instead, the sky will settle ominously before they arrive, washing the world with a sickly shade of yellow before disaster struck. I had seen my last yellow sky in 1981, just before a funnel cloud dropped a mile from my childhood home and blew apart the theater where I had seen *The Empire Strikes Back*. Today's sky looked gray, heavy, and wet: an annoyingly persistent rainstorm and nothing more. In a lull, we dashed to our car, still planning on an afternoon of damp thrifting.

I clicked on the radio. The public radio announcer declared, breathlessly, that the Evangelical Lutheran Church of America's national convention and its ongoing debate over consecrating gay clergy had been interrupted by reports of a funnel cloud that had appeared near the Minneapolis Convention Center. *Give me a break*, I thought. *How long until some kook declares that this is God's wrath upon them?* I failed to recognize the real-time relevance of this report until the newscaster took a call from a resident who verified that a funnel cloud had plopped down in his neighborhood just to the south, where the rainbow flags flew whether the Evangelical Lutheran Church of America liked it or not.

Was it possible? I thought. *No. It couldn't be.*

My knuckles cracked audibly as I increased my grip on the steering wheel. As the callers' addresses trailed southward from downtown, my breath grew even shallower. The names of streets and intersections meant nothing to my kids, who appeared fascinated by the hammer of the rain against the increasingly enfeebled windshield wipers.

"Mom," Elliott peeped from the back seat. Miriam was singing to herself and paying absolutely no attention. "What county do we live in?"

"Hennepin, honey," I said, eager to give him reassurance as well as the truth. "We live in Hennepin County."

"Good," he said, obviously relieved. Dakota and Goodhue had just been announced as the counties in the path of the storm; I hadn't realized he was paying attention.

As the two radio men discussed the pattern of the storm as it moved from west to east, excitedly mulling the prospect of a tornado hitting a metropolitan neighborhood—*my* neighborhood—I quivered, fighting mightily against the adrenaline rocketing through my veins.

Was it possible? No. It couldn't be.

The first true emergency siren of our very quiet summer had blared only two weeks earlier, tripped when a stray funnel cloud was spotted in our large county's northern environs. I'd just snuggled two hyperactive children down to sleep, so when the news report showed that the storm was wide of us, I didn't bother dragging them to the basement. The siren, based at the middle school four blocks away, annoyed the neighborhood for several minutes until its *woooooooooooo* trailed off into silence. "Better safe than sorry," everyone said. "Better known than unknown."

I believe in this system. I always have. I happily explained its logic to my college classmates, transplants who shook with terror at one o'clock in the afternoon on the first Wednesday of the month. "That's just the regular tornado drill," I announced to confused Bostonians and Portlanders looking to the sky for signs of a prairie air raid. Sturdy Midwesterners trust in the natural order of things, living in unglamorous environs for a reason. Without mountains, we avoid volcanoes and earthquakes; without oceans, we escape hurricanes. We learn that even our homegrown dangers are predictable: tornadoes, while scary, announce themselves to trained meteorologists, who set off the emergency sirens, which send attentive mothers and children into basements statewide. Everyone is safe; everyone is happy.

By the time I pulled the car into our neighborhood, I was trembling all over, fighting the tornadic force of my own anxiety and the even stronger pull of my desire to keep my shit together in front of my children. The clash dizzied me momentarily, before obligation to Elliott and Miriam leveled me out: these two people depended on me for protection, both physical and emotional. Upon returning, I looked again at the uprooted tree I had seen on our way out, its trunk sucked from the ground with such force that hunks of the sidewalk came with it.

It was not only possible; it was undeniable: *I drove my kids into the path of a tornado.*

To protect my son from dust mites, I nearly drove him into a *funnel cloud.*

And if that weren't awful enough, I gave him false confidence about an emergency alert system that *failed.*

Elliott sneezed, twice, and I handed him a Kleenex from the small pack we kept in the dashboard cup holder. "What are you looking at, Mom?" he asked, dabbing at the snot from his left nostril.

"A big mess," I said.

Around dinnertime, the rain stopped and the clouds blew east. Our neighborhood glowed a healthy, vibrant yellow, the color of the sun, of summer, of safety. The kids pulled on vinyl boots for protection against puddles, but I went out in my canvas Chuck Taylors. I didn't feel invincible; I felt humbled. If my feet got wet, I could handle it.

Out of the picture
Mamalode, June 23, 2015

My second piece at Mamalode *was a remembrance of my friend Pam and how much I had taken her presence at the bus stop for granted. I did have my daughter take pictures of me on the last day of school. I looked sweaty and weird, but I did it!*

Parents like me avail ourselves of every opportunity to photograph our children, particularly at all of the relevant firsts—smile, tooth, haircut, Christmas, and birthday. As our kids grow older and milestones grow farther apart (and our presence with the Canon PowerShot grows more embarrassing), we limit the photo ops to yearly obligations or, as my friend and neighbor Pam called them, "traditions!" She announced photo sessions with a smile and a corny wink, but her firmly set jaw warned even the surliest preteens that compliance was not optional.

We knew we'd miss the children one day, when they left our street for college, jobs, and families of their own; too late, we realized how much we would miss the grownups, too.

On January 30, 2013, fourteen months after she was diagnosed with brain cancer, my friend Pam passed away. In the days that followed her death, I spent hours combing through thousands of photos in an increasingly desperate drive to see her again, especially as I remembered her, before radiation burned her scalp and medication distorted her face.

I wanted to hold a picture of her smile, broadening as I walked nearer to the bus stop outside her front door. I wanted to watch that smile harden into a grimace when she learned that another member of the block's Girl Scout troop snatched up my quota of Thin Mints for the year. I wanted her glow of relief when she saw that I wouldn't leave her alone with Hank, the sweat-stained dad who meant well but said "shit" in front of the grade schoolers a few too many times. I wanted tangible evidence of her smirk as she shared news about a neighbor's wife leaving in the middle of the night, screaming obscenities and taking the dog. She loved gossip almost as much as she loved photography.

Pam took traditions and their documentation extremely seriously. Every year she shot SD cards full of the first and last days of school, Halloween costumes, National Night Out parties, and all manner of annual activities (snowman building, mud-puddle splashing, sprinkler dashing, leaf-pile destroying) that marked the passage of time on our block in South Minneapolis.

In picture after picture, Pam's two daughters smile and occasionally wince beside my own son and daughter and up to a dozen other squirrelly children. We parents told ourselves that these pictures, hundreds and hundreds of them, could offer a glimmer of hope in our futile effort to slow down our kids' race towards adulthood. After all, we said every September, wasn't it only yesterday that Kelcy loved Elmo more than One Direction? That Miriam rode a tricycle? That Campbell had two front teeth?

If Pam appeared in a photo at all, she was looking away from the camera, spooning a sticky pile of macaroni and cheese onto a child's paper plate. Occasionally she'd be captured in conversation with another parent, her face contorted mid-sentence, her eyes blazing red from the camera's flash or closed entirely. Her voice snarks in my ear, disparaging that woman's awkwardness and begging for a better, more glamorous way to be remembered.

Adults can usually be relied upon to photograph one another on birthdays and major holidays, especially when a member of the family is euphemistically referred to as "getting up there." We too easily forget the people who fill in the days in between, the friends and neighbors, those who are woven so tightly into the fabric of our everyday lives that it takes a deep, irreparable tear for us to realize how bound together we really are.

From September 2005, when our oldest children entered kindergarten, until November 2011, when she was admitted to the ER, I saw Pam every weekday at seven in the morning and two in the afternoon at the bus stop, where we continued to congregate long after our jittery kindergarteners needed our presence. I never photographed Pam while we gossiped, complained about mitten-losing children and husbands who rarely cooked dinner, or moaned about mercurial Minnesota weather. I didn't think to document the quiet moments on which our friendship was built.

My daughter is in her last year of elementary school, a fourth grader who does not need me to join her at the corner of East Forty-ninth Street. Yet I walk down to the end of the block every day, in a ritual that I both cherish and resent.

Sometimes I stare the back door of Pam's house and remember her stumbling out, running fingers through gray-rooted, ash-blonde hair, pushing her toes through her daughter's pink-flowered flip-flops in her haste to meet the bus on time. We would talk of volunteering for Field Day or who was going home on that night's episode of *American Idol*. Why didn't I take a picture then?

The uncomfortable truth I confront as I flip through thousands of pictures is that permanence is an illusion; neither digital file nor 4x6 slip of Kodak paper can reanimate the people we love. Pam's own scrapbooks, displayed at her memorial service, did little to heal her mourners' grief. And in those pictures, carefully curated by the woman herself, she looked flawless—every hair in place and every smile relaxed and genuine.

She is perfect; she is gone.

If our lives unfold as planned, my last walk to greet the elementary school bus will occur on a warm afternoon this June. I'll have a camera in my hand, Kleenex in my pocket, and a bit of the wisdom that is earned from grief. I expect that my hair will be a mess, but my smile will be exquisite as I ask my daughter to take a picture . . . of me.

Fed up!
Minnesota Women's Press, September 2015

Another column about food, this time about keeping up with food trends, especially ones that will win us points in the Mommy Wars. I mock the low-sugar craze in this piece, but the truth is I dropped five pounds as soon as I stopped adding nonorganic chocolate soymilk to my morning coffee. Fed up, indeed!

"Have you heard of the movie *Fed Up?*" I asked my teenage son as we scrolled through our Netflix queue.

"Yeah, it's about how sugar is destroying America," he replied, slurping on a Sprecher's Grape Soda. "We saw it in health class." Suddenly I no longer felt smug about serving my child pop from an independent Wisconsin brewery and not a can of Crush. I looked at the label: 66 grams of sugar per artisanal glass bottle. Yikes!

First fat, then cholesterol, then carbs, and now sugar—every decade has its verboten food product, blamed for everything from heart disease to cancer to something called "Feel Like Crap Syndrome," a non-scientific term invented by the author of an anti-sugar tract called *The Blood Sugar Solution* that I found at the library. The book lists so many vague symptoms (irritability, fatigue, achiness) that earning a diagnosis seems suspiciously inevitable.

When I felt crappy twenty years ago, fat was the cause and sugary Snackwell's cookies were the remedy. Science doesn't always get it right, especially when "it" is something as slippery as good health. How does one define such a thing? Longevity? *Not* feeling like crap? Or feeling like crap, yet still thin enough to be a runway model?

After streaming *Fed Up*, I crashed harder than a toddler after downing a grande mocha Frappuccino (61 grams of sugar); the film forced me to confront the long list of all the sugar-filled foods I handed my kids in the course of a day. I'm not talking about Twinkies (19 grams of sugar per cake)—I mean the "healthy" stuff I used to tuck in lunchboxes with a clear conscience, like strawberry Yoplait (18 grams of sugar per tub).

As a feminist, I'm very aware of the socioeconomics of food trends as well as the manipulative tactics employed by corporate America to tug at the moral conscience of our nation's mothers. In practice, however, I'm just another mom trying to raise healthy kids while saving a buck at Target.

I'm extremely fortunate that I have the money to buy food from the periphery of the grocery store, as well as the time to cook it. Many do not, a point made with heart-wrenching clarity in *Fed Up*, though you don't need to see the film to know that fresh food is increasingly out of reach for American families; all you need is a trip to the grocery store and a calculator.

As of this writing, a shopper at Cub Foods in Minneapolis can choose between two breakfast options: Honey Nut Cheerios with 2 percent milk for fifty cents a serving, or two organic eggs and a nitrite-free pork sausage patty for $1.29 a serving. One is less expensive and more convenient in the short term but has possibly devastating consequences in the long term. Nothing makes a mom feel more like crap than fearing for her child's future!

When I stopped buying our favorite cold cereals, my kids asked for frozen waffles instead (3 grams of sugar each, but essentially a syrup-delivery device). When I refused, they asked for another favorite breakfast, Greek vanilla yogurt (15 grams sugar) with granola (14 grams). "Why won't you eat eggs?" I wailed.

"Are you cooking them?" my son asked. The last time he boiled a pot of noodles, he didn't notice the electrical cord under the gas burner until the acrid smoke nearly killed us all.

If you need me, I'll be in the kitchen until the next food movement arrives.

Forty-four is the new forty-four
Radical Housewife blog, November 5, 2015

I did not include my darkest, most depressing birthday blog posts in this compilation, because they are just too much, even for me.

It was my birthday last week. Back when I was a prolific, several-times-a-week blogger, I offered reports on my birthday, all of them terrible. For years I was convinced that my birthday was a day set aside to haunt me, to remind me of the constant specter of death.

This is why people don't usually invite me to parties.

Miraculously, though, I *was* invited to a party this Halloween! I dressed as the most irritating character on *Orange is the New Black*, Alex Vause. No one at the party watched the show.

Do you ever feel like you're that person at the party? The one who mentions death at the dessert table? The one whose costume is a little bit off?

I've been blogging as The Radical Housewife since 2006. A lot has changed in the last decade, including the rise and fall of blogging as media outlet and platform or, as some call it, "brand." From the jump I loved writing about the things that interested me: feminism, parenting, pop culture, grief, joy, reproductive rights, Minnesota politics, body image, Courtney Love, Hillary Clinton, NOW, and books, books, books—especially my own.

People don't read or write blogs that much anymore. I know I don't. When my attention span is short and cranky, I go to Twitter. When I want the luxury to post four sentences and a photo of my kids doing something cute, I go to Facebook. There doesn't seem to be as much space for the long-form noodling that connected so many interesting people via MySpace, Blogger, and LiveJournal back in the day.

Take me, for example: I never wrote to make a living off of ad revenue, but I *did* want to connect. I *did* want to build something of a "brand," which I assumed would lead to the ego fulfillment that I felt was my American birthright. In the blogosphere, I could create my own costume! I deserved to be invited to all the parties, dammit!

I was invited to a few, and for that I am very grateful. I found my nonfiction voice and an audience, and I did what my high school yearbook promised I'd do (that would be "get published," not "marry Holden Caulfield").

This isn't my goodbye post, by the way. A presidential election is less than a year away—do you think I want to squander that opportunity to build my brand . . . er, join the party?? In fact, I might just throw myself a party to celebrate the ten-year anniversary of The Radical Housewife.

Don't worry, you'll be invited.

About the author

Shannon Drury is the author of the memoir *The Radical Housewife: Redefining Family Values for the 21st Century*, winner of a 2015 USA Book Award. A longtime columnist for the *Minnesota Women's Press*, her personal and political essays have appeared in print magazines, online news outlets, and literary anthologies.

She is married to a great feminist guy and they share a house in Minneapolis with two cats, two kids, three computers, hundreds of vinyl records, thousands of books, millions of Lego pieces and billions of dustbunnies.

www.ingramcontent.com/pod-product-compliance
Lightning Source LLC
Chambersburg PA
CBHW022227010526
44113CB00033B/640